D1076326

A
WISDEN
COLLECTION

A
WISDEN
COLLECTION

EDITED BY GRAEME WRIGHT

BLOOMSBURY

First published in 2004 by
Bloomsbury Publishing Plc
38 Soho Square
London W1D 3HB

www.bloomsbury.com/reference

This title is published by Bloomsbury under licence from
John Wisden & Co Ltd

A copy of the CIP entry for this book is available from the British Library

ISBN 0 7475 7435 9

10 9 8 7 6 5 4 3 2

All papers used by Bloomsbury Publishing are natural, recyclable products made from wood grown in well-managed forests. The manufacturing processes conform to the environmental regulations of the country of origin.

Index by Hilary Bird
Typeset by RefineCatch Ltd, Bungay, Suffolk
Printed and bound in Great Britain by Clays Ltd, St Ives plc

CONTENTS

DEDICATION

In memory of
Sir Paul Getty

INTRODUCTION

"No man, who knows nothing else, knows even his Bible," Matthew Arnold argued in his 1869 essay, *Culture and Anarchy*. The same might be said about *Wisden*, though unlikely by Matthew Arnold in 1869. *The Cricketers' Almanack* was then in only its sixth edition, still a year away from being *John Wisden's Cricketers' Almanack*, and had yet to establish itself as "the cricketers' bible". Not till the 1938 makeover did it become today's *Wisden Cricketers' Almanack*.

While not carrying John Wisden's name in its original title, the Almanack had in fact been his project from the start, published and sold by his company "at their cricketing and British sports warehouse, 2 New Coventry Street, Haymarket". The price was one shilling, the extent 112 pages. It is still published by John Wisden & Co but, 141 editions on, it has grown to 1,648 pages. That, coincidentally, is 112 fewer pages than the 140th edition, something of an achievement in these inflationary times for international cricket.

It is no secret that a quarter of Wisden's first Almanack was unconnected to cricket, or that little of the cricket related to the previous season. That doesn't stop this slim volume commanding a price in excess of £6,000. However, *Wisden* is nothing if not evolutionary. Soon there were averages for the principal teams and, before long, match reports to flesh out the scorecards. In time *Wisden* became a talking-shop, with prominent players airing their views on the cricket issues of the day, and as it grew in size it grew in stature. Under the successive editorship of brothers Charles and Sydney Pardon, *Wisden* became an authority on cricket, valued for its independence and integrity. The public, press and the game's politicians turned to *Wisden* for answers, references and quotations, just as the men of God looked to their Bibles.

From the day he opens a newspaper and reads "*Wisden* says . . ." every new editor of the Almanack quickly realises what he has taken on. The reference might be nothing more than a comment on a pitch. It could as easily be his thoughts on the future of county cricket, his concern about the legitimacy of a bowler's action, or an old cricketer's reminiscences on bygone days. The editor and his contributors are conscious that the words they write sit solid in their volumes down the ages, ready to be recalled not once but time after time.

I came to *Wisden* not as a cricket writer but as a book editor with some knowledge of cricket and cricketers. Until then, the late 1970s, I had never owned a *Wisden*. Occasionally, and it was only occasionally, I had used it as a reference book, but I couldn't say I knew it well. My first task was to familiarise myself with the way *Wisden* worked, and the best way to do that was by reading it. However, as anyone who has picked up a *Wisden* will tell you, you are lost from the moment your eyes first flicker over the pages.

"The chief joy of reading *Wisden*," Rowland Ryder wrote in his 1965 Almanack article, "The Pleasures of Reading *Wisden*", "is also the chief snare – once you have picked up a copy you cannot put it down." Familiar names leap from the page, names that are familiar even if you don't follow cricket all that closely. Something quirky usually catches the eye; *Wisden* can be delightfully idiosyncratic. Browse through the schools section of earlier *Wisdens*, say, and you'll find the name of a best-selling novelist or an Oscar-winning director, a rugby or soccer international or a politician; even a cricket writer or two. Matthew Arnold's edict begins to have a resonance. To get the most out of *Wisden*, it helps to know more of the world than the world of *Wisden*. With a few extra-parochial interests, *Wisden* becomes more than a cricket book; it becomes entertaining; an amusement.

Like cricket itself, *Wisden* is an English institution. That doesn't mean it has to be taken unduly seriously – or, for that matter, that it should take itself too seriously. It deserves to be respected for what it sets out to do, for what it achieves and for what it means to the tens of thousands who buy it every year. But it's also a book to savour, whether for its writing, the memories it fires or the reminiscences it inspires. It can be history, both social history and cricket history – and for those who understand such things there are numbers and statistics to configure and refigure. Generations of schoolboys and schoolgirls, to the consternation of editors, have added, subtracted, multiplied and divided score-cards in an attempt to prove that *Wisden*, along with Homer, has nodded. One editor became so exasperated at letters pointing out that a county's averages didn't tally with the figures in its score-cards that he requested the headmaster of the school concerned to supervise his young charges better during prep. Then again, think what *Wisden* was doing for their arithmetic.

Scorecards and averages don't feature much in this collection. The intention is to give a taste of *Wisden* through its writing. That's how its style has developed; it's how editors have stamped their imprint; and it's where *Wisden*'s humour resides, whether intentionally or unintentionally. Some of the irony is certainly unintentional, the irony coming only with the years. Take, for example, Sir H. D. G. Leveson Gower's 1937 recollection of his time as Oxford captain in 1896.

> During the lunch interval on the last day, when I was none too happy of our prospects of victory – three good wickets were down for just over 70 – this spectator approached me and said, "I'm afraid Oxford's prospects of victory are very poor. What do you think?" My answer, given rather abruptly, was "We shall win all right." "What?" said my interrogator, "are you sure? I have been laid 8 to 1 against Oxford, shall I take it?" "Certainly," I said, anxious to get away from this rather adhesive person. Ten days afterwards I received a registered envelope with a sapphire pin enclosed – and the following letter: "Thank you so much for your very valuable information. I collected a very nice sum but I knew it was a certainty as it came from 'The Horse's Mouth'."

All jolly innocent; a cameo of an era when cricket and betting were carefree bedfellows – or so we were taught to believe. One hundred years on, Australians Shane Warne and Mark Waugh received considerably more than a sapphire pin for their off-the-record information to a betting man – and were handsomely fined for their troubles by the Australian Cricket Board. Hard to imagine a latter-day "Shrimp" Leveson Gower being so forthright in his admission. The good lord Condon and his cohorts would be on his case in the time it takes the ICC to cobble together an email. Post-Cronje, "information" has become virtually synonymous with match-fixing, sad to say.

History, if not strictly repeating itself, has a happy knack of coming round again with minimal variations. It is one more reason why a consistent, independent book of record is so important. Cricket has never been backward when it comes to controversies, and *Wisden* has dealt with them courageously both in the present and for posterity. John Wisden can't have known what he was setting in motion with his "little wonder" of 112 pages in 1864, but subsequent editions have left successive editors in no doubt of their responsibility to the Almanack and to the game it records so diligently.

EDITORS OF WISDEN, 1864–2004

W. H. Crockford* and W. H. Knight*	1864–1869
W. H. Knight*	1870–1879
George H. West*	1880–1886
Charles F. Pardon	1887–1890
Sydney H. Pardon	1891–1925
C. Stewart Caine	1926–1933
Sydney J. Southerton	1934–1935
Wilfrid H. Brookes	1936–1939
Haddon Whitaker	1940–1943
Hubert Preston	1944–1951
Norman Preston	1952–1980
John Woodcock	1981–1986
Graeme Wright	1987–1992, 2001–2002
Matthew Engel	1993–2000, 2004–
Tim de Lisle	2003

* *Exact dates and roles unconfirmed.*

ACKNOWLEDGEMENTS

In the Preface to the 1904 *Wisden*, editor Sydney Pardon names just ten men as having a share in the compilation of his 682-page Almanack. By 2004 the List of Contributors is a veritable roll-call, running to more than 250 men and women, possibly boys and girls, with the editor acting as Chief of the General Staff. Named or not, the contributors over 141 editions have made *Wisden* possible. By extension, this *Wisden Collection* would not have seen the light of day without them.

Certainly my fondest memory of editing *Wisden* remains the enthusiasm and generosity of everyone who contributed in whatever way to the Almanack, their friendship and the pride they took in being part of something unique. As I compiled this book, I realised they were maintaining a long tradition of the sung and unsung. In recognising the importance of this tradition, I also acknowledge with humility as well as thanks everyone since 1864 whose affection for cricket and *Wisden* has kept the Almanack alive for each new generation to taste, savour, collect and, yes, contribute to.

Graeme Wright
July 2004

NOTES: The edition of *Wisden Cricketers' Almanack* from which an extract has been taken is indicated by the year that appears either above the extract, or alongside its heading or the name of its author.

In tables and other statistics, an asterisk next to a score denotes not out.

JOHN WISDEN

1885

John Wisden, born at Brighton, September 5th, 1826, died April 5th, 1884.

A splendid all-round cricketer in his day: a good bat, a fine field, and as a bowler unsurpassed. A quiet, unassuming, and thoroughly upright man. A fast friend and a generous employer. Beloved by his intimates and employees, and respected by all with whom he came into contact.

As a given man in the North v South match of 1850, John Wisden performed the unrivalled feat in a first-class contest of clean bowling the whole of his opponents [the South] in their second innings. As an instructor of our national game he was most successful, and during the time he was cricket tutor at Harrow the school team were never beaten by Eton.

In 1852, in conjunction with James Dean, he formed the United All England Eleven, and in 1859, with George Parr, took a team of cricketers to Canada and the United States, and thus inaugurated a movement which has had a most important bearing on the prosperity of the game.

In 1855, in partnership with Frederick Lillywhite, he established the cricket outfitting business which for so many years was conducted by him personally, and which is now carried on by those who managed it for many years and enjoyed his fullest confidence. In 1857 he was appointed secretary to the Cricketers' Fund Friendly Society, and continued to act in that capacity until his death.

In 1864 he issued the first number of the "Cricketers' Almanack", a very primitive production consisting of scores only, but which, thanks to the enthusiasm of subsequent editors, has now been accorded the title of "the most accurate and authentic record of the game" published.

John Wisden was one of the smallest of men who have become famous as cricketers, his height being but 5ft 4½in, and his weight in his prime being only seven stone. Owing to his diminutive size, and prowess as a cricketer, he earned the sobriquet of "The Little Wonder".

by Sir Spencer Ponsonby Fane, 1913

I knew Jack Wisden very well and played with or against him for about ten years in the important matches of those days, for which I was able to get away from the Foreign Office, such as Gentlemen and Players, North and South, Kent and England, etc. He was a very fine and accurate bowler, perfect length, but with little work, except what the ground gave it. He was a fast medium, but I think he was classed as a fast bowler – and played on that side in the match, Fast v Slow.

He was a delightful bowler to play against, but required very careful watching, for he was apt to send in occasionally a very fast shooter, then so fatal on Lord's ground. I have no recollection of his bowling a "yorker", called a "Tice" in those days – a mode of attack not in vogue at the time. I believe he was the first of the players to play in a straw hat, instead of the white topper worn by the older players. He was a good field, and an excellent bat, which was rather exceptional for a bowler at that time, when bowlers were not expected to be very able performers with the bat. He was a genial, pleasant and respectable fellow in every way, liked and respected by every one with whom he came in contact.

THE WISDEN WOODCUT

The Wisden woodcut, with its two nineteenth-century cricketers in tall beaver hats, first appeared on the cover of *Wisden Cricketers' Almanack* in 1938. Since then it has become not only the Almanack's but also John Wisden & Co Ltd's trademark, recognisable wherever cricket is played and followed. Not always as well known, or appreciated, is that the woodcut is the work of an especially gifted English artist, Eric Ravilious.

Ravilious studied at the Royal College of Art in the early 1920s – Paul Nash was one of his tutors – and initially worked as a wood engraver. As his reputation grew, so too his techniques became more diverse, embracing lithography, decorative designs for glass, ceramics and textiles, and water-colours. The mid-1930s saw Ravilious begin his series of patterns for Wedgwood; with the outbreak of World War II he became an official war artist. He was killed, aged thirty-nine, on a Coastal Command reconnaissance flight over Iceland in September 1942.

The flattened circle containing the two cricketers is a feature of Ravilious's wood engravings. So is the hint of nostalgia in the evocation of cricket's rural origins, a reminder that Ravilious was an essentially English artist. "Provincially English" was how David Gentleman described Ravilious's outlook in a *Times* article on him in November 2002. But there is more to the Wisden woodcut than nostalgia; it is also emblematic. It represents the traditions and values of cricket that *Wisden* upholds and continues through the standard of its writing, reporting and recording.

"Sixty years after his death," Gentleman wrote, "Ravilious's work wears very well. It was admirably wide-ranging . . ."

As is the Almanack adorned by his woodcut.

BALL AND BRUSH 2003

Lawrence Toynbee mixed his playing experience as a cricketer with his artist's gift for conveying the movement and spirit of sport in an acclaimed series of cricket paintings. These include *Hit to Leg*, *Cricket at Canterbury* and *Cricket in The Parks*, all of which may be viewed at Lord's, and *The Nursery End at Lord's*. Toynbee, a lively medium-fast bowler from his days in the Ampleforth XI, knew The Parks well. He had been Oxford's leading wicket-taker in 1942, when he gained a wartime blue, and was disappointed not to be given a chance to play first-class cricket on his post-war return to Oxford to train at the Ruskin School of Drawing. Perhaps an Oxford side flush with former servicemen was circumspect about the accuracy of a fast bowler whose tank had reputedly taken out a French cow and run over a wounded British soldier.

CLASSROOM TO
COUNTY GROUND

He was a comic-book hero, the stuff of *Boy's Own* stories. The school crack called from the classroom to play for – and ultimately, of course, save – the county. Nor was he simply the fantasy of a writer's imagination. Writers could draw on real-life precedents that *Wisden* had been recording since its earliest editions.

The 1873 Almanack reports the visit of MCC and Ground to Norwich to play Norfolk and Norwich Club, and tells how "the feature with the ball was the bowling of young Mr Davies – a lad not seventeen years old – who bowled 47 [four-ball] overs for 47 runs and six MCC wickets – four 'bowled'. His fellow students of the Grammar School were so elated at their comrade's success that they hoisted him shoulder high and carried him in triumph round the ground." So essential, that shoulder-high circuit of the ground. No comic-book story could end without it.

Today's schoolboy is most likely to play out his *Boy's Own* moment – assuming he gets the chance at all – in front of family and a handful of county members who wouldn't know him from Adam or the Australian assassin with a Lithuanian passport. *Wisden* didn't even mention that Miles Robinson was still a Shrewsbury schoolboy when he opened the Sussex bowling in two 1947 Championship games. But then he didn't take a wicket, and elsewhere in the relevant Almanack E. M. Wellings, the schools correspondent, decreed that there was "no likelihood of him improving materially with his present style". Wellings was spot on. Robinson never played first-class cricket again.

As for Dunedin schoolboy Glenn Turner, not a mention in *Wisden* of his six games for Otago in 1964/65 (highest score 28). Mind you, given that he once spent a whole morning's session scoring just three runs, it's unlikely his schoolmates hung out at Carisbrook waiting for the shoulder-high circuit. They were more likely hanging ten at St Kilda, trying to impress the beach bunnies.

On the Asian subcontinent, youngsters are already playing Test cricket at an age when English schoolboys are more distracted by GCSEs, let alone by A levels. Not that *Wisden* divulges whether they attend school or not, preferring primly to caution that the ages of these boy cricketers "should be treated with extreme caution . . . owing to deficiencies in record-keeping" in countries such as Bangladesh and Pakistan.

No such deficiencies, one hopes, in the case of Karachi-born Owais Shah, whose age was given as seventeen when he made his debut for Middlesex in 1996. "When school commitments allowed," *Wisden* enthused, "he made five Championship appearances, with two fifties, and was taken to Australia by England A." Two fifties and not a mention of the shoulder-high circuit! The lads from Isleworth and Syon School must have been preoccupied down at the mall.

Sometimes, though, the romance has to be diluted with a dose of realism. Owais Shah didn't just drop into county cricket. He was groomed through an age-group process providing the stepping-stones to success. So, too, was an earlier Middlesex schoolboy, Ian Bedford, albeit in a less structured way. A pupil at Woodhouse Grammar School in Finchley, he too was seventeen, with another year of school ahead of him, when Championship-chasing Middlesex drafted him in to bowl his leg-breaks and googlies against Essex. Bedford responded with six for 134, Middlesex went on to take the title, and he finished the season second in their averages with 25 wickets at 19.36 apiece.

But, as the pragmatic Wellings points out in *Wisden*: "This was not really an example of a boy being rudely pitchforked into county cricket. For the previous three years Bedford had been carefully nursed by the wise men at Lord's, among whom Archie Fowler, the chief coach, and G. O. Allen should be mentioned. From the time he played his first game at Lord's, against the Cross Arrows three years before, he was groomed for bigger things. By 1947 he was by skill and temperament, which was surprisingly equable in such a young boy, ready for the trial that Middlesex gave him. I will say no more than that he was fully worthy of his success, which held out the very highest promise for the future. He has length, flight and spin; he has bowling brains, and I can see only one danger – that he will allow himself to be overworked before he is muscularly set."

As it happened, the promising future never came to fruition. Bedford played a few more games in 1948 and was disappointing in 1950 when he came back from National Service. That, in fact, might have been his lot in county cricket but in 1961, when Middlesex wanted an amateur as captain, he answered the committee's call and led the side for two seasons. In 1966, still only thirty-six, he collapsed while batting for Finchley in a club game at Buckhurst Hill and died on the way to hospital.

Looking at the schools cricket of 1947, the *Wisden* reader soon notices the centuries flowing from the bat of P. B. H. May of Charterhouse, the outstanding schoolboy batsman of his generation. Yet three years passed before he first played for Surrey. On the other hand, David Sheppard, who played alongside Peter May and Ian Bedford in the Lord's schools games, did turn out for Sussex that summer. Similarly, Colin Cowdrey played for Kent in his first summer out of school, 1950, but only with the same moderate return as Sheppard. No one doubted these were England cricketers to come; it's just that their headlines were still in the making, and *Wisden* mentioned their county appearances, if at all, only in passing.

The cricketers who follow made an immediate impression. Ian Bedford's debut is not included in this section, as it coincided with one of Denis Compton's hundreds and so may be found in the chapter entitled "The Summer of Centuries". In some instances the players had just left school, but by making their

name in their first summer out, it seems to me that they qualify as
going from classroom to county ground.

A LITTLE HELP FROM HIS FRIENDS 1976

In 1902/03 Arthur Ongley appeared for a Westland (New Zealand)
XXII against Lord Hawke's English team and captured eight wickets
for 36 in an innings of 69 with his leg-spinners. Sir Pelham Warner in
Cricket Across The Seas wrote, "Ongley, a boy of nineteen, who had
some coaching from Albert Trott, bowled slow right-hand with a
break both ways, the ball coming off the matting very quickly, but he
derived much assistance from his 16 fielders."

ARCHIE MacLAREN 1891
SUSSEX v LANCASHIRE

At Brighton, Thursday, Friday, Saturday, August 14, 15, 16, 1890.
The innings of Lancashire was mainly remarkable for the outstanding success of Mr A. C. MacLaren, the Harrow captain,
who made his first appearance in the county team and scored 108
in splendid style. It was probably quite without parallel for a
schoolboy to make over a hundred in his first important county
match, and he more than justified the high opinions that had
been formed of him in the contest between Eton and Harrow. He
made his 108 in two hours and ten minutes, without giving a
single chance, and hitting nine fours, six threes and 15 twos.

Sussex 86 (A. Watson three for 23, A. Mold six for 59) **and 100**
   (C. A. Smith 39; A. Watson five for 41, A. Mold four for 52).
Lancashire 248 (A. C. MacLaren 108, J. Briggs 54; G. L. Wilson four for
   47, W. A. Humphreys three for 42).

Archibald Campbell MacLaren (1871–1944) enjoyed a long career lasting altogether to 1923, during which he captained Lancashire and England, in 22 of his 35 Tests. "An immaculate batsman possessing the
grand manner, he would have gained still higher renown on the playing
field but for periods of poor health and the calls of business," said
Wisden 1945. "Expert knowledge, obtained by careful study of every
intricacy of the game, might have made him supreme as captain, but

he lacked the buoyant optimistic temperament so necessary for complete success in cricket and was easily upset by disagreement with selectors in being given players whom he did not consider suitable to the occasion." MacLaren's 424 for Lancashire against Somerset at Taunton in 1895 was the highest first-class score until W. H. Ponsford's 429 in 1922/23.

SAMMY DAY 1898
GLOUCESTERSHIRE v KENT

At Cheltenham, Monday, Tuesday, Wednesday, August 9, 10, 11, 1897. For two days this game was extremely well contested, but on Wednesday Gloucestershire gained the upper hand and won by 63 runs. There was some capital batting, but everything was dwarfed by the remarkable performance of the Malvern schoolboy, S. H. Day, who was playing his first county match. In making his 101 not out, he was at the wicket for three hours without giving a chance and hit 11 fours. But for him, Kent would have cut a sorry figure in their second innings.

Gloucestershire 205 (R. W. Rice 57, A. G. Richardson 51; W. Wright three for 28) **and 249** (W. G. Grace 58, H. Wrathall 32; F. Martin three for 60, J. R. Mason four for 49).

Kent 190 (S. H. Day 8, H. C. Stewart 64; G. L. Jessop three for 71, C. L. Townsend three for 49, W. S. A. Brown four for 39) **and 201** (S. H. Day 101 not out, F. Marchant 37; G. L. Jessop three for 41, C. L. Townsend four for 69).

Samuel Hulme Day (1878–1950) went on to win a blue in all four years at Cambridge, captaining them in 1901, and played for Kent until 1919. An excellent footballer, at inside-forward for the Corinthians, he won three England caps in 1906. His younger brother, Arthur, also played for Malvern and Kent.

REGGIE SPOONER 1900

While the breakdown of Briggs and Hallam cast something like a gloom over the Lancashire team last summer, the season had its brighter side in the discovery of two players of distinct promise. These cricketers were R. H. Spooner, the Marlborough captain,

and John Sharp, a good bowler who had previously been chiefly
known as an Association Football forward. [Right wing for
Everton, Sharp was capped by England at cricket and soccer.]
Spooner was not tried until the middle of August, but his first
appearance was almost as great a triumph as that of A. C.
MacLaren had been nine years previously. He had made scores
of 69 and 198 against Rugby [at Lord's], and followed these suc-
cesses with 158 for Lancashire second eleven against the Surrey
second eleven at Old Trafford. Naturally, this brilliant work
earned him a trial for Lancashire, and amply did he justify his
inclusion in the side, scoring 44 and 83 against Albert Trott and
J. T. Hearne. It was a disastrous match for Lancashire, but
Spooner covered himself with glory. A batsman possessed of a
splendid style and plenty of strokes he should have a great future
before him. It was the opinion of one famous veteran that he was
as good a bat as A. G. Steel when the great Cambridge cricketer
left Marlborough 22 years ago.

MIDDLESEX v LANCASHIRE

At Lord's, Thursday, Friday, Saturday, August 17, 18, 19, 1899.
Middlesex wound up their season at Lord's with a triumph,
beating Lancashire in the easiest fashion by ten wickets. There
were some sad failures in batting on the Lancashire side, but
R. H. Spooner, the Marlborough captain, made a brilliantly successful first appearance for the county and Albert Ward played a
very fine second innings. Spooner was batting an hour and 20
minutes for his 44 and less than two hours for his 83. Splendid
off-driving – very hard and always on the ground – was the great
feature of his cricket.

Middlesex 406 (P. F. Warner 78, F. J. G. Ford 71, C. M. Wells 59,
   G. MacGregor 61, extras 36; A. Mold six for 160) **and 42** for no wkt.
Lancashire 184 (R. H. Spooner 44; A. E. Trott eight for 91) **and 262**
   (R. H. Spooner 83, A. Ward 83 not out, extras 40; A. E. Trott four for
   77, F. J. G. Ford six for 56).

Reginald Herbert Spooner (1880–1961), a tall and stylish opening
batsman, epitomised the classical amateur of cricket's Edwardian

golden age. "There was nothing ferocious or brutal in Spooner's bats-manship," Sir Neville Cardus wrote. "It was all courtesy and breeding." *Wisden* said: "He drove with special skill to the off, often at the expense of fast bowlers, and strong wrists enabled him to invest his strokes with surprising power when playing back." Spooner played for Lancashire between 1899 and 1921, and in ten Tests for England, but service in the Boer War and business commitments restricted his first-class career. As elegant a centre-threequarter as he was batsman, he also played rugby for England.

FREDDY KNOTT 1911
by C. Toppin

The doings of the Tonbridge XI centre almost entirely around that wonderful cricketer, F. H. Knott. Seldom, if ever, have the doings of a schoolboy caused so much interest in the cricket world. An aggregate of over 1,100 runs, containing six centuries, for his school season, with an average of 80, and a jump straight into the strongest county side of the year, where he was not on mere trial, but seemed rather indispensable to its success, would seem to predict that some day in the near future he will take his place among the giants of the game. He appears to have most of the known strokes at his command, but the two points, which I consider are the strongest features of his play, are his watchful-ness and the strength of his back play. He seems to be one of very few batsmen who nowadays, in playing back, attempt to force the ball past the bowler to the boundary. His future as a cricketer will be a matter of great interest.

KENT v WORCESTERSHIRE

At Dover, Monday, Tuesday, August 15, 16, 1910. The outstand-ing feature of this return engagement was the remarkable batting triumph of F. H. Knott, the Tonbridge schoolboy, who, only introduced into county cricket a week previously, succeeded on the occasion of his third appearance for Kent in putting together a delightful innings of 114. The young cricketer, playing with admirable skill and confidence, obtained his score in two hours and a quarter without, so far as could be seen, giving a chance.

He drove finely on each side of the wicket and got the ball away cleverly on the leg side. He and Humphreys, after Worcestershire had given a very tame display, made 160 for the first Kent wicket in an hour and three-quarters.

Worcestershire 120 (A. Fielder three for 30, C. Blythe three for 36) **and 171** (F. Pearson 32, H. K. Foster 30; D. W. Carr four for 38).

Kent 310 (F. H. Knott 114, E. Humphreys 66, C. V. L. Hooman 55; R. D. Burrows four for 105, E. G. Arnold five for 91).

Frederick Hammett Knott (1891–1972) failed to win a blue in his freshman year at Oxford in 1911 but did so in his next three years and was captain in 1914 when, *Wisden* 1915 said, "He captained a winning side against Cambridge and at the most critical part of the match played with admirable skill and nerve. His whole career at Oxford was, of course, a sad disappointment ... the hopes of his schooldays have never been fulfilled." The outbreak of World War I and an eye problem meant he played no more county cricket for Kent. His brother, C. H. Knott, followed him to Tonbridge, Oxford and Kent and, as master-in-charge of cricket at Tonbridge, had a significant say in the development of the young Colin Cowdrey.

WILFRED TIMMS 1922
NORTHAMPTONSHIRE v ESSEX

At Northampton, Saturday, Monday, Tuesday, June 11, 13, 14, 1921. Only on one other occasion in the season did Northamptonshire show such batting form and, though overwhelmed on the first day and compelled to follow on against a huge balance of 381, they avoided defeat in splendid style. The honours were divided by Haywood and the young public school batsman, W. W. Timms. Haywood hit 15 fours in his 132 and, so far as could be seen, gave no chance. Timms, who was taking part in his second county match, had the luck to be missed at backward point at the start of play on the third morning, but apart from this and another chance when 43 he played extraordinarily well. His success delighted the crowd, and at the end of the game he was carried off the field shoulder-high by his fellow schoolboys. He was batting five hours and three-quarters.

Essex 604 for seven dec. (A. C. Russell 108, J. R. Freeman 286, P. A. Perrin 77, G. Carter 44, J. G. Dixon 49, extras 33; C. N. Woolley four for 90).

Northamptonshire 223 (W. W. Timms 23, G. J. Thompson 69, K. G. Ball 49; J. G. Dixon three for 53, P. Toone four for 96, A. D. Martin three for 43) **and 445** for five (C. N. Woolley 50, R. A. Haywood 132, W. W. Timms 154 not out, G. J. Thompson 58, extras 33).

Wilfred Walter Timms (1902–1986), captain of Northampton Grammar School in 1921, had been given leave by the school to play for Northamptonshire in their home games against Kent and Essex. Later that season he played for the county during the summer holidays, on occasion captaining the side, and he continued to play for them until 1932 when his schoolteaching duties allowed. He taught Spanish and French, and was master-in-charge of cricket at Charterhouse from 1932 to 1946. "He was of great assistance to me in developing the basics of my batting," Peter May wrote in *Wisden* 1987.

DENYS WILCOX 1930
MIDDLESEX v ESSEX

At Lord's, Wednesday, Thursday, August 14, 15, 1929. Quite the feature of the opening day was the batting of D. R. Wilcox, a Dulwich boy, who had met with marked success in a Schools' match the previous week [scoring 78 for The Rest against Lord's Schools]. Wilcox went in at a most anxious moment, Essex having lost four wickets for 25 and Russell being disabled. He rose to the occasion in great style, settling down to such a sound, yet punishing, game that he remained for an hour and three-quarters and, chiefly by driving and pulling, made 71 out of 120. Middlesex obtained 81 for three wickets, but then H. T. O. Smith, a fast-medium bowler associated with the Midland Bank, disposed of Mann, D. Russell and Robins in four balls. Hendren, however, was seen at his best and in their second innings the Essex batting against Peebles was strangely weak. Middlesex knocked off the 121 runs for victory in 95 minutes, H. E. Carris, an Old Millhillian, showing both freedom and power.

Essex 152 (D. R. Wilcox 71; T. J. Durston three for 32) **and 165** (H. W. F. Franklin 77, D. R. Wilcox 11; I. A. R. Peebles five for 56).

Middlesex 197 (H. W. Lee 38, E. H. Hendren 89, G. E. Hart 33;
  H. T. O. Smith four for 50, J. O'Connor three for 43) **and 123** for four
  (H. E. Carris 67 not out).

Denys Robert Wilcox (1910–1953) became an important influence on the development of young cricketers before his early death at forty-two, both as headmaster of Alleyn Court prep school at Westcliff-on-Sea and as a coach. With Trevor Bailey, one of his former pupils, he wrote *Cricketers in the Making*, which drew on his involvement with the Essex coaching scheme. Sadly he did not live to savour the literary success of another pupil, John Fowles, a contemporary and friend of Bailey, whose novels include *The Collector*, *The Magus*, *Daniel Martin* and *The French Lieutenant's Woman*. A stylish right-hand bat, Wilcox had first played for the county in 1928, and on going up to Cambridge he won his blue from 1931 to 1933, being captain in his last year. Although teaching duties subsequently limited his opportunities for first-class cricket, he was joint-captain of Essex from 1933 to 1939, and in 1946 he shared in an Essex eighth-wicket record partnership of 263 with Reg Taylor.

TREVOR BAILEY 1943

The discovery of an all-rounder of high class in T. E. Bailey, the Dulwich College captain, tempered the misfortunes of Essex. Born at Westcliff, Bailey came under the notice of D. R. Wilcox when at school, and the forecast of the Essex captain that the youth would go far was justified by his debut in first-class company at Lord's. His fast and accurate bowling for Middlesex-Essex against noted opponents in the Kent-Surrey team earned considerable praise. Bailey also bowled remarkably well in opposition to well-known players in a charity match at Chichester, where he clean bowled five of six victims. He joined the Royal Marines at the end of the season.

MIDDLESEX AND ESSEX v KENT AND SURREY

At Lord's, August 3, 4, 1942. Drawn. A splendid match, worthy of the players engaged, produced much fine cricket, sensational incidents, and a finish that compensated for the inconclusive result which came after a glorious effort to snatch victory. Trevor Bailey, the Dulwich College captain, put enthusiasm into a Bank Holiday crowd of 22,000 people – 16,693 paid for admission – by dismissing three batsmen in his first over. G. O. Allen gave way at 33 to Bailey, whose second ball beat Bennett; Ames hit a three to the on, but the seventh delivery got Bridger leg-before and the next sent Todd's middle stump flying. Ames prevented Bailey doing the hat-trick. Carefully nursed by G. O. Allen, Bailey resumed after lunch and bowled Bedser.

Kent and Surrey 193 (Flt-Lieut L. E. G. Ames 34, Major E. R. T. Holmes 39, Sgt T. G. Evans 55; Sgt Instr M. S. Nichols four for 47, T. E. Bailey four for 36) **and 277** for six dec. (J. R. Bridger 41, Major E. R. T. Holmes 114 not out; T. E. Bailey two for 42).

Middlesex and Essex 281 (Cpl S. M. Brown 58, Sqdrn-Ldr W. J. Edrich 46, PC L. H. Compton 33, Sgt Instr M. S. Nichols 51, T. E. Bailey 0; Sgt A. V. Bedser four for 72, Sgt F. G. Pierpoint four for 42) **and 186** for four (Cpl S. M. Brown 34, Sqdrn-Ldr W. J. Edrich 73, Sgt Instr D. C. S. Compton 57).

Trevor Edward Bailey (1923–) fulfilled all his early promise. Even "Bailey batted 80 minutes for a painstaking 40" for F. M. McRae's XI v Cross Arrows in *Wisden* 1943 adumbrated his legendary back-to-the-wall innings for England, the most famous of which came against Australia at Lord's in 1953 when he batted four and a quarter hours for 71 to save a seemingly hopeless cause. "There was something faintly improbable about Bailey's appearance when he first came on the scene," John Woodcock wrote in *Wisden* 1969. "His hair was almost too curly; his gestures were elaborately histrionic; his run-up seemed unnecessarily long; his approach was fastidiously anatomical." He played for Essex from 1946 to 1967, captained them with skill and imagination, and in 61 appearances for England became the fourth player from any country to score 2,000 runs and take 100 wickets in Tests. He was cricket correspondent of the *Financial Times* and a member of the BBC *Test Match Special* commentary team.

STATISTICIAN'S NIGHTMARE 1978

Alfred Samuel Bensimon had a short but very interesting first-class career. He played a single match for Western Province in 1931/32, making his debut at the advanced age of forty-five, and he played three more matches for them in 1933/34 when he was over forty-seven. He was the captain on these three occasions and bowled his leg-breaks so effectively that he took 17 wickets for only 177 runs. These four matches constituted his whole first-class career. As it happened Bensimon proved a statistician's nightmare, for his younger brother, Abel, had the identical initials, A. S., and he made his first-class debut in 1912/13, 20 years before his elder brother; his career ended in 1923/24. Not surprisingly, it was assumed that they were one and the same person.

DAVID BAIRSTOW 1971
YORKSHIRE v GLOUCESTERSHIRE

At Bradford, June 3, 4, 5, 1970. Gloucestershire won by nine wickets [and] gained their first Championship victory in Yorkshire since 1947. Yorkshire suffered their third successive Championship defeat. David Bairstow, an eighteen-year-old schoolboy, on the second day of his Championship debut, took his A level examinations at 7 a.m. by special arrangement and later held four catches at the wicket in an innings, but there was little other satisfaction for Yorkshire.

Yorkshire 267 (B. Leadbeater 70, P. J. Sharpe 62, D. L. Bairstow 15, C. M. Old 34; M. J. Procter six for 38) **and 152** (G. Boycott 45, J. H. Hampshire 42, D. L. Bairstow 2; D. A. Allen three for 43, M. Bissex five for 34).

Gloucestershire 304 (D. M. Green 69, M. Bissex 53, M. J. Procter 35, D. R. Smith 38; C. M. Old three for 92, A. G. Nicholson three for 84, D. Wilson three for 59) **and 116** for one (R. B. Nicholls 79 not out).

David Leslie Bairstow (1951–1998) remained Yorkshire's wicket-keeper until 1990, by which time he had made 1,099 dismissals in first-class cricket, along with 13,961 runs, and equalled the world record of 11 catches in a match (Yorkshire v Derbyshire, Scarborough, 1982). "His fighting qualities overrode any technical deficiencies," *Wisden* 1998 recorded: "He was at his best when batting in one-day games when victory was improbable but just short of impossible." "Bluey" Bairstow played in four Tests and 21 one-day internationals for England.

MARK RAMPRAKASH 1988

Nobody with [Middlesex's] future at heart wanted to overpraise Mark Ramprakash, who made his debut at seventeen in the first match, but he entranced watchers with his exquisite, powerful strokes. Next day he was back at college. After term, however, there were more glowing innings, plus the inevitable ducks. "Do not burden him with expecting too much," Gatting asked, but it must be recorded that Ramprakash displayed the strokes and authority of Gatting at a similar age.

MIDDLESEX v YORKSHIRE

At Lord's, April 25, 26, 27, 1987. Yorkshire won by two wickets ... Middlesex, 45 for two at the second-day close, were taken out of trouble by Roseberry and Ramprakash, whose hundred partnership was laced with boundaries. Ramprakash hit one six and seven fours off 99 balls and made a glowing impression on his first-class debut. Then it was back to school the following day for the seventeen-year-old, who had come in because of injuries to Gatting, Radley and Butcher.

Middlesex 292 for seven dec. (W. N. Slack 84, A. J. T. Miller 69,
    M. R. Ramprakash 17, P. R. Downton 59 not out; P. W. Jarvis three for
    44, P. Carrick three for 41) **and 198** for five dec. (M. R. Ramprakash 63
    not out, M. A. Roseberry 52; A. Sidebottom four for 54).
Yorkshire 227 (K. Sharp 56, D. L. Bairstow 34; J. E. Emburey four for 38)
    and 267 for eight (M. D. Moxon 30, R. J. Blakey 44, K. Sharp 75,
    A. Sidebottom 32 not out; P. H. Edmonds three for 85, A. R. C. Fraser
    three for 55).

Mark Ravin Ramprakash (1969–) played for Middlesex until 2000, including three seasons as captain, then crossed the Thames to join Surrey. His picture-perfect strokeplay in county cricket elicited comparisons with past masters, but an intensity of personality rarely allowed

his talents full rein in his 52 Tests for England. "There was compensation in the form of an emotional and redemptive maiden Test century
from Mark Ramprakash," *Wisden* reported on the Fifth Test between
West Indies and England in 1997/98. "Coming after 37 innings in his 21
previous Tests had produced only three fifties, his virtuoso 154 proved
once and for all that he is capable of reproducing his dominant county
form for England. It also transformed him from a fringe player into an
outside bet as Atherton's successor [as England captain]." In the event
it was not to be, and there was only one other Test hundred to counter
further disappointments.

TWINNING 1982

Alec Bedser, who died in June 1981, aged 33, in a motor accident in
Johannesburg, was a right-arm medium-pace bowler who played for
Border in the Currie Cup in 1971/72. Like his twin brother, Eric (they
were named after the famous English cricketing twins), Alec was a
distinguished all-round sportsman. Another car accident, several
years earlier, had curtailed his cricket career.

CRICKET ON ICE

1880

All England will remember, with a shiver and a shudder, the long, sad, and severe winter of 1878/79, commencing, as it did in October '78, and continuing – with more or less severity – up to the middle of May '79; and even then the cold, nipping, bronchitis-creating winds seemed loth to leave the land they had so sorely stricken with distress, disease and death. But there is no black cloud without its silver lining, and one bright spot in this dark winter was that its severity and length enabled more

CRICKET MATCHES ON THE ICE

to be played than were ever before played in the course of one winter. In chronicling the following matches played on the ice in the winter of 1878/79, the compiler wishes it to be understood that the summary does *not* comprise *all* the matches so played, but only those kindly brought to his notice by correspondents, or extracted from the newspapers; and he regrets that he is unable to give space for the full scores of several of these matches.

[The 12 matches recorded by *Wisden* included the following.]

CRICKET MATCH ON THE ICE BY MOONLIGHT

About the time Lord Harris's team were playing one of their matches under the bright and burning sun of an Australian summer, an English team were playing their game in the dear old country at home under the bright and brilliant beams of the new year's full moon.

This match by moonlight came about this wise. The moon was full on the 8th of January, shining with unclouded and truly splendid brightness throughout that evening and night. At the same time a sharp, keen, thoroughly old-fashioned frost was setting the ice in capital form for skating and other icy pastimes. The next day being bright, frosty and fine, the skating cricketers of the royal borough of Windsor duly announced that

> *"A Cricket Match would by played by Moonlight on the Ice in Windsor Home Park at 7 o'clock that evening."*

Consequently several hundred spectators assembled, and the match *was played by moonlight*. "The game (says the chronicler) caused no end of amusement owing to the difficulties encountered by the players while bowling, batting and fielding."

Mr Bowditch's Side (*only nine men batted*) 15; Mr Gage's Side (*ten men batted*) 17.

CHESTERFIELD v SHEFFIELD

Played on the Ice on a Dam near Brampton, January 22, 1879. About one thousand people assembled to witness this match, which was played on the understanding that when a man had made 25 runs he was to retire. The Sheffield men had much the best of the battle when "time" was called; but as William Mycroft, H. Charlwood, J. Rowbotham and other celebrated cricketers played, it will be more satisfactory to give the score; here it is:

Chesterfield 113 (H. R. J. Charlwood 25, C. H. Trown 25; J. Rowbotham 4 wkts).

Sheffield 125 for seven (S. Blyde 25, R. Gillott 25, W. Shearstone 25, J. Rowbotham 25).

LORD HENRY NEVILL'S SIDE v MR WILLIAMS' SIDE

Played on the Ice at Eridge Castle, Kent, February 1, 1879. The Marquis of Abergavenny, with that considerate courtesy characteristic of his race, had the gates of his park thrown open to all who chose to enter and witness the grand *Fête* on the frozen water of the great lake at his lordship's seat – Eridge Castle. The Marquis and a distinguished company were present, and some 2,000 other visitors assembled, who appeared to heartily enjoy the jolly games of hockey, played at one end of the lake, and cricket at the other. As to the cricket match both captains were (as captains should be) well in front of their men, Lord Henry Nevill taking the lead with 70 not out – pronounced by the critics "A remarkably good innings, his lordship having been frequently applauded for the dexterity he displayed, and the command he evinced over skates and bat." But Mr Williams ran a close second to his lordship, both as to skill on skates and run-getting, for he scored an innings of 68 in good form; and if it could have been played out to the pleasant end, the game would doubtless have had a most interesting finish, for when the early darkness stopped play Mr Williams' side had two wickets to fall, with only 53 runs to make to win.

Lord H. Nevill's Side 228 (Stephenson 49, Lord H. Nevill 70 not out;
   Mr Stafford 3 wkts).
Mr E. S. Williams' Side 176 for eight, including five run outs
   (E. S. Williams 68).

This was the last match played on the ice in that terribly severe and distressing winter, for on the following day (Sunday, February 2) a rapid thaw set in, continuing throughout the Monday; and although winter and rough weather subsequently returned, and discomfortingly continued with us up to the middle of May, there was no further frost sufficiently severe to form and fix ice capable of playing cricket on; and so, with Lord Henry Nevill's match at Eridge Park, was ended the never-to-be-forgotten CRICKET ON THE ICE SEASON of 1878/79.

TALENT SPOTTING

"If not for every taste," Robert Shelton wrote in the *New York Times* in 1961, "his music-making has the mask of originality and inspiration, all the more noteworthy for his youth. Mr Dylan is vague about his antecedents and birthplace, but it matters less where he has been than where he is going, and that would seem to be straight up."

If you're going to pick 'em, pick winners. Maybe Shelton was hedging his bet a shade with "would seem to be" instead of "is". But as Bob Dylan and the decades rolled on in anything but harmony, Shelton could have dined on that notice without having to eat his words.

Wisden's correspondents also knew a talent when they saw it. And like Shelton, as Almanacks over the years record, they had the confidence to back their intuition in print. To paraphrase Kenneth Tynan, you don't have to be able to drive the car to know the way.

Not that *Wisden* always encouraged crystal-gazing. After all, as Bob Dylan put it in one of his *Blonde on Blonde* tracks, "Time will tell, just who fell, and who's been left behind." But then, at the start, John Wisden didn't encourage any comment at all. "We of course make no comments upon the matches," his first editor wrote in 1864, "leaving the cricketer to form his own opinion with regard to the merits of the men, since a great many of our readers are at least equal, if not superior, to ourselves in arriving at a right judgment of the play."

It does mean we're given only the scorecard of W. G. Grace's first match at Lord's, three days after his sixteenth birthday. But in the long run, does it really matter? His half-century says it all. The rest, as they say, is history.

W. G. GRACE

William Gilbert Grace (1848–1915), Gloucestershire, London County and England.

First-class career 1865–1908.

	M	Runs	Avge	100s	Wkts	Avge	10w/m	5w/i	Ct/St
F/c	879	54,896	39.55	126	2,876	17.92	66	247	887/5
Test	22	1,098	32.29	2	9	26.22	–	–	39

Highest score: F/c 344   MCC v Kent, Canterbury, 1876.
              Test 170 England v Australia, The Oval, 1886.
Best bowling: F/c 10–49 MCC v Oxford University, Oxford, 1886.
              Test 2–12 England v Australia, Lord's, 1890.

by Sydney Pardon, 1916

Of Mr Grace's cricket from the time of his first appearance at Lord's in July 1864, for the South Wales Club against the MCC, down to the end of 1876, columns could be written without exhausting the subject. He was picked for the Gentlemen, as a lad of seventeen, both at Lord's and The Oval in 1865, the honour being conferred upon him quite as much for his medium-pace bowling as for his batting. A year later, however, he proved himself, beyond all question, the best batsman in England, two wonderful innings at The Oval establishing his fame. He was, in the main, quite orthodox in style, his bat being as perfectly straight as Fuller Pilch's, but he greatly enlarged the domain of orthodoxy, playing a far more aggressive and punishing game than any of the classic batsmen who came before him.

W. G. developed the art of batting to an extraordinary degree, but he was not, like [his brother] E. M., a revolutionist. There is his own authority for stating that he did not indulge in the pull till he was forty. A splendid all-round hitter, he excelled all his predecessors in his power of placing the ball on the on-side. When the wicket was difficult and the ball turning, Mr Grace

1865

At LORD's, July 21 and 22, 1864

South Wales Club

J. J. Sewell, Esq b Hearne	3	– c Winslow b Teape	3
E. M. Grace, Esq b Teape	0	– b Nixon	4
J. Lloyd, Esq c Nixon b Hearne	8	– c Royston b Hearne	5
W. G. Grace, Esq b Teape	50	– c Swain b Hearne	2
W. J. Price, Esq c and b Hearne	13	– b Hearne	26
F. R. Price, Esq b Hearne	27	– c Winslow b Hearne	4
Capt. Homfray lbw b Hearne . .	6	– b Hearne	5
Capt. R. Jones c Infelix			
b Hearne	65	– b Hearne	7
C. Bishop, Esq b Hearne	10	– not out	8
D. G. Davies, Esq b Nixon	2	– b Hearne	6
W. Crawshay, Esq not out	0	– b Nixon	7
Byes 12, l-b 12, w 3	27	Byes 2	2
	211		79

MCC and Ground

A. Infelix, Esq c F. R. Price			
b W. G. Grace	47	– not out	10
E. Ellis, Esq c Davies			
b E. M. Grace	16		
T. Hearne c and b F. R. Price . .	59	– not out	12
S. Teape, Esq b E. M. Grace . . .	13		
W. Swain b W. J. Price	23		
Viscount Royston c and			
b E. M. Grace	0		
Hon. G. Milles st Lloyd			
b E. M. Grace	4		
Marquis Bowmont			
b W. J. Price	11		
L. S. Winslow, Esq b W. J. Price	1		
S. P. Fraser, Esq st Lloyd			
b E. M. Grace			
H. Nixon not out	0	– run out	0
Byes 10, wide 1	11	Bye 1, wides 5	6
	186		28

Drawn.   Umpires – Fennell and G. Chatterton.

trusted for defence to that strong back play which, even in his
boyhood, convinced his people at home that he would be a
greater batsman than E. M. Mr Grace's batting from 1868
onwards quite overshadowed his bowling, and yet during his
career he took many hundreds of wickets. Indeed, old Bob
Thoms, the umpire, always contended that if he had not been
such a wonderful batsman he would have been the best slow
bowler in England. He bowled medium pace with a purely
round-arm action in his young days, but slackened his speed
about 1872.

His superb strength and health enabled him to stand any
amount of cricket, but in his best two years as a bowler – 1875
and 1877 – his batting fell off 50 per cent. He did not rely much
on break, only turning in a little from leg, but he had great command over his length and very seldom indeed pitched short. His
chief strength lay in head work. No one was quicker to find
out the weak points of a batsman or more certain to lure an
impetuous hitter to his doom. When he first appeared for the
Gentlemen, Mr Grace was a splendid outfield, capable of throwing the ball a hundred yards, but as time went on he took to
fielding near the wicket and for many years he had no superior at
point except his brother E. M.

by Lord Harris, 1916

I suppose it has been difficult for the present generation, who
have seen occasionally at Lord's or in some country match his
massive form, to realise that in the seventies he was a spare and
extremely active man. My old comrade, Mr C. K. Francis,
reminded me when we attended his funeral that in 1872, when
Mr Fitzgerald's team of Gentlemen visited Canada and the
United States, W. G.'s playing weight was no more than 12
stone 7 lbs.

HE AIN'T HARRY, HE'S MY BROTHER 1934

MIDDLESEX v SOMERSET

H. W. Lee c F. S. Lee b J. W. Lee . . . 82 – run out . . . 14

NOTE: London-born brothers, Harry, Jack and Frank Lee all played for Middlesex at one time, but the younger two, Jack and Frank, seeing no opening with the county, migrated to Somerset. Opening the batting for their adopted county, they once put up a hundred together three times in four days. Frank Lee, when his playing days were over, became a first-class umpire and stood in 29 Tests.

WILFRED RHODES

1899

Beyond everything else, the feature of Yorkshire's season was the discovery of Wilfred Rhodes. The enforced retirement from the eleven, under rather painful circumstances, of Robert Peel had left a splendid opening for a new slow bowler, and the hour brought forth the man. It was indeed a piece of great fortune for the Yorkshire executive to find exactly at the right moment the very bowler they wanted. Whatever he may do in the future, Rhodes proved himself last summer, as a left-handed slow bowler, the legitimate successor in the Yorkshire eleven to Peate and Peel. To say this is only to do him the barest justice, for as a matter of fact neither Peate nor Peel on first coming out made half such a sensation. To find an exact parallel to Rhodes's doings in this his opening season, one must go back to 1878 when Mr A. G. Steel, in his first year at Cambridge, jumped at once to the top of the tree.

Young, strong and possessing an easy natural action, which seems literally part of himself, Rhodes has everything in his favour. He was of course highly fortunate in getting a start on bad wickets, but it says much for his skill that he should have been able to take full advantage of his opportunities. His first match – against the MCC at Lord's – established him, and so long as the weather remained unsettled he never looked back, each succeeding game finding him more and more formidable. Naturally enough, when the hard wickets came, he was far less effective, but he nearly always bowled well and it was only on the rarest occasions that he met with anything like severe punishment. In the 26 county matches he took 126 wickets at a cost of less than 14 runs each – an astonishing record indeed. He was called upon to do far more work than any other bowler on the side, delivering 1,000 overs as against 747 by Haigh and 697 by Mr Jackson.

It was ill-naturedly suggested that if the summer had been a fine one all the way through, very little would have been heard of the new bowler, but we regard such criticisms as this as both shallow and ungenerous. Like all other slow bowlers, Rhodes is bound to do better in wet seasons than in dry ones, but we cannot think it possible he would have met with such success unless he had possessed first-rate ability. There is no bowler in England whose doings in 1899 will be watched with a more eager interest.

It was not alone as a bowler that Rhodes did good work for Yorkshire as, with eight not outs to help him, he came out seventh in the batting list with the capital average of 21. We have heard it said that in his local club he was more highly rated as a batsman than a bowler, and it is quite possible that, like Peel before him, he may develop into a great run-getter. It is to be hoped, however, that he will not improve his batting at the expense of his more valuable qualification for county cricket. Yorkshire's batting is nearly always strong, but a first-rate slow bowler is a pearl of price not often found.

Wilfred Rhodes (1877–1973), Yorkshire and England.
First-class career 1898–1930.

	M	Runs	Avge	100s	Wkts	Avge	10w/m	5w/i	Ct
F/c	1,107	39,802	30.83	58	4,187	16.71	68	287	764
Test	58	2,325	30.19	2	127	26.96	1	6	60

Highest score: F/c 267* Yorkshire v Leicestershire, Leeds, 1921.
                Test 179 England v Australia, Melbourne, 1911/12.
Best bowling: F/c 9–24 C. I. Thornton's England XI v Australians, Scarborough, 1899.
                Test 8–68 England v Australia, Melbourne, 1903/04.

by Sir Neville Cardus, 1974

Wilfred Rhodes was Yorkshire cricket personified in the great period of the county's domination, shrewd, dour, but quick to seize opportunity. When he was not playing for Yorkshire, in his spare time, so to say, he played for England. In his first Test match he was last in the batting order, and at Sydney in the 1903/04 rubber he took part in England's most persistent and prolific Test match last-wicket partnership to this day; he helped R. E. Foster to add 130 for the tenth wicket, his share 40 not out. Eight years afterwards he went in first for England at Melbourne, and against Australia he was the partner of Hobbs in the record first-wicket stand of 323. In 1902 he had gone in last for England at Kennington Oval when 15 runs were wanted to beat Australia; George Hirst, with whom he always opened Yorkshire's attack, was holding the wicket at the other end. England won by one wicket. Twenty-four years afterwards, Rhodes in his forty-ninth year was recalled to the England eleven and was one of the main causes of Australia's defeat and England's emergence from years in the wilderness.

He was a great player, one of the greatest in cricket's history, not only for his all-round performances denoted by the statisticians. He was great because his cricket was redolent and representative of Yorkshire county. In his old age he lost his eyesight and found his tongue. He accepted his affliction philosophically, and consoled himself by a flow of genial chatter never before heard from him.

JACK HOBBS
1906

A Cambridgeshire man by birth and the best bat for that county in 1904, Hobbs had duly qualified for Surrey by two years' residence and at the opening of the 1905 season it was known that a great deal was hoped of him. His early play exceeded all expectations and by the end of May he had established his reputation, his scoring for three or four weeks being extraordinary. It cannot be said that he kept up his form, but inasmuch as he made 1,004 runs in county matches alone he may fairly be regarded as the best professional batsman Surrey have brought forward in recent seasons. Easy and finished in style he is particularly strong on the on-side, scoring in front of short leg with great skill and certainty. His comparative falling off as the season advanced may have been due to the strain of having two first-class matches a week nearly the whole summer, but he certainly developed a tendency to play too much with his legs. He is a cricketer from whom a great deal may be expected, but he should endeavour to brighten up his fielding. Though a safe catch, he is not at present very quick on his feet.

Sir John Berry Hobbs (1882–1963), Surrey and England.
First-class career 1905–1934.

	M	Runs	Avge	100s	Wkts	Avge	5w/i	Ct
F/c	826	61,237	50.65	197	107	25.00	3	334
Test	61	5,410	56.94	15	1	165.00	–	17

Highest score: F/c 316*   Surrey v Middlesex, Lord's, 1926.
                Test 211   England v South Africa, Lord's, 1924.
Best bowling: F/c 7–56   Surrey v Oxford University, Oxford, 1911.
                Test 1–19 England v South Africa, Cape Town, 1909/10.

by Herbert Strudwick, 1964

On any type of wicket, he was the best batsman in my experience, a first-class bowler if given the chance, and the finest cover-point I ever saw. He never looked like getting out and he was just the same whether he made 100 or nought.

1964

Early in his career Hobbs fielded at third man and in the long-field, but he became a cover-point of universal renown for accuracy and speed. In 11 matches in Australia (1911/12) his returns to the wicket brought about the dismissal of 15 batsmen.

by Matthew Engel, 2000

Jack Hobbs scored more runs than anyone else in the history of first-class cricket: 61,237. He scored more centuries than anyone else, 197. Most astonishingly from a modern perspective, the last

98 came after his fortieth birthday. However, his career batting average is 50.65, which does not even put him in *Wisden*'s top fifty.

Only 16 of his hundreds were double-hundreds. One says "only" with trepidation, because just four men have surpassed that. But the figure does not remotely compare with Bradman's 37 or Walter Hammond's 36. Hobbs was not primarily interested in scoring runs for their own sake. For much of his career he would go in at the top of a strong Surrey batting order on good Oval pitches. His job was to get the innings started. He would frequently be out for a-hundred-and-few, and was content enough himself with 60 or 70, though he liked to please his friends who took such things more seriously. But there were other times, when wickets had fallen and the ball was flying: "That was the time you had to earn your living," he said. More than that, it was when he earned his undying reputation, his knighthood and his place as a Cricketer of the Century. He was never as dominant as Bradman; he never wanted to be. But his contemporaries were in awe of his ability to play supremely and at whim, whatever the conditions.

There was another aspect to his mastery. There seems no record of any unkindness in his make-up. He was neat and cor-rect and moral, yet never humourless (indeed, he was a renowned dressing-room joker). He shied away from the limelight without ever resenting it. More than anyone else, he lifted the status and dignity of the English professional cricketer.

FRANK WOOLLEY
1907

The colt, Woolley, deserves more than a passing notice. It was unfortunate that he had to be left out of some matches after he had established himself in the Kent team, but this was only an accident due to the super-abundance of capable players. Good as he already is, Woolley will no doubt, with increased physical strength, go far ahead of his first season's doings. It is quite possible that within two or three years he will be the best left-handed bat in England. Against Somerset at Gravesend, and Sur-rey at The Oval, he bowled uncommonly well, but as the summer advanced he was regarded more and more as a batsman. His bowling – slow to medium-pace left-hand – has evidently been modelled on that of Blythe.

Frank Edward Woolley (1887–1978), Kent and England.

First-class career 1906–1938.

	M	Runs	Avge	100s	Wkts	Avge	10w/m	5w/i	Ct
F/c	979	58,969	40.75	145	2,068	19.85	28	132	1,018
Test	64	3,283	36.07	5	83	33.91	1	4	64

Highest score: F/c 305* MCC v Tasmania, Hobart, 1911/12.
                    Test 154 England v South Africa, Manchester, 1929.
Best bowling: F/c 8–22 Kent v Gloucestershire, Maidstone, 1921.
                    Test 7–76 England v New Zealand, Wellington, 1929/30.

by Bob Arrowsmith, 1979

Frank Woolley was a slow left-arm bowler with a beautiful action and was at one time perhaps the best of his type in the world. He caught during his career far more catches than anyone else, except wicket-keepers, yet it is as a batsman that he is primarily remembered. Few now alive have seen a player who approached him in ease and grace, and his average rate of scoring has been exceeded only by Jessop and equalled by Trumper. His philosophy was to dominate the bowler. "When *I* am batting," he said, "*I* am the attack." This was made possible not only by his wonderful eye and sense of timing but by his range of strokes. He had every orthodox stroke at his command and no preference for one over another. Like W. G., he simply employed the one the occasion demanded. In defence, too, his back stroke, certainly in his maturer years, was a model of soundness.

All types of bowler came alike to him personally, but, if he saw his partner in trouble, he would make it his business to "settle" the bowler responsible. The feelings of an opposing captain on such occasions were succinctly expressed by Woodfull: "He made the game look so untidy." It appeared as if the wrong bowlers were on and the fieldsmen all in the wrong places. One can see why Woolley could be a far greater menace than players with higher averages. And if some statistically minded reader says,

"But wouldn't he have been a greater player had he exercised a bit more caution?" I am sure that all who saw him and, even more, all who played with him would answer firmly, "No."

WALLY HAMMOND
1924

Of far more importance in its bearing on the future was the fine form shown by Hammond – checked in 1922 by the discovery that he was not properly qualified for Gloucestershire. Here we have in all likelihood one of the best professional batsmen of the future. Irreproachable in style and not yet twenty-one years of age, Hammond has all the world before him, and there is no telling how far he may go. He led off in wonderful fashion last summer with scores of 110 and 92 against Surrey at Bristol. This exceptional standard he naturally could not keep up in later matches, but he finished with an aggregate of 1,300 runs and an average of 28. Honoured with an invitation to appear for the Players against the Gentlemen at The Oval, he scored 46 and 19, making an excellent impression.

Walter Reginald Hammond (1903–1965), Gloucestershire and England.
First-class career 1920–1951.

	M	Runs	Avge	100s	Wkts	Avge	10w/m	5w/i	Ct/St
F/c	634	50,551	56.10	167	732	30.58	3	22	819/3
Test	85	7,249	58.45	22	83	37.80	–	2	110

Highest score: F/c $\Big\}$ 336* England v New Zealand, Auckland, 1932/33.
Test

Best bowling: F/c 9–23   Gloucestershire v Worcestershire, Cheltenham, 1928.

Test 5–36   England v South Africa, Johannesburg, 1927/28.

by Neville Cardus, 1966

"Wally" indeed was cricket in excelsis. You had merely to see him walk from the pavilion on the way to the wicket to bat, a blue handkerchief peeping out of his right hip pocket. Square of shoulder, arms of obvious strength, a beautifully balanced physique, though often he looked so weighty that his sudden agility in the slips always stirred onlookers and the batsmen to surprise.

His career as a batsman can be divided into two contrasted periods. To begin with, when he was in his twenties, he was an audacious strokeplayer, as daring and unorthodox as Trumper or Compton. Round about 1924 I recommended Hammond to an England selector as a likely investment. "Too much of a 'dasher'," was the reply. Like Hobbs he modulated, as he grew older and had to take on heavier responsibilities as a batsman, into a classic firmness and restraint. He became a classical player, in fact, expressing in a long innings the philosophy of "ripeness is all". It is often forgotten that, on a bad wicket, he was also masterful.

He could, if he had given his mind constantly to the job, have developed into a bowler as clever as Alec Bedser himself with a new ball. Here again, he was in action the embodiment of easy flowing motion – a short run, upright and loose, a sideway action, left shoulder pointing down the wicket, the length accurate, the ball sometimes swinging away late. I never saw him besmirching his immaculate flannels by rubbing the ball on his person, rendering it bloody and hideous to see.

As a slip fieldsman his easy, lithe omnipresence has not often been equalled. He held 78 catches in a single season, ten in one and the same match. He would stand at first slip erect as the bowler began to run, his legs slightly turned in at the knees. He gave the impression of relaxed carelessness. At the first sight, or hint of, a snick off the edge, his energy swiftly concentrated in him, apparently electrifying every nerve and muscle in him. He became light, boneless, airborne. He would take a catch as the ball was travelling away from him, leaping to it as gracefully as a trapeze artist to the flying trapeze.

HEDLEY VERITY
1931

A notable event in Yorkshire's season – possibly one fraught with great importance to the future of the county – was the appearance of Verity. A slow left-handed bowler, with command of both spin and length, Verity also sends down a fastish ball that runs on with his arm and, if he develops the powers which he displayed last summer, would appear to be the natural successor to Wilfred Rhodes. Fairly tall, strongly built, and possessed of a happy temperament, he may, if he avoids the swerving heresy and devotes his energies to spin and accuracy and to those subtle variations of pace and flight which the great bowlers learn by continuous practice, attain the highest honours of the cricket field.

Hedley Verity (1905–1943), Yorkshire and England.
First-class career 1930–1939.

	M	Runs	Avge	100s	Wkts	Avge	10w/m	5w/i	Ct
F/c	378	5,605	18.08	1	1,956	14.90	54	164	269
Test	40	669	20.90	–	144	24.37	2	5	30

Highest score: F/c 101   Yorkshire v Jamaica, Kingston, 1935/36.
                Test 66*   England v India, Manchester, 1936.
Best bowling: F/c 10–10 Yorkshire v Nottinghamshire, Leeds, 1932.
                Test 8–43 England v Australia, Lord's, 1934.

by R. C. Robertson-Glasgow, 1944

Hedley Verity, Captain, The Green Howards, died of wounds a prisoner-of-war in Italy on July 31, 1943, some two months after his thirty-eighth birthday. He had been reported wounded and missing, and the news of his death came on September 1, exactly four years after he had played his last match for Yorkshire and, at Hove, taken seven Sussex wickets for nine runs in one innings, which finished county cricket before the war.

Judged by any standard, Verity was a great bowler. Merely to watch him was to know that. The balance of the run-up, the high ease of the left-handed action, the scrupulous length, the pensive variety, all proclaimed the master. He combined nature with art to a degree not equalled by any other English bowler of our time. He received a handsome legacy of skill and, by an application that verged on scientific research, turned it into a fortune. There have been bowlers who reached greatness without knowing or, perhaps, caring to know just how or why; but Verity could analyse his own intentions without losing the joy of surprise and describe their effect without losing the company of a listener.

In each of his nine full English seasons he took at least 150 wickets, and he averaged 185 wickets a season; thrice consecutively (1935–36–37) he took over 200 wickets. His average ranged from 12.42 to 17.63. He headed the first-class English bowling averages in his first season and in his last, and never came out lower than fifth.

by Don Bradman, 1944

It could truthfully be claimed that Hedley Verity was one of the greatest if not THE greatest left-hand bowler of all time. Most certainly he could lay just claim to that honour during the 1918–1939 period. No doubt his Yorkshire environment was of great assistance, for left-hand bowling seems to be in the blood of Yorkshiremen. It is one of their traditions and inalienable rights to possess the secrets of the art.

LEN HUTTON
1935

One of the most promising of the younger brigade was Hutton who, with a nice style, showed himself master of most of the strokes. There is clearly a bright future for this young cricketer.

1936

Hutton, because of ill-health, was seldom in the eleven.

1937

Hutton completed his thousand runs (1,108), with an average of 29.94. These were by no means exceptional figures for a batsman who, at the age of eighteen in 1934, was hailed as an embryo England player. When he batted seven hours at Leeds for his one century of the season, Hutton revealed a wealth of defensive skill, but his stubborn resistance greatly flattered the same Surrey bowling that Leyland at times flogged unmercifully. Serious defects in Hutton's technique, however, were never noticeable. Perhaps far too much was expected of him, and until he executes his strokes with greater freedom he might well be regarded as being some distance from the point of maturity. As Sutcliffe may bat lower down in the order next season, much depends upon Hutton, and all Yorkshire enthusiasts hope and believe he will rise to the standard of his mentor.

Sir Leonard Hutton (1916–1990), Yorkshire and England.
First-class career 1934–1960.

	M	Runs	Avge	100s	Wkts	Avge	10w/m	5w/i	Ct
F/c	513	40,140	55.51	129	173	29.51	1	4	400
Test	79	6,971	56.67	19	3	77.33	–	–	57

Highest score: F/c ⎫
　　　　　　　 Test ⎭ 364 England v Australia, The Oval, 1938.

Best bowling: F/c　6–76 Yorkshire v Leicestershire, Leicester, 1937.
　　　　　　　 Test　1–2 England v Australia, Sydney, 1954/55.

by John Woodcock, 1991

Being chosen for Yorkshire when still a month short of his eighteenth birthday made Hutton the youngest player to appear for the county since George Hirst in 1889. He came into a side that had won the Championship for the previous three years – Yorkshire had not been out of the first four since 1911 – and to play regularly for them in those days gave a young man a distinct advantage. In Hutton's case, the transition from callow youth, cap steeply tilted, to one of the world's most accomplished batsmen was achieved in an extraordinarily short time. Yorkshire colts getting a game for the county side in the middle 1930s were left in no doubt that they were there to be seen and not heard. It was an austere school and Hutton was an astute observer. Within four years of joining it he had become a household name. Nothing was more remarkable about his *tour de force* at The Oval [making a world-record 364 for England v Australia] than that he was only just twenty-two at the time.

Then came the war, claiming several summers when Hutton's play would still have carried the bloom of youth, and leaving him, as the result of a training accident, with his left arm two inches shorter than the right. With the return of peace, the mantle that had been Hammond's passed to Hutton, whose batting, despite having been laid up for so long, had matured. Between 1934 and

1939 he had scored 11,658 runs at an average of 48.98. From 1945, when he played his next first-class innings, to his retirement in 1955 he made another 28,292 at 58.81.

For the benefit of those who never saw Hutton bat, I have been trying to think of someone playing today who puts one in mind of him, and I am not sure that I can. This is surprising, for he was essentially orthodox and resolutely conventional. Except that he gives the impression of hitting the ball, and less of stroking it, than Hutton did, Stephen Waugh, the gifted Australian of similar build, probably comes as near as anyone. Mohammad Azharuddin is another who possesses that intuition which gives the great natural players such a start to life.

SLEEPWALKING 1986

Leonard Cullen, a good natural all-round games-player, quick on his feet, had 18 matches for Northamptonshire in 1934 and 1935 but made only 253 runs and his five wickets cost 59.09 runs each. His career was virtually ended by an extraordinary accident. Playing against Glamorgan at Llanelli in 1935, he fell out of a window in his hotel while walking in his sleep. Even this did not wake him, and when he came to he was some way from the hotel and had to ask his way back. His injuries kept him out of the side for some weeks, and after one more appearance he returned to South Africa.

DENIS COMPTON
1937

Of perhaps greater importance than the continued excellence of Hendren – because of its bearing upon the future – was the leap into prominence of Denis Compton. In 1935, Compton played three innings for Middlesex second eleven without accomplishing anything of note. Last season, at the age of eighteen, he made his county debut in the Whitsuntide engagement with Sussex at Lord's and, going in last, scored 14. From that point, he never looked back, not only commanding a regular place in the team but embarking upon a gradual ascent in the batting order. To him fell the distinction of scoring

1,000 runs in his first season in big cricket, a feat he completed in his last match before commencing training with Arsenal Football Club, for whom he is an outside-left of outstanding skill.

In the batting figures he finished second only to Hendren of the regular members of the eleven, and Mr P. F. Warner, chairman of the Test Match Selection Committee, paid him a deserved tribute when he described him as "the best young batsman who has come out since Hammond was a boy". Once only did Compton reach three figures, scoring in 105 minutes exactly 100 not out against Northamptonshire at Northampton, but he was a model of consistency. Eminently sound in defence, he displayed discretion in picking the ball to punish, and he employed the drive, pull and square-leg hit with splendid effect. Here was a batsman who really hit the ball and timed his strokes to a nicety, and if one fault could be urged against him it was a lack of certainty in his footwork when hooking. This did not affect the stroke itself, but it often threatened the loss of his wicket, as it did at Hove when he trod on his stumps. In various positions, he proved himself a fieldsman of conspicuous merit, and also a left-hand bowler of some pretensions; he finished off the Hampshire second innings at Lord's by taking three wickets for 11 runs.

Denis Charles Scott Compton, CBE (1918–1997), Middlesex, Holkar and England.

First-class career 1936–1964.

	M	Runs	Avge	100s	Wkts	Avge	10w/m	5w/i	Ct
F/c	515	38,942	51.85	123	622	32.27	3	19	416
Test	78	5,807	50.06	17	25	56.40	–	1	49

Highest score: F/c 300 MCC v North-East Transvaal, Benoni, 1948/49.
Test 278 England v Pakistan, Nottingham, 1954.
Best bowling: F/c 7–36 MCC v Auckland, Auckland, 1946/47.
Test 5–70 England v South Africa, Cape Town, 1948/49.

by Neville Cardus, 1958

Denis Compton counts amongst those cricketers who changed a game of competitive and technical interest to sportsmen into a highly individual art that appealed to and fascinated thousands of men and women and boys and girls, none of whom possessed a specialist clue, none of whom could enter into the fine points of expert skill. He lifted cricket into an atmosphere of freedom of personal expression. The scoreboard seldom told you more than half the truth about what he was doing on the field of play. In an age increasingly becoming standardised, with efficiency the aim at the expense of impulse – for impulse is always a risk – Compton went his unburdened way, a law to himself.

Compton fascinated all lovers of cricket, informed or uninformed, whether he was making runs or not, or whether he was taking wickets or not. In fact, whenever Compton seemed seriously in trouble and under the necessity to work hard he was then even a more arresting spectacle than usual. As we watched him groping and lunging and running out of his ground before the ball was released, we were more than ever aware that here was no merely talented cricketer; here was one under the sway and in the thrall of incalculable genius. For it is certain that Compton often was as much in the dark as the rest of us as to why and how he came by his own personal achievements, how he added to a fundamentally sound technical foundation an unpredictable inspiration, as though grace descended on him.

GODFREY EVANS
1943

Once more, Sergeant T. G. Evans, of the Army and Kent, showed very fine form as wicket-keeper. A discovery indeed.

D. Compton, going out to drive [Alec] Bedser, was neatly stumped by T. G. Evans who, with 55 in the first innings of Kent and Surrey, showed that he is not only a good wicket-keeper.

Thomas Godfrey Evans, CBE (1920–1999), Kent and England.
First-class career 1939–1969.

	M	Runs	Avge	100s	Wkts	Avge	Ct/St
F/c	465	14,882	21.22	7	2	122.50	816/250
Test	91	2,439	20.49	2	–	–	173/ 46

Highest score:	F/c	144 Kent v Somerset, Taunton, 1952.
	Test	104 England v West Indies, Manchester, 1950; v India, Lord's, 1952.
Most match dismissals:	F/c 9	(8ct, 1st) Kent v New Zealanders, Canterbury, 1949.
	Test 7	England v South Africa, Lord's, 1955 (6ct, 1st); v Australia, Lord's, 1956 (6ct, 1st); v West Indies, Nottingham, 1957 (all ct).

by Neville Cardus, 1960

Godfrey did not just wait for chances which any competent keeper could take. He was creative. With abnormal anticipation and agility he could turn a brilliant leg-glance, a certain four most times, into a batsman's fatal error. Such a wicket-keeper is a positive force in the attack. With Evans behind the stumps, the greatest batsmen hesitate to attempt strokes which, with stumpers of average ability behind them, they would have put into execution confidently.

Evans was not a keeper in the classic style, not all quiet balanced outlines, like Bertie Oldfield, who used to catch or stump in a flash and yet appear the embodiment of politeness and almost obsequious deportment, as though saying to his victim: "Awfully sorry, but it is my painful duty – Law 42, you know." Evans was modern in the almost surrealistic patterns achieved by his motions. He seemed to get the ball by leaving out physical shapings and adjustments which ordinary human anatomies have to observe. He was a boneless wonder. Did he play to the gallery? If he did so, the quicksilver snapdragon leapings, dartings and flickerings of him were second nature. Nobody could pose with Evans's accuracy and get away with it.

The crowd hailed him with glee as he walked out to bat. He won the usual and easy laughs by darting in and out of his crease, pretending to go for unsafe runs. As a fact, he could be a very dangerous and even a beautiful driver, as the West Indies discovered at Old Trafford in 1950 when he came to the crease in England's first innings with the score 88 for five. While Bailey defended, he attacked and scored his maiden century of 104 out of 161 put on for the sixth wicket. As proof that Evans is not all "fun and games" but a true cricketer, we can point to his wonderful adaptation and self-discipline at Adelaide in January 1947. In their second innings England had lost eight wickets for 255, Compton not out. Evans actually did not score a run until he had driven Bradman and the Australian attack almost to desperate measures for 95 minutes. In all, Evans obstructed for two hours and a quarter. He and Compton scored 85 together and, without being separated, saved the match, Evans not out 10, made from seven of the 98 balls he received. The innings was evidence of the serious side of Evans who, as with every born and skilful man of comedy, knew, and still knows, how to time a laugh.

BRIAN CLOSE
1950

Looking to the future, perhaps of even more importance was the discovery of Close, a fine all-rounder who in his first season in county cricket completed the "double". He was the youngest player to accomplish this feat as well as to play for England. In fact Brian Close, at the age of eighteen, stood out as the most remarkable find for many years. About six feet tall, with exceptional physique, and still growing, he would open the bowling with pace and swerve, then use the ball for right-arm off-breaks. He batted left-handed and could control his play to suit the occasion. Moreover he fielded magnificently near the wicket.

Dennis Brian Close, CBE (1931–   ), Yorkshire, Somerset and England.
First-class career 1949–1986.

	M	Runs	Avge	100s	Wkts	Avge	10w/m	5w/i	Ct/St
F/c	786	34,994	33.26	52	1,171	26.42	3	43	813/1
Test	22	887	25.34	–	18	29.55	–	–	24
ODI	3	49	16.33	–	0	–	–	–	1

Highest score: F/c 198   Yorkshire v Surrey, The Oval, 1960.
　　　　　　　　Test 70   England v West Indies, Lord's, 1963.
　　　　　　　　ODI 43   England v Australia, Lord's, 1972.
Best bowling: F/c 8–41   Yorkshire v Kent, Leeds, 1959.
　　　　　　　　Test 4–35 England v India, Leeds, 1959.

by Bill Bowes, 1964

Because he was senior professional with the club, and the job was
his by right, Yorkshire in 1963 offered the captaincy to their all-
rounder Brian Close, who hitherto had never quite accomplished
what was expected of him. It was a trial appointment. Nobody
quite knew how it would work out. The result was astonishing.
Almost overnight it seemed that Close matured. He showed a
knowledge of his own team and the play of opponents which
immediately stamped him as a thinker and tactician. His field
placings were as intelligent and antagonistic as any seen in the
county for 25 years and, like Brian Sellers before him, if a fieldsman was required in a "suicide position" the captain himself was
first for the job. Determination and purpose came into his own
cricket. He regained his place in the England team and won
national approval for the unflinching way he played the West
Indies fast bowlers, Hall and Griffith. To his own great delight he
saw Yorkshire, in their centenary year, to their 28th outright
Championship success.

Notes by the Editor, *Wisden*, 1967

Brian Close, the latest England captain, was the third player to
cover himself with glory on a belated return to the Test team.
Back in 1949 he was the youngest cricketer at the age of eighteen to appear for England, the youngest Yorkshireman to gain
his county cap and the youngest player to accomplish the
double. Since then his Test career has been intermittent. MCC

took him to Australia in 1950 – his only overseas tour – and on his single appearance at home against Australia at Manchester in 1961 his Test career seemed to have been completed when he was assailed on all sides for alleged reckless strokeplay. Yet he was back in 1963 and batting courageously against the fiery bumpers of Hall and Griffith in all five Tests with West Indies. But strangely England did not pick him again until a captain was needed last August for the final Test at The Oval. He had proved his ability as a leader for Yorkshire and he led England in the same positive way; his bowling changes were successful and his personal example close to the batsman at short leg made an aggressive set of fielders who took all the catches offered. Perhaps, luck did go his way for once. This forthright Yorkshireman was certainly the hero of the hour and appears destined to lead England in the West Indies next winter.

1968
WARWICKSHIRE v YORKSHIRE

At Birmingham, August 16, 17, 18, 1967. Drawn. This was the match with tremendous repercussions. The last hour and 40 minutes, in which Warwickshire had to score 142 to win and failed by nine runs, led to allegations of delaying tactics against Yorkshire and to the eventual censuring of their captain, Close.

by E. M. Wellings, 1969
MCC IN WEST INDIES, 1967/68

The MCC team had been chosen in the midst of controversy. The Board of Control selectors made public the fact that they wanted Close as captain, although he had been censured for his conduct of the Yorkshire team in their match against Warwickshire. The MCC committee overruled them and decided that the offence for which he was censured barred him from the tour captaincy.

1972

The signing of the former Yorkshire and England captain, Close, brought greatly increased interest and zest to the Somerset cricket scene in 1971 and the confidence of the supporters was largely justified by the event. Somerset moved up six places in the County Championship and ten places in the John Player League. He enjoyed a triumphant year after his previous injury troubles. He did not miss a match and made five centuries, including one against Yorkshire as well as one against the eventual champions, Surrey, the day after he had suffered a severe facial injury. His death-defying fielding positions brought him many astonishing catches and he took his place in the team splendidly. His forceful example should make his captaincy as useful to Somerset as previously it has been to others.

Notes by the Editor, *Wisden*, 1977

It is customary in England for the captain to be co-opted on the selection committee and he usually gets his way in the final choice of players. So when forty-five-year-old Brian Close stood up boldly to the hostile West Indies bowlers and made 88 for Somerset while the Test Trial was in progress a few miles away at Bristol, Greig pleaded for him to be recalled. Close justified the move with an average of 33.30 in three Tests and in partnership with John Edrich (39) at Manchester made the highest combined age of any Test opening pair since 1930, when G. Gunn (50) and A. Sandham (39) opened for England in the West Indies and J. B. Hobbs (47) and F. E. Woolley (43) started the batting against Australia at Lord's.

It was in trying to solve one of their deepest problems that the selectors asked Close to open at Manchester, where on the Saturday the West Indies fast bowlers, and particularly Holding and Daniel, gave a display which was unsavoury as well as being bad cricket. England were at their mercy. Yet by ducking out of the way of the numerous bouncers or taking the ball on various parts of their anatomy, Close and Edrich were able to see out the last 80 minutes of the day. They nudged 21 runs, 11 of them from the bat, off 17 overs, three of which were bowled by the off-spinner Padmore, who had to be brought on to cool things down. Condemnation to a man in both the printed and spoken word brought sense to the Monday play, to the advantage of the transgressors. The fast men aimed at the stumps and were vastly more effective for the remainder of the tour. Close and Edrich were not to appear again, and probably they were not sorry about that.

Eric Hill, 1978

Ian Terence Botham, aged twenty-one, took five Australian wickets on his first day of Test match cricket. By an apposite twist of chance, that day brought Brian Close's announcement of his retirement 28 years after his first England appearance at eighteen years of age. Botham has tremendous respect for Close, his county captain, with whom he has much in common. He says "He kept me in order" and avers stridently "We were always a better side with him there". They share a fierce determination to succeed, besides outstanding courage.

PETER MAY
1950

The feature of the [Combined Services] season was the splendid batting of Writer P. B. H. May, the former Charterhouse School captain, whose average of 63.18 for 11 completed innings was surpassed only by Hardstaff and Hutton in the first-class list. May, who is qualified for Surrey, took a major share of the credit for the victory over Worcestershire, making 97 and 175.

Peter Barker Howard May, CBE (1929–1994), Cambridge University, Surrey and England.

First-class career 1948–1963.

	M	Runs	Avge	100s	Ct
F/c	388	27,592	51.00	85	282
Test	66	4,537	46.77	13	42

Highest score: F/c ⎱
               Test ⎰   285* England v West Indies, Birmingham, 1957.

by John Woodcock, 1971

When Peter May announced his retirement from first-class cricket in 1962, at the young age of thirty-two, it was hoped that he might one day play again. That he has never done so is the reason for an appreciation such as this having been delayed so long.

May was fortunate in the pitches on which he learnt to bat. On the hill at Charterhouse they were fast and true, and at Fenner's they were even truer. In 1950, his first year at Cambridge, four of the University side – John Dewes, Hubert Doggart, David Sheppard and May – were chosen for the Test Trial at Bradford, and by the end of 1951 they had all played for England. May did so for the first time against South Africa at Headingley in 1951, and in his first Test innings he made 138. By the winter of 1953/54 he was in the West Indies under Len Hutton; by 1954/55 he was Hutton's vice-captain in Australia and New Zealand; and when Len gave up the captaincy it was handed on to May. Still only twenty-six, he wasn't really ready for it; but Trevor Bailey had been passed over, and May's place in the England side was assured for years to come. All things considered he did it well, although I am not sure that we gave him credit for that at the time.

His chief qualities as a captain were his courtesy and his intensity of purpose. He was also unwaveringly straight. His players knew exactly where they were with him, and if at times he was too lenient for their own good that was a fault they enjoyed. In only five years he led England 41 times, more than any captain of any country; under him England won 20 Test matches, drew 11 and lost 10.

On the few occasions that May can still be persuaded to take a bat in his hand, either for charity or a friend, he plays in a different dimension from anyone else in the game. To see him is to be reminded of his class. The on-drive was his particular glory. Though one of the hardest of all strokes to play, he scored many runs with it even as a boy. From wide mid-on to cover-point, off front foot and back, his shots had great power, the result of timing rather than strength. The most remarkable stroke I ever

saw him play was at Lord's, when from the middle of the ground
he hit a medium-pacer high into the Mound Stand, over extra
cover and off the *back* foot.

WE'RE OFF 1937
SUSSEX v NOTTINGHAMSHIRE

Sussex had all the best of the match. With five minutes of the extra
half-hour remaining, they went in to get nine runs for victory. The
first over yielded seven runs; then slight rain began and Heane [the
Notts captain], having appealed to the umpires, led his team from the
field. A threat by Sussex to cancel fixtures arose out of this incident
but the trouble was smoothed over.

NOTTINGHAMSHIRE REVIEW

Closer still to defeat were Nottinghamshire at Hove where Sussex
with all their wickets in hand required only two runs for victory when,
a few minutes from time, the umpires agreed to Heane leading his
men off the field because of rain. There followed a threat by Sussex to
cancel fixtures, and the Nottinghamshire committee replied to the
effect that they did not uphold the action taken but expressed their
confidence in Heane as captain. In that way ended an occurrence that
caused a stir for several days. Considering all the circumstances, it
seemed that the umpires were the sole judges in the matter after
Heane appealed to them.

BRIAN STATHAM
1951

The new fast bowler, Statham, possessed a lively run-up and,
having finished his Army service, he should prove a great asset to
the side. His opening overs in the return match with Yorkshire
bordered on the sensational.

LANCASHIRE v YORKSHIRE

At Manchester, August 5, 7, 8, 1950. Drawn. The match produced keen and exciting cricket. The first thrill came when
Statham disposed of Lowson, Lester and Watson for 13 runs,
and Yorkshire faltered to such an extent that they lost half their

wickets for 47. [Later] Statham dismissed Halliday and Coxon in three balls.

John Brian Statham, CBE (1930–2000), Lancashire and England.
First-class career 1950–1968.

	M	Runs	Avge	100s	Wkts	Avge	10w/m	5w/i	Ct
F/c	559	5,424	10.80	–	2,260	16.37	11	123	230
Test	70	675	11.44	–	252	24.84	1	9	28

Highest score: F/c 62   Lancashire v Leicestershire, Manchester, 1955.
Test 38   England v India, Lord's, 1959.
Best bowling: F/c 8–34   Lancashire v Warwickshire, Coventry, 1957.
Test 7–39 England v South Africa, Lord's, 1955.

by Matthew Engel, 2001

Brian Statham was one of the best of all English fast bowlers, and beyond question the best-liked. A gentle man who had to be persuaded to bowl a bouncer, he was the mainstay of the England team in its vintage period between 1951 and 1963. His name will be forever coupled with that of Freddie Trueman, though they actually played together in only half his Tests. Statham's name always came second because he was the foil to Trueman's sabre – and the more reticent man. In cricketing folklore he is remembered primarily for his accuracy. "If they miss, I hit," he would say. This diminishes his astonishing skill. He was indeed accurate; so are many fast-medium bowlers. Statham kept his line and length at a very high pace indeed, comparable with all but the very fastest of Test match bowlers. A batsman hit by Statham – even on the foot, which was more likely than the head – knew all about it. In Statham's case the area around off stump was more a corridor of certainty than uncertainty, but if the ball hit the seam it jagged back in very sharply. The results were always formidable, and occasionally devastating.

He was, year after year, Lancashire's leading bowler. And lacking anyone to give him the support he himself provided so unstintingly for England, until the emergence of Ken Higgs in 1958, he sometimes had to do all the work himself. At Coventry in 1957, he bowled Lancashire to an innings win with match figures of 15 for 89. Though he dipped in and out of the England team, through injuries and the whims of selection, his form remained remarkably constant.

His methods remain a matter of some debate. His action was certainly too chest-on to be accepted as classical. He swung the ball only rarely, and perhaps never by design. Part of the secret seems to have been that Statham was not merely supple but double-jointed. "He could put his right arm round his face and touch his right ear and do the same with his left arm and left ear at the same time," said an admiring Geoff Pullar. He was certainly an impressive athlete: a beautiful outfielder and an occasionally effective left-handed tailender. His bowling quality was never in dispute. Nor was his character: he had an enchantingly easy-going temperament.

FRANK TYSON
1954

Tyson did enough to suggest that he might become a very fine fast bowler.

Frank Holmes Tyson (1930–   ), Northamptonshire and England.
First-class career 1952–1960.

	M	Runs	Avge	100s	Wkts	Avge	10w/m	5w/i	Ct
F/c	244	4,103	17.09	–	767	20.89	5	34	85
Test	17	230	10.95	–	76	18.56	1	4	4

Highest score: F/c 82   Northamptonshire v Sussex, Hove, 1960.
              Test 37*   England v Australia, Brisbane, 1954/55.
Best bowling: F/c 8–60   Northamptonshire v Surrey, The Oval, 1957.
              Test 7–27 England v Australia, Melbourne, 1954/55.

by E. Eden, 1956

Not for a long time has a star burst upon the cricket firmament with such startling suddenness as has been the case with Frank Tyson, the Northamptonshire and England fast bowler. Tyson established himself as a regular member of the county team in 1954. That year, too, began his notable partnership as opening bowler for England with Statham, of Lancashire, for Tyson was chosen to play in the final Test match with Pakistan in which he distinguished himself by taking four wickets for 35 runs in the first innings. Four times in county engagements he disposed of five batsmen in an innings. Even so his choice as a member of the MCC team to tour Australia during the winter came as something of a surprise.

In the First Test match in Australia, Tyson took only one wicket and that at a cost of 160 runs, and it looked as though the selectors had made a mistake in choosing him. Then he shortened his run by three or four yards with remarkable results. In the Second Test at Sydney he took four wickets for 45 and six for 85, and in the Third at Melbourne achieved his best performance by dismissing seven men for 27 runs in the second innings. His place in the England side was thus assured and, including the two matches with New Zealand, his Test record for the tour read 39 wickets, average 17.25. Such was his pace that Australian journalists gave him the pseudonym "Typhoon Tyson".

Essentially a quiet and modest man, whose thinning hair makes him look older than his twenty-five years, Tyson owes his triumphs to perseverance. Whether in League cricket or when playing in the Army, he went on learning all the time. He discovered that fast bowling was a question not so much of strength as of rhythm. When finding himself engaged in three-day matches, he considered a longer run would help to conserve energy; yet in Australia he owed his success to the fact that he returned to the methods he employed earlier in his career.

by Richie Benaud, 1977

Tyson and Statham were the first really fast bowlers I batted against in first-class cricket. I played in the Australian XI game against MCC in Melbourne in 1954 and Statham was on his own then. He posed enough problems for me and the other Australian batsmen on trial, and I had a fair guide to his pace because I had hit a century off Ray Lindwall in Brisbane a couple of weeks earlier. It was a rude shock to find that Statham was making me hurry my shot a little. It was an even ruder shock the following week to bat at No. 3 against Tyson at the Sydney Cricket Ground and find him sliding at me from 20 yards at the Randwick End and having to fend one away from my chin to first slip. Frank was never quite the same again after that tour, but it was no real pleasure to bat against him and Brian Statham in those Tests, on at least two pitches that were difficult. The Sydney pitch was so green it could hardly be distinguished from the rest of the square, and the Melbourne one so dry that it was thought necessary to give it a subtle hosing on the rest day.

DEREK UNDERWOOD
1964

Of the [Kent] bowlers, Underwood was the most successful, taking 101 wickets in his first season. This eighteen-year-old medium-pace bowler was considered one of the discoveries of the year.

Derek Leslie Underwood, MBE (1945–   ), Kent and England.
First-class career 1963–1987.

	M	Runs	Avge	100s	Wkts	Avge	10w/m	5w/i	Ct
F/c	676	5,165	10.12	1	2,465	20.28	47	153	261
Test	86	937	11.56	–	297	25.83	6	17	44
ODI	26	53	5.88	–	32	22.93	–	–	6

Highest score: F/c 111   Kent v Sussex, Hastings, 1984.
　　　　　　　Test 45*   England v Australia, Leeds, 1968.
　　　　　　　ODI 17   England v Pakistan, Birmingham, 1974.
Best bowling:　F/c 9–28   Kent v Sussex, Hastings, 1964.
　　　　　　　Test 8–51   England v Pakistan, Lord's, 1974.
　　　　　　　ODI 4–44 England v West Indies, Sydney, 1979/80.

by Doug Ibbotson, 1988

The full significance of Derek Underwood's retirement from first-class cricket will not properly be manifest until four o'clock, or thereabouts, on the last day of a moribund Championship match at Canterbury. Many of the faithful will be departing for Evensong, and seasoned correspondents will have advised their sports editors that the inevitable draw warrants no more than a brief litany.

Doubtless they will be right. Whereas, in the foregoing 25 years, the remarkable Derek Leslie Underwood frequently proved them wrong. For, in his capacity and determination to take, rather than buy, wickets on an unresponsive pitch, Underwood was a rare bird among spin bowlers. Whereas, against the average slow bowler, batsmen were principally alert to the prospect of punishing loose balls, when facing Underwood they steeled themselves against the unexpected – often to discover that, when it came, neither temperament nor technique was adequate. Not the least of their problems was that he was not strictly a slow bowler in the traditional sense.

Underwood would peel off his sweater, trudge out his flat-footed run-up and wheel in to bowl. Alas, to elder statesmen deck-chair deep in disconsolation, it was not an edifying sight: the approach too long, the delivery too flat. Yet, even as they "hrrumphed" to the heavens in the name of Alfred Percy Freeman, Underwood's unique talents were at work. The obdurate batsman pushes forward and is caught off the handle. He takes his leave, a sadder – though little wiser – man, to be replaced by another who, already impregnated with doubt, dithers, dabbles and departs. In this typical scenario lay the real mark of a master bowler: a measure of the professionalism too often overlooked when, in league with a spiteful pitch, Underwood became virtually unplayable.

Most memorable, perhaps, was his match-winning seven for 50 at The Oval to square the 1968 series against Australia. Here was the young Underwood in his element. Torrential rain in the morning flooded the outfield, scores of volunteers joined the groundstaff in mopping up, and so began an agonising race against time that ended with five minutes to spare as the England spinner took his fourth wicket in 27 balls. A splendid statistic but, in perusing the Underwood curriculum vitae, it is equally pertinent to consider his analysis for the first innings of that same match – played on a pitch which yielded 494 runs for England and 324 for Australia. Underwood claimed only two wickets but, in so doing, conceded fewer than 1.7 runs for each of his 54 overs; a degree of economy, not to mention stamina, that seldom deserted him.

ALAN KNOTT

1965

Two newcomers to the [Kent] side during the season were Knott, a capable young wicket-keeper who kept Catt out of the side during the latter part of the programme; and Graham, a 6ft 8in medium-fast bowler from Northumberland. Knott batted stylishly and kept wicket with enough skill to augur well for the future.

1966

Perhaps the most encouraging aspect of the season was the magnificent form of young Knott, considered in the highest circles to possess the ability to succeed Ames and Evans as another great Kent and England wicket-keeper. At nineteen, Knott showed remarkable ability, holding many fine catches, particularly down the leg side. In all he claimed 84 victims and scored 559 runs. His 49 not out against Sussex at Tunbridge Wells was an innings worthy of a master.

Alan Philip Eric Knott (1946–   ), Kent, Tasmania and England.
First-class career 1964–1985.

	M	Runs	Avge	100s	Wkts	Avge	Ct	St
F/c	511	18,106	29.63	17	2	43.50	1,211	133
Test	95	4,389	32.75	5	–	–	250	19
ODI	20	200	20.00	–	–	–	15	1

Highest score: F/c 156 MCC v South Zone, Bangalore, 1972/73.
                     Test 135 England v Australia, Nottingham, 1977.
                     ODI 50 England v Australia, Lord's, 1972.

Most match   F/c 9   Kent v Leicestershire, Maidstone, 1977.
dismissals: Test 7   England v Pakistan, Nottingham, 1967 (all ct); v Pakistan, Leeds, 1971 (6ct, 1st); v India, Manchester, 1974 (6ct 1st).
                 ODI 4   England v New Zealand, Swansea, 1973 (all ct).

by Mike Brearley, 1986

Alan Knott was a great cricketer. In my view he was also the best wicket-keeper of his time. He had a good physique for the job – short, low-to-the-ground, agile and quick (though he himself foresees a new breed of tall keepers by analogy with tall goalkeepers, and maintains that he had to stretch so much because he was not particularly supple, especially in the hips). He had marvellous hands. Physically he kept himself extremely fit, and was an assiduous practiser. His technique was not classical; he took catches with one hand when he might have got two to the ball, and he sometimes dived when he could have reached the ball without falling. He had a sound reason for both – simply that for him these methods were more natural and more effective. His judgment about what to go for was unerring. Though brilliant, he eschewed the flamboyant. He stood back to medium-pacers more than his predecessors, not at all for safety-first or to avoid error, but as the result of a cool calculation as to the overall effectiveness to the side.

He would have been in my book a more or less automatic selection for any team on the strength of his keeping alone. When his batting was put in the scales, all doubt fell away. For he was also a genius – a minor genius – with the bat. Here, too, he was no purist for the sake of orthodoxy. Against fast bowling he realised that he had a better chance of playing a lifting delivery if he changed his grip so as to have his top hand behind the handle; this enables the batsman to hold his hands in front of his face and keep the bat straight. He evolved a kind of French cricket technique for use when he first went in against the quickest bowlers; but soon took every opportunity to attack, clipping the ball square on either side of the wicket and cutting deftly, often, intentionally, over the slips' heads. He played a sort of off-glide to good effect, particularly against off-spinners. His sweeping was unique, his secret to get low, watch the ball, and not try to hit it too hard. I remember an innings against India at Bangalore in 1977. The pitch had deteriorated to the point where good spinners were almost unplayable. Yet "the flea" kept dancing down the pitch to Bedi and Prasanna and chipping them over mid-wicket or extra cover. The cheek and verve of this innings were unmatched in my experience.

Behind all his extravagances as a batsman – as with his idiosyncrasies as a keeper – there were the basic skills. His head was always steady, and he was capable of long defensive innings as well as of impish aggression. He was completely unselfish. He was courageous, too. But the courage that marked him out, for me, was of a more broad-based kind. He had the guts, the confidence and occasionally the stubbornness to stick to his method if he felt that he was right. I cannot think of any cricketer, with the possible exception of Ian Botham, whose game has given me more pleasure.

GRAHAM GOOCH
1975

Gooch, a home-grown youngster from Leytonstone, really blossomed in the last few weeks of the season. The highlight of his career so far came with a superb not out century which sent Leicestershire to defeat at Chelmsford. He still has some way to go to confirm his promise, but certainly appears to be blessed with the ability to succeed.

Graham Alan Gooch, OBE (1953–   ), Essex, Western Province and England.
First-class career 1973–2000.

	M	Runs	Avge	100s	Wkts	Avge	10w/m	5w/i	Ct
F/c	581	44,846	49.01	128	246	34.37	–	3	555
Test	118	8,900	42.58	20	23	46.47	–	–	103
ODI	125	4,290	36.98	8	36	42.11	–	–	45

Highest score: F/c ⎱ 333 England v India, Lord's, 1990.
                Test ⎰

                ODI 142 England v Pakistan, Karachi, 1987/88.
Best bowling: F/c 7–14 Essex v Worcestershire, Ilford, 1982.

                Test 3–39 England v Pakistan, Manchester, 1992.

                ODI 3–19 England v Pakistan, Cuttack, 1989/90.

by Christopher Martin-Jenkins, 1998

The golfer Joyce Wethered was once playing a crucial shot in a major championship when an express train suddenly thundered past. "Didn't the train put you off?" she was asked later. "What train?" she replied. The ability to forget the clutter of everything else and concentrate this completely is surprisingly rare, even among great performers in sport. But Graham Gooch had it in full measure. And this skill, more the result of mental steel than any natural gift, was the single most important reason for the fact that, by the time he started his final match for Essex on July 23, 1997, Graham Alan Gooch, born at Whipps Cross in Leyton-stone exactly 44 years before, had become the most prolific player in history.

One had sensed that he must be somewhere near, when all his limited-overs runs had been added to his final tally of 44,841 in first-class games at an average of 49.11,* but it took the computations of Robert Brooke to confirm for *Wisden* this stupendous fact. No single batsman, not Grace, nor Hobbs, nor Woolley, nor Boycott, nor any of his contemporaries in an age of proliferating fixtures, had made so many runs in top-class cricket as the pink-faced, heavy-limbed yeoman of Essex. He had, in fact, unnoticed, overtaken Jack Hobbs's total of 61,237 runs when he reached 67 in a Benson and Hedges game between Essex and Gloucestershire at Chelmsford on May 9, 1995. He finished with 65,928 at 45.81.* It is hard to imagine who might ever overtake him.

It is the all-round consistency, the excellence of his figures against all types of bowlers – Terry Alderman's supremacy over him in 1989 was the result of a technical fault assiduously worked out and corrected – and, above all, in all types of cricket, which placed him above the players of his own era. Of the top ten scorers in one-day internationals, all have played county cricket and know what it is to switch so often between first-class games and one-day matches of differing lengths. But when the totals of the modern greats are totted up, Haynes, Richards, Greenidge, Boycott, Amiss, Javed Miandad, Salim Malik, Border, Jones, Boon and the rest all fall short of Gooch.

All this does not, of course, make Graham Gooch the greatest player of his time but, even if we judge him only by the timeless yardstick of first-class cricket, ignoring the mind-wearying, sinew-stretching demands of the limited-overs game, his stature is clear. After the reduction in Championship matches in 1969, he alone scored above 2,000 runs in more than three seasons. He did so in five. Another 56 runs in his last full season, 1996, would have made it six. Moreover – and this makes his achievement all the more remarkable – Gooch belongs truly with the entertainers: he was a magnificent sight in full sail. This was no dabber of singles, no delicate leg-glancer or specialist in the smooth caress of a half-volley through extra cover. On the contrary, he was a bold, imposing player: a mighty driver and fierce square-cutter, who looked at the crease to be taller and bulkier than he actually was, with a bat apparently broader than the law permits.

* Gooch scored a further five runs in 2000 for MCC v New Zealanders at Oxford, taking his overall total to 65,933 at an average of 45.75.

VIV RICHARDS AND IAN BOTHAM
by Eric Hill, 1975

Two newcomers were the twenty-two-year-old Vivian Richards, from Antigua, and the eighteen-year-old Ian Botham, from Yeovil, previously of the Lord's groundstaff. Richards, a wonderful phenomenon, made the biggest impact of any player since Gimblett in 1935. Fresh from club cricket, he glowed with good humour and glorious batting adventure, his broad grin belying the withering force of his exquisitely timed strokes. His happy desire to hit the ball, of course, got him out often when he should have built a big innings. Perhaps the West Indies tour to India and Pakistan will train him to temper his zest without diminishing his enormous attraction. He is a beautiful fielder 30 yards from the bat.

Botham, forced into service by Cartwright's injuries, also showed star quality. His lively right-arm swing bowling, clean flowing driving, and the ability to field magnificently anywhere were soon evident. His successful fight to win the Benson and Hedges quarter-final at Taunton showed technical abilities underlined by courage and temperament of the highest order.

Notes by the Editor, *Wisden*, 1975

Likely England Talent

To return to England's problems. Players have to be found this summer to take part in the Prudential (World) Cup and the four Test matches that will follow against Australia. Personally, I was disappointed that England relied on so many of the old brigade for the tour of the Antipodes. The side was rich in experience, but the three youngest, Willis, Old and Hendrick, were twenty-five. I would particularly like to see Botham given a chance while he is young and enthusiastic.

Sir Isaac Vivian Alexander Richards (1952–   ), Leeward Islands, Combined Islands, Somerset, Queensland, Glamorgan and West Indies. First-class career 1971/72–1993.

	M	Runs	Avge	100s	Wkts	Avge	10w/m	5w/i	Ct/St
F/c	507	36,212	49.40	114	223	45.15	–	1	464/1
Test	121	8,540	50.23	24	32	61.37	–	–	122
ODI	187	6,721	47.00	11	118	35.83	–	1	100

Highest score:	F/c 322	Somerset v Warwickshire, Taunton, 1985.
	Test 291	West Indies v England, The Oval, 1976.
	ODI 189*	West Indies v England, Manchester, 1984.
Best bowling:	F/c 5–88	West Indians v Queensland, Brisbane, 1981/82.
	Test 2–17	West Indies v Pakistan, Port-of-Spain, 1987/88.
	ODI 6–41	West Indies v India, Delhi, 1989/90.

Ian Terence Botham, OBE (1955–   ), Somerset, Worcestershire, Queensland, Durham and England. First-class career 1974–1993.

	M	Runs	Avge	100s	Wkts	Avge	10w/m	5w/i	Ct
F/c	402	19,399	33.97	38	1,172	27.22	8	59	354
Test	102	5,200	33.54	14	383	28.40	4	27	120
ODI	116	2,113	23.21	–	145	28.54	–	–	36

Highest score: F/c   228   Somerset v Gloucestershire, Taunton, 1980.
               Test 208   England v India, The Oval, 1982.
               ODI 79   England v New Zealand, Christchurch,
                          1991/92.
Best bowling: F/c   ⎱
               Test ⎰ 8–34 England v Pakistan, Lord's, 1978.
               ODI 4–31   England v Australia, Sydney, 1991/92.

by John Woodcock, 1994

With the retirement last season, within a few weeks of each other, of Ian Botham and Vivian Richards, first-class cricket lost two of the greatest of all its stars. Botham and Richards were good companions. Brought together by cricket, they became firm enough friends to spend a part of their winters going round the halls, exchanging banter with much the same abandon as they showed on the field. They had no particular talent for the stage, I think; but their prowess as cricketers deserves to be remembered for as long as the game is played.

Before Richards, Antigua had yet to be recognised as a nursery of prodigiously talented cricketers. That it now has a Test match ground and a quarter of a million tourists a year owes much to Richards. If Nelson put Antigua on the map by making it the base from which he sallied forth to do battle with the French in the Caribbean, Richards came to glamorise it by looking and batting as he did. He had the countenance to go with his style. In 1976 alone he scored 1,710 runs in Tests (just think of it!) at an average of 90, culminating in an innings of 291 against England at The Oval – and he was still only twenty-four.

For most of the next two years Richards was lost to Test cricket while on the road with the Packer Circus. There was an intolerance, a belligerence about the way World Series Cricket was played which either hardened its adherents or flustered them. In the event, it confirmed Richards's supremacy. In a way, it made a man of him.

Ian Botham, meanwhile, was fast becoming the talk of English cricket. He was very strong, patently irrepressible and cheerfully insubordinate. By the time Richards joined Somerset in 1974, Botham, although almost four years his junior, was already on the staff there. They made a flamboyant, ultimately ungovernable pair. After a while Somerset hardly knew what had hit them. Botham played the first of his 102 Test matches, against Australia, at Trent Bridge in July 1977, when he was twenty-one. By the end of his fourth he had taken five wickets in an innings three times, made the first of his 14 Test hundreds and run out his captain, Geoffrey Boycott, because he thought he was scoring too slowly if the match, against New Zealand at Christchurch, were to be won (which, eventually, it was). Within two years and one month Botham had scored 1,000 runs and taken 100 wickets in Test matches – no one has ever done that in a shorter time – and was well on the way to becoming a sporting legend.

Botham's brushes with authority, whether they concerned cricket or the law, in England or elsewhere, may have been evidence of a free spirit, but they were really no more excusable for that. Richards, for his part, had a temper to contend with, which was behind a swingeing two-year suspension, imposed in his late teens, from playing cricket in Antigua, and was another reason for his being held in fairly universal awe. To Botham, the colour of a man's skin was of small account. To Richards it mattered much more; more, sometimes, than was helpful. Botham was quite without artifice. You got what you saw. Richards was proudly and defiantly black. The swagger with which he walked to the wicket, flashing that Rastafarian wristlet; the air with which he looked round the field, the conviction with which he twiddled his bat, the condescension with which from time to time he failed, were all a part of one of the supreme acts in the history of the game. He was stamped with "the image of a king". As he ruled, so too he raged, and so, in his tranquil moments, he responded to affection.

Viv was a hard cricketer, but a chivalrous, warm-hearted and unselfish one. In the years of his maturity his love of the game and still unwavering determination inspired Glamorgan to a season to remember. Botham was just as fiercely competitive, just as chivalrous and chauvinistic, and just as contemptuous of averages. The marathon walks undertaken to raise funds for leukaemia have been magnificent, and reflect an abundantly generous spirit. He, too, "sounded forth the trumpet that shall never call retreat". They are two of the immortals, and it is an honour to salute them as such.

GRAEME HICK
1985

One name to watch out for in 1985, if Worcestershire can find ways of getting him into the side, is the Zimbabwean batsman, Graeme Hick. He emerged as a prolific scorer for the second eleven and for Kidderminster in the Birmingham League, and marked his Championship debut with an unbeaten 82 after going in at No. 9 in the last game against Surrey.

1986

Then there was Graeme Hick, the prolific young Zimbabwean who looks set to follow in Glenn Turner's footsteps and become Worcestershire's leading overseas batsman. He started the summer with seven centuries outside the first-class game before joining up with the Zimbabweans. For them he scored 230 in the opening game against Oxford University, one of the highest maiden first-class centuries ever made, and followed this with 192 against Glamorgan. On returning to Worcestershire he hit his first Championship century, an innings of 174 not out against Somerset, to which he added 128 against Northamptonshire.

Graeme Ashley Hick (1966–   ), Zimbabwe, Worcestershire, Northern Districts, Queensland and England.
First-class career 1983/84 to August 30, 2004.

	M	Runs	Avge	100s	Wkts	Avge	10w/m	5w/i	Ct
F/c	468	37,343	53.50	126	231	44.61	1	5	592
Test	65	3,383	31.32	6	23	56.78	–	–	90
ODI	120	3,846	37.33	5	30	34.20	–	1	64

Highest score: F/c 405*   Worcestershire v Somerset, Taunton, 1988.
Test 178   England v India, Bombay, 1992/93.
ODI 126*   England v Sri Lanka, Adelaide, 1998/99.

Best bowling: F/c 5–18 Worcestershire v Leicestershire, Worcester, 1995.

Test 4–126 England v New Zealand, Wellington, 1991/92.

ODI 5–33 England v Zimbabwe, Harare, 1999/2000.

by Peter Roebuck, 1999

Upon the abandonment of the match in which he scored his 100th hundred, Graeme Hick walked across a damp and emptying ground in Worcester and into the arms of his daughters. It was an ordinary thing to do, but it was noticed because it said something about a cricketer who had once seemed a fearless gladiator, but whose confidence had slowly been eroded. Always he had seemed distant. A fellow could watch him bat a hundred times and still not feel close. Suddenly he seemed human, warm and vulnerable, a quiet man in a noisy place. Watching him, it was hard to believe he really wanted to throw himself back into the hurly-burly.

It may be his fate to be remembered as a remarkable cricketer and a monumental scorer of runs, as a player fit and reliable, yet incapable of taking the extra step; in short, a player whose finest moments came along at times of their own choosing. Considering his achievements, it might seem a harsh judgment. More leeway is given elsewhere. Sport forgives those who cannot contain themselves on the field, whose careers consist of flashes of brilliance, calling them charming and romantic and misunderstood. Sport also forgives those who must scrape around for their runs. But it will not smile upon those who do not deliver upon their promises, even if they did not make those promises themselves.

It was Hick's fate to be given an ability that did not suit his temperament. It took him on a long journey, across the world and into himself, took him further than he cared to go. His upbringing was simple and secure, and did not prepare him for the conflict. He has always been a performer rather than a downright competitor.

Happily, there is much to be said on Hick's behalf. His cultured and forceful strokeplay has given enormous enjoyment to crowds across the world. He has hardly ever let his supporters down, or his team-mates, or the game itself. He has scored a mountain of runs, few of them given away. The regularity with which hundreds came along said much about his fitness, discipline and concentration. He has been an impressive and largely impassive professional, one of the heaviest scorers to appear in the last 20 years, and one of the best tall batsmen. His accomplishments are extraordinary. Only in Test cricket has Hick been found wanting, and even there his record is not so bad. None the less, something was missing, a spark, an ability to be himself in the most demanding situations.

MICHAEL VAUGHAN
1995

Vaughan established himself as Moxon's opening partner in his first full season, displaying an impressive range of strokes. He was prepared to take calculated risks in an attempt to dominate the bowling and, inevitably, some critics suggested that he lacked self-discipline. But, overall, Yorkshire surrendered the initiative too often and it would be a mistake to interfere too much with Vaughan.

by Ralph Dellor, 2000

ENGLAND A IN ZIMBABWE AND SOUTH AFRICA, 1998/99

The whole ensemble was drawn together by Michael Vaughan. On his third A tour but with limited experience of captaincy, he emerged as an accomplished batsman and a natural leader. He was rewarded with total support from his team, which he repaid with several important innings. The coach, John Emburey, a former England captain himself, had no hesitation in marking him as one for the future. If the players under his command develop as hoped, Vaughan could one day lead some of them out in a Test match.

NOTE: Michael Vaughan's England A touring party included Andrew Flintoff ("made the most rapid strides of all"), Steve Harmison ("struggled at the outset but, as the tour progressed, gained control without

losing pace, and troubled good batsmen with channelled aggression")
and Chris Read ("next in line as England's wicket-keeper if the choice
was made purely on keeping").

Michael Paul Vaughan (1974–   ), Yorkshire and England.
First-class career 1993 to August 30, 2004.

	M	Runs	Avge	100s	Wkts	Avge	10w/m	5w/i	Ct
F/c	209	13,336	38.54	36	113	45.06	–	–	100
Test	50	3,777	45.50	13	5	97.40	–	–	32
ODI	49	1,035	24.06	–	8	39.62	–	–	10

Highest score: F/c ⎫
                Test ⎬ 197 England v India, Nottingham, 2002.
                ODI 83   England v South Africa, Birmingham, 2003.
Best bowling: F/c 4–39   Yorkshire v Oxford University, Oxford, 1994.
                Test 2–71 England v India, Nottingham, 2002.
                ODI 4–22 England v Sri Lanka, Manchester, 2002.

by David Hopps, 2003

Michael Vaughan began 2002 keenly aware of the impatience for
him to prove his worth as a Test batsman. If it emanated less
from the England management than from the media, none the
less the time was nigh for Vaughan to establish himself as a senior
player and a worthy opening partner for Marcus Trescothick.
Such was his response that, by the year's end, he was not just
established, but had become England's most accomplished
performer since the heydays of Gooch and Gower.

He was Test cricket's leading run-getter in 2002, an impressive
feat, if not the most meaningful one in England, where the cricketing year, like the financial, traditionally begins in April. Even
more impressive was the style in which he made his runs. He had
always been technically sound, but a reflective, somewhat potter-
ing, even stressful air in his formative years encouraged some to
harbour suspicions that he would be overpowered by attacks of
the highest class. He answered that in wonderfully emphatic style.
In 2002, cricket grounds in England and Australia resounded to a
new Michael Vaughan, a batsman more confident in his method

and much more forceful in his strokeplay. Deliveries that were once sneaked into the covers now pummelled the boundary boards. Short balls, and some not very short, were pulled and hooked in a manner that must have surprised even Vaughan himself. By the end of the year, his habit of touching the peak of his helmet, like a classical batsman of old respectfully touching the peak of his cap, had become a familiar sight. Throughout, he played with a dignity that signalled him a player of true worth.

AN UMPIRE'S BEST FRIEND 1961

Occasionally the joke went against Alec. In a game in 1948 he turned down a strong appeal by the Australian touring team. A little later a dog ran on to the field, and one of the Australians captured it, carried it to Skelding and said: "Here you are. All you want now is a white stick."

HOWZAT?

It's the thirties that get them. There was a time, early last century, when the twenties did the business, but the Laws of Cricket have been rewritten a few times since then. These days Laws 30 (Bowled) to 39 (Stumped) define the ten ways a batsman can be sent on his way.

Back in 1900 there were only nine. The parvenu is "Timed Out", and even that has been tweaked from the 1980 code to the 2000 revision. Where once the incoming batsman was permitted two minutes to get on to the field of play after the fall of a wicket – in other words, across the boundary – he now gets three minutes to reach the wicket and take guard. Former umpire Don Oslear, author of *Wisden: The Laws of Cricket*, likened this amendment to subjecting the batsman "to a time-trial before being allowed to start his innings". Not that a few minutes here or there would have made any difference to West Indian fast bowler Vasbert Drakes in September 2002. His flight from Colombo was delayed and he was still making his way to East London, to join his Border team-mates in their game against Free State, when the umpires decided they wouldn't wait for him any longer. *Wisden* records him as the second-ever victim of Law 31 (Timed Out) in first-class cricket. The other two can be found on the following pages.

Of all the Laws concerning dismissals, Leg Before Wicket (LBW) has had more angels dancing on pinheads than any other. The Hon. R. H. Lyttelton, brother and uncle of some famous cricketers, published pamphlets and wrote passionately in *Wisden* on the subject. "The true principle – it cannot be too often repeated," he thundered in the 1921 Almanack, "is that the bat, and the bat only, is the weapon to play the ball with, and if the legs are put in front of the wicket they are put there at the batsman's risk. Personally I should like to go further, and a batsman should be given out if the ball hits any part of his person, except his hand, that is between wicket and wicket, and whether the ball would have hit the wicket or not should not be a consideration at all unless it is too high."

"Praise be to Mr R. H. Lyttelton," the egalitarian "Crusoe" Robertson-Glasgow wrote in *Wisden* 1951, "who, after crusade and brochure, persuaded the law-givers to award the bowler what he had earned. A year or two before this Charter of Liberty was granted, I remember a Somerset bowler saying, with so quiet a voice and smile, to a certain batsman from the North, 'Excuse me, but is there anything in the nature of stumps between you and the wicket-keeper?' "

"Crusoe" was a bowler. Cricket's professional philosophers, needless to say, the men who know their paso doble from a Texas two-step, were batsmen: Thomas Case of Oxford and Middlesex, Mike Brearley of Cambridge, Middlesex and England, and Edward Craig of Cambridge and Lancashire. So maybe it's not too surprising that, after all the years of lobbying and lawmaking, LBW still leans towards the batters when it comes to their last – sometimes first – line of defence against the bowlers' wiles.

Notes by the Editor, *Wisden*, 1935

Everyone will remember that last season an incident which did not sound nice occurred at Eastbourne in the match between Sussex and Lancashire. James Parks of Sussex, not hearing the umpire and under the impression that he had been given out for a catch at the wicket made by Duckworth standing back, walked away and when he was out of his ground Duckworth ran up and put down the wicket; Parks was thereupon given out by the other umpire. We will admit that Parks, before walking away, should have made certain if the umpire put his finger up or not, but that does not really concern the point I wish to raise. It has been the custom – in my opinion a very bad one – for some years now for umpires when answering an appeal in the negative to turn their heads away; look towards the sightscreen and say nothing, or else tell the bowler or wicket-keeper to "get on with it". In its simplest interpretation this gesture has always appeared to me to be of a contemptuous nature and unnecessary on the cricket field. I would urge the MCC to issue an instruction that when an answer to an appeal is in the negative, the umpire must clearly and audibly say: "Not out." There ought never to be any misunderstanding over the affirmative reply, which is the raising of the index finger above the head; equally there should be none when the answer to the appeal is in the batsman's favour.

CAPTAIN'S CALL
by Charles Stewart Caine, 1933

A characteristic story of Lord Harris used to be told by George Hearne. Joining his captain, who was well set and batting in fine form, Hearne, almost directly he went in, found himself called upon to attempt a sharp single. To Hearne's idea there existed no chance of a run being obtained and he momentarily hesitated but, seeing Lord Harris coming, Hearne responded and, as he expected, was run out by several yards. As he retired from the wicket, Hearne had to pass Lord Harris who – very hot tempered as a young man – muttered "Damn little fool. Serve you jolly well right. Why the devil don't you come when you're called?" Having sacrificed his own wicket to save that of his captain, Hearne naturally thought these words rather hard. Some time later Lord Harris got out and walked across to where Hearne and the other professionals were sitting. "George," said he, "that was no run." "No, my lord," replied George, "I didn't think it was." "Why then did you come?" he was asked. "Well, I saw you coming and thought your wicket was worth more than mine." "Another time I do a silly thing like that," said Lord Harris, "don't you come. I beg your pardon."

AIRBORNE
by R. C. Robertson-Glasgow, 1975

Such a man [Alan Watt of Kent] was born to be a hitter. Coming in at No. 10 he hit me five or six times from the middle wicket to the square-leg boundary. Suddenly, he played a relatively calm stroke, missed, and was stumped. This was difficult to understand. I asked the square-leg umpire what had happened. "Well, you see," he answered, "he had both feet off the ground at once."

HARDLY CRICKET 1920
SOMERSET v SUSSEX

An extraordinary and in some respects very regrettable incident marked the first of the Taunton matches last season. On the second afternoon Sussex, with the score at a tie, had a wicket to fall, the remaining batsman being Heygate who was crippled by rheumatism. It was understood when the innings began that he would not be able to bat and, as there was some doubt as to whether he would come in, one of the Somerset players – not J. C. White, the acting-captain – appealed to Street, the umpire, on the ground that the limit of two minutes had been exceeded. Street pulled up the stumps and the match was officially recorded as a tie. The matter gave rise to much discussion and the MCC committee, when the question was referred to them, upheld the umpire's decision. Whether or not Heygate would have been able to crawl to the wicket, it was very unsportsmanlike that such a point should have been raised when there remained ample time to finish the match. Up to the time of the incident the game was a very good one, the ball beating the bat on the second day.

NOTE: Law 45 (1914 revision). The umpires shall allow two minutes for each striker to come in, and ten minutes between each innings. When they shall call "Play", the side refusing to play shall lose the match.

NO BOY SCOUT 2004
NOTTINGHAMSHIRE v DURHAM UNIVERSITY CCE

The students were comfortably outclassed, and Shafayat made an early bid for the fastest hundred of the season – 73 balls – but the most remarkable incident was only the third case of a player being timed out in first-class cricket. Nottinghamshire were delaying the declaration for Read's century, but No. 10 Charlie Shreck lasted just three balls on first-class debut. Harris, nursing a groin strain, had not expected to bat and by the time he had strapped on his pads, and raced part-way down the pavilion steps, the fielders were heading his way – he had already exceeded the three minutes now allowed for players to arrive at the crease under Law 31.

SITTING IT OUT 1999
ORISSA v TRIPURA

Tripura No. 11 Hemulal Yadav became the first player ever to be given timed out, under Law 31, in first-class cricket. A drinks interval had been called at the fall of Tripura's ninth wicket, during which Yadav sat near the boundary, but the umpires said that he made no attempt to come to the crease after the break and they upheld Orissa's appeal against him.

SECOND CHANCE 1937
RUGBY v MARLBOROUGH

Next morning Walford hit out spiritedly and the Rugby total reached 161. Inglis, the last man, was run out in a curious way. He lifted a ball to Graham, who held the ball momentarily before dropping it. Several of the players began walking to the pavilion, but the umpire did not leave his position and on appeal gave "not out". Then the ball was thrown to the wicket-keeper who, before Inglis regained his crease, put down the wicket.

OVER AND (NOT) OUT 1951

While batting for Hampshire against Somerset at Southampton in August 1889, Delme-Radcliffe was concerned in a curious incident. Thinking he was out stumped, he began to walk to the pavilion, but the appeal had not been upheld. Then a fieldsman pulled up a stump and he was given out "run out", but in the meantime the other umpire had called "over" so the batsman continued his innings.

A POTHECARY'S LAMENT 1920
HAMPSHIRE v GLOUCESTERSHIRE

A very curious incident marked this drawn match of heavy scoring. On the second day, just at the close of Hampshire's first innings, Pothecary played a ball into the top of his pad and shook it out into the hands of Smith, the wicket-keeper. He was given out "caught", contrary to Law 33b, which states: "If the ball, whether struck by the bat or not, lodges in the batsman's clothing, the ball shall become dead". All through the game the batting on a beautiful wicket completely beat the bowling, 1,167 runs being scored in two days. Far surpassing anything that he had done before, Smith made two separate hundreds.

LAW FOR ONE, LAW FOR ANOTHER
Notes by the Editor, *Wisden*, 2000

In two different Tests in New Zealand in 1996/97, similar incidents occurred in which the ball got trapped amid the batsman's equipment and was then caught before hitting the ground. Andrew Caddick was given not out at Christchurch; Romesh Kaluwitharana was out at Dunedin. The Caddick ruling will apply.

A BIT OF A BLOW 1935

Mr Alexander Merlin Corbett appeared for Yorkshire v Gloucestershire at Bramall Lane, Sheffield, in 1881 when, in his one match for the county, he was dismissed twice without scoring. In the first innings he had an unusual experience, for he played forward to a ball which got up, went off his bat to his forehead and straight into the hands of W. G. Grace; the bowler was W. Midwinter.

BAILED OUT 1894
MIDDLESEX v SUSSEX

An extraordinary incident marked the first day of the match, Foley, on an appeal by the bowler, being given out by Henty for picking up one of the bails and replacing it while the ball was in play. The decision was so preposterous that Murdoch, the Sussex captain, went into the pavilion and succeeded in persuading Foley to resume his innings.

NICE PAINT JOB 1957

Against MCC and Ground at Lord's in 1902, Nottinghamshire's James Iremonger was the central figure of an unusual incident. For the first time in a big match, white enamelled stumps were being used – and the enamel was not quite dry. Iremonger received a ball which moved a stump to which the bail adhered! He went on to score 100.

IN THE RIGHT SPIRIT 1928
MIDDLESEX v NOTTINGHAMSHIRE

A remarkable match ended in favour of Notts by ten wickets. On Saturday, although the wicket kicked awkwardly, Notts had 210 runs registered and only three men out when first Lilley and then Payton had temporarily to retire through injury. The game changed to 251 for eight wickets, but Flint and Larwood hit up 127 in 70 minutes. Flint treading on his wicket, neither umpire curiously enough could see what happened. Flint apparently knew he was out and gave his wicket away next ball.

NOT IN THE RIGHT SPIRIT 1997
by Matthew Engel
SOUTH AFRICA v ENGLAND, CAPE TOWN

England's main resistance came from Thorpe, whose innings ended in extraordinary circumstances. He attempted a single off Adams but Hudson hit the stumps with a direct throw from backward square leg. Umpire Dave Orchard turned down the appeal. But the spectators in the hospitality boxes, who all had access to TV sets, watched the replay, which suggested Thorpe should have been given out, and began baying for Orchard to change his mind. The South African captain Cronje approached Orchard, who consulted his colleague Steve Randell and then called for the TV replay, which confirmed the majority view. In a narrow, technical sense, justice was done, but this was perilously close to mob rule. Orchard, who was not a member of the international panel and standing in only his second Test, was later quoted as saying he had momentarily forgotten the replay was available. The referee, Clive Lloyd, fined Cronje half his match fee for appealing to the replay, against ICC regulations.

AUSSIE RULES 1988
ENGLAND v PAKISTAN, PERTH

In Pakistan's innings a blind spot in the umpires' knowledge of the Laws cost Ramiz Raja his wicket. Not hearing umpire Crafter's no-ball call, Ramiz began walking out when he clipped Gatting to Athey at wide mid-on, whence after hesitation Athey lobbed the ball to Richards. On appeal Ramiz was given out by umpire French at square leg in contravention of Law 38(2): "If a no-ball has been called, the striker shall not be given run out unless he attempts to run." Rarely as such an eventuality arises, two Test umpires should have known the Law.

OWN GOAL 1936
ETON v HARROW

All the while F. G. Mann defended stubbornly, and Cassavetti, missed at the wicket while the position was still critical, helped him to place Eton out of any danger. Mann's dismissal provided another strange incident. He played a ball from Duveen just in front of him, and when it came to rest tapped it back to save the wicket-keeper the trouble of fetching it. The wicket-keeper, however, did not take the ball, which hit the stumps and on appeal Mann was given out ["bowled Duveen"].

AND AGAIN 2003
by David Hopps
INDIA v ENGLAND, BANGALORE

The chief talking point on the first day was the controversy when Vaughan became the seventh batsman in Test cricket to be dismissed for handling the ball. His reputation as a perpetually blighted Test batsman – one he would do well to ignore – had arisen largely because of some freakish injuries, but here a mental aberration undid him. Vaughan was batting with more authority than at any time in his Test career when, on 64, he missed a sweep at the off-spinner Sarandeep Singh. As the ball became tangled beneath him, he first smothered it, then brushed it away from his crease, a lapse that would be condemned in a club match. The ball was not heading for the stumps, but that was irrelevant under Law 33. India were entitled to appeal, although Vaughan complained, unwisely, that it was "against the spirit of the game". Hussain's admission that he would have appealed himself "nine times out of ten" put this gripe into perspective. Had Vaughan simply tossed the ball to a fielder, an appeal would have been unlikely.

OF COURSE NOT 1927
ENGLAND v AUSTRALIA, THE OVAL

With Richardson in, Collins was guilty of a strangely foolish action. A ball from Tate bounced back off Strudwick's gloves. Collins caught it and threw it back to the wicket-keeper. Had an appeal been made against Collins for handling the ball when in play, the umpire could scarcely have avoided giving the batsman out under Rule 29.

HORSE SENSE 1938

Of Walter Brearley's many characteristics which delighted spectators, nothing attracted more attention or aroused more amusement than his hurried walk to the wicket when, as customary, he went in last to bat. Sometimes if, as at The Oval, he was not sure of the position of the gate on the field, he would vault the pavilion rails. It was said at Old Trafford that when Walter Brearley hurried to the wicket, the horse walked between the shafts ready to drag the heavy roller for use at the end of the innings.

THE SUMMER OF CENTURIES

For many war-worn Britons, still getting over the coldest winter in decades and limited in many of life's pleasures by rationing, the 1947 cricket season would live in their memories the way the 1967 summer of love was immortalised by their children. "In every way [it] bears favourable comparison with any year within living memory," editor Hubert Preston wrote in his Notes to the 1948 *Wisden*. Not that the sun always shone; the match reports that follow show that. At Worcester, where the ground had barely recovered from the worst flood on record, the touring South Africans were treated to snow. But then the summer of love wasn't all sex and *Sergeant Pepper* either, except in our imaginings.

Just as Lennon and McCartney provided the motif for the baby-boomers, so Compton and Edrich established 1947 in the minds of their parents. Bill Edrich was a war hero, a decorated bomber pilot; Denis Compton was a free spirit whose billboard-poster good looks and dashing strokeplay pushed war and privation into the background. Thousands quit their office desks and schoolboys played truant when the word spread that Compton was in.

Men took girlfriends to watch him bat by way of courting, as if Compton was England's answer to Clark Gable. That golden summer he was. One couple, selling me 20 years of *Wisdens* many years later, reminisced how their relationship might have foundered when he first took her to Lord's to see "the famous Denis Compton everyone was talking about". The famous Compton was dismissed in his first over and she burst out laughing. Middlesex heads turned in fury in their direction. Compton out in his first over was no laughing matter.

As with the summer of love, the cloudless skies soon darkened. In 1968 Lennon and McCartney gave way to Jagger and Richards; 20 years earlier Compton and Edrich had come up against Lindwall and Miller and all of a sudden head-banging was all the rage. The summer of centuries was stomped on by Bradman and his invincible Australians.

COMPTON AND EDRICH 1948
by R. C. Robertson-Glasgow

In their cricket, it is what Compton and Edrich are that matters far more than what they have done. They stand, in these eyes at least, for something which has no place prepared in the books of scores and record. In that territory which lies outside the microcosm of numerals, already they are kings; benevolent kings appointed and acclaimed by like-minded subjects; champions in the fight against dullness and the commercial standard. They are the mirror of hope and freedom and gaiety; heroic in the manner of the heroes of school stories; the inspiration and quarry of the young because, in a game that threatens to become old in the saddest sense, they do not outgrow the habit, the ideals, the very mistakes of youth.

Most cricketers enjoy doing well, though I could name great ones who had a queer way of showing their enjoyment. But Denis Compton and Bill Edrich are of that happy philosophy which keeps failure in its place by laughter, like boys who fall on an ice-slide and rush back to try it again. They give the impression, whether batting, bowling or fielding, that they are glad enough merely to be cricketing for Middlesex and England – "Fate cannot harm me, I have played today." And they seem to be playing not only in front of us and for us, but almost literally with us. Their cricket is communicative. We are almost out of breath at the end of an over by Edrich. We scratch our heads perplexedly at a googly from Compton which refuses to work. We smile with something near to self-satisfaction when, with easy vehemence, he persuades a length ball from the leg stump to the extra-cover boundary.

That such players should break records is inevitable rather than relevant. Numbers can be such silly things. They excite many and prove nothing, or nothing that matters. In summer 1947, records made by the great Surrey and England pair, T. Hayward and J. B. Hobbs, were knocked down. Compton's 18 centuries in a season beat Hobbs's 16 centuries in a season of 22 years before; his 3,816 aggregate beat Hayward's 3,518 scored in 1906. And Hayward was also beaten by Edrich with 3,539. Very well done, too. But let us not therefrom deduce comparisons of skill; for, if we were to try anything in this line, we should have to bring up the subject of modern and ancient bowling, and that would lead us not only far from our brief but also to an inescapable, if unpalatable, conclusion. Let us, rather, flatter by inconclusiveness, and meditate on the analogy that Blackpool with 2,000,000 holidaymakers would not necessarily be an improvement upon Blackpool with 1,468,749.

MOST HUNDREDS IN A SEASON
Eighteen: D. C. S. Compton 1947.
Sixteen: J. B. Hobbs 1925.
Fifteen: W. R. Hammond 1938.
Fourteen: H. Sutcliffe 1932.
Thirteen: G. Boycott 1971, D. G. Bradman 1938, C. B. Fry 1901, W. R. Hammond 1933 and 1937, T. W. Hayward 1906, E. H. Hendren 1923, 1927 and 1928, C. P. Mead 1928, H. Sutcliffe 1928 and 1931.

Wisden, 2004

Touching upon this question of records, I received at the end of summer, 1947, a letter from an Australian, a friend of cricket and of mine. "As one of Compton's admirers," he wrote, "and doubtless all who see or meet him get that way, I hardly expected him to score 18 hundreds in a season. I thought him too good a player for that sort of thing. Am I right in assuming that Denis played his usual cricket and the 18 hundreds just happened in the process?" Well, my Sydney friend *is* right, or very nearly.

Compton cannot help it. He has the habit of batting, as the sun has the habit of journeying from east to west; and the fielders are his satellites. Hardest-working of them, and most perplexed, is cover-point. Other batsmen of our time have been severer on the stroke. Walter Hammond could leave the nimblest cover motionless or just flickering as by token. But Compton uses cover-point as a game within a game, tantalises him with delayed direction and vexes him with variety. He is for ever seeking fresh by-products of the old forward stroke and has not yet, I fancy, come to the end of the experiment. He finds it so amusing and so profitable. He outruns the traditional and discovers new truth. Compton is the axiom of tomorrow.

MOST RUNS IN A SEASON

	Season	Inns	NO	Runs	HS	100s	Avge
D. C. S. Compton	1947	50	8	3,816	246	18	90.85
W. J. Edrich	1947	52	8	3,539	267*	12	80.43
T. W. Hayward	1906	61	8	3,518	219	13	66.37
L. Hutton	1949	56	6	3,429	269*	12	68.58
F. E. Woolley	1928	59	4	3,352	198	12	60.94
H. Sutcliffe	1932	52	7	3,336	313	14	74.13
W. R. Hammond	1933	54	5	3,323	264	13	67.81
E. H. Hendren	1928	54	7	3,311	209*	13	70.44
R. Abel	1901	68	8	3,309	247	7	55.15

NOTE: 3,000 in a season has been surpassed on 19 other occasions. W. R. Hammond, E. H. Hendren and H. Sutcliffe are the only players to achieve the feat three times. M. J. K. Smith (3,245 in 1959) and W. E. Alley (3,019 in 1961) are the only players except Compton, Edrich and Hutton above to have reached 3,000 since World War II.

Wisden, 2004

Compton has genius, and if he knows it he doesn't care. Edrich has talent; or, more truly, he started with a number of talents and has increased them into riches. Compton, in essence, has not altered from the lad of just eighteen who scored 100 not out at Northampton in 1936 while numbers 10 and 11, Sims and Peebles, admired and defended at the other end. His whereabouts in artistry cannot be doubted. His effect silences question. But

Edrich has, as they say, gone through it. He rose, half fell, and rose again to a place higher and less slippery. The cost and the lesson are expressed in his concentration. With bat and ball he is an all-in cricketer; no funny stuff here; no holidays of mind or body. Compton is poetry; Edrich is prose, robust and clear. Far more than Compton, Edrich uses the practical and old-fashioned methods and areas of attack. He likes the straight hit, and that pull-drive which gave old E. M. Grace so many runs and W. G. so many moments of reflective beard-stroking. Old-fashioned, too, is Edrich's high backlift in preparation for stroke. He gives the idea of a height and a reach beyond fact. But also he is a hooker, nearly as vicious as his great forerunner, Pat Hendren.

Edrich and Compton are fitting adornments and exponents of a game that was meant not as an imitation of, but as a refreshment from, the worldly struggle.

DENIS COMPTON'S RECORD RUN

NOTE: Just in case the mention of Manns in the following match reports causes any confusion, the one on the English side is F. G. (George) Mann of Middlesex, the other is N. B. F. (Tufty) Mann of South Africa, a tauntingly accurate left-arm slow bowler. When the South Africans played Middlesex, "Tufty" Mann dismissed George Mann in both innings, prompting the incomparable John Arlott to muse upon "Mann's inhumanity to Mann".

MIDDLESEX v WORCESTERSHIRE

At Lord's, May 21, 22, 23, 1947. Middlesex won by 234 runs. Two splendid innings by Denis Compton and admirable bowling by Edrich, who took five wickets in each innings, earned this success. On a cheerless day Compton, missed at the wicket off Howorth when four, hit 11 fours in his not out 88. Worcestershire bowled splendidly, but in the Middlesex second innings Jackson was absent suffering from cramp. Brown hit one six and eight fours in a brilliant display before Compton made the first of his 18 centuries in this memorable season. He was rarely in trouble, and in a grand partnership with Edrich added 118 in 80 minutes. Rain caused a long hold-up on the last day, when Middlesex claimed the extra half-hour. Not until then did Mann call on Sims, and he finished the match with 20 minutes to spare by dismissing Perks and Jenkins.

Middlesex 207 (S. M. Brown 42, W. J. Edrich 34, D. C. S. Compton 88 not out; R. T. D. Perks three for 71, P. F. Jackson three for 45) **and 314** for seven dec. (J. D. Robertson 43, S. M. Brown 61, W. J. Edrich 48, D. C. S. Compton 112; R. Howorth three for 71).

Worcestershire 134 (L. H. Gray three for 37, W. J. Edrich five for 61) **and 153** (R. O. Jenkins 42; L. H. Gray three for 42, W. J. Edrich five for 69).

MIDDLESEX v SUSSEX

At Lord's, May 24, 26, 1947. Middlesex won by ten wickets. Robins [the Middlesex captain], who made his first appearance of the season, claimed the extra half-hour on the second day. Edrich, in splendid form, and Denis Compton made 223 together in the one complete batting mastery of the match. Mann showed most freedom, hitting nine fours during 70 minutes of admirable batting. Sussex lost four wickets for 43 on Saturday and, though Griffith stayed 70 minutes, they never showed signs of recovery against a cleverly managed attack and brilliant fielding. Edrich helped to dismiss eight men, taking four wickets and four catches, and Gray bowled a good length with sustained speed. Nearly 17,000 people paid for admission on Saturday, and the crowd on Whit Monday numbered nearly 30,000.

Middlesex 380 (W. J. Edrich 106, D. C. S. Compton 110, F. G. Mann 69; James Langridge four for 38, C. Oakes three for 70) **and 21** for no wkt.

Sussex 139 (S. C. Griffith 45; L. H. Gray four for 28, W. J. Edrich three for 34) **and 259** (C. Oakes 32, James Langridge 85, G. Cox 65; L. H. Gray three for 42, J. M. Sims four for 46).

MIDDLESEX v SOUTH AFRICANS

At Lord's, May 31, June 2, 3, 1947. Drawn. Edrich and Denis Compton took batting honours for Middlesex, who on the last day struggled to avoid defeat on wearing turf. The South Africans batted unevenly on Saturday. Mitchell stayed four hours ten minutes, hitting ten fours by cuts and leg-side strokes, and the

---

COULD NOT BAT 1935

ESSEX v WORCESTERSHIRE

On Whit Monday morning Nichol, the Worcestershire batsman, was found dead in bed – a sad event that marred the enjoyment of the match but did not prevent Worcestershire gaining first-innings lead.

DID NOT BAT 1999

In August 1939 Lionel Lister, Lancashire captain since 1936, was padded up at Northampton when he was summoned by his territorial regiment. He said goodbye to his team-mates (he was recorded as "absent . . . 0"), and never played another first-class match.

---

strong-driving Nourse, whose figures included 12 fours, helped to add 147 in 90 minutes. Viljoen, in just over two and a half hours, hit 14 fours, mostly to leg. Middlesex lost two men for 40. Then Compton and Edrich added 147, and Leslie Compton helped his brother put on 103. Denis Compton hit 19 fours, drives and pulls, in four hours' faultless batting. Mann declared 108 behind, and the South Africans lost eight wickets for 112, Sims performing the hat-trick when dismissing Ovenstone, Rowan and Tuckett. Harris, with two sixes and 12 fours, scored 76 in 65 minutes, and Middlesex needed 326 to win. Edrich, staying three and a quarter hours, hit 13 fours when few other batsmen shone.

South Africans 424 (B. Mitchell 109, A. D. Nourse 92, K. G. Viljoen 104, A. M. B. Rowan 36; J. M. Sims four for 148, J. A. Young four for 52) **and 217** (A. Melville 42, T. A. Harris 76, N. B. F. Mann 30; J. M. Sims six for 89).

Middlesex 316 for eight dec. (W. J. Edrich 67, D. C. S. Compton 154, L. H. Compton 32; A. M. B. Rowan four for 130) **and 226** for six (W. J. Edrich 133 not out, D. C. S. Compton 34).

ENGLAND v SOUTH AFRICA
First Test Match

At Nottingham, June 7, 9, 10, 11, 1947. Drawn. How England fought back from a seemingly hopeless position will cause this match to be a subject of cricket discussion for a long time.

Surprisingly dismissed on a perfect batting wicket for 208, England lost four men for 170 after following on 325 behind, so that when Yardley joined Compton 155 runs were needed to avoid an innings defeat with Evans the only recognised batsman to come. Yet England made such a complete recovery that South Africa were denied a victory their earlier superiority deserved, and in fact, for one brief moment on the last day, faint visions were raised of a South African defeat.

In view of the harvest of runs previously gathered by county batsmen at Trent Bridge, it was expected that bowlers would face an unusually difficult task. So events proved and, in spite of England's first-innings failure, batsmen were so much in their element that the four days produced 1,458 runs while 31 wickets fell. Several records were established, of which the most notable were: (1) The 319 stand by Melville and Nourse beat the previous highest for the third wicket in any Test and was a South African Test record for any wicket. (2) South Africa's total of 533 was their best ever in Test cricket. (3) Melville became the first South African to score two separate centuries in a Test, and his 189 stood as the biggest individual score for his country against England. Including his 103 at Durban in 1938/39, he thus made three centuries in successive innings against England. (This became four in the Second Test, at Lord's.) (4) Compton and Yardley shared in the highest Test fifth-wicket stand in England – 237.

[After South Africa's massive first innings] England shocks followed quickly. Hutton and Washbrook were out for 48; but an unbroken partnership of 106 by Edrich and Compton to the end of the second day gave hope of a big reply. Though 86 overs were delivered, Melville preferred to wait for the new ball till his bowlers were fresh in the morning. The mental effect of this probably cost Compton his wicket. At any rate he made a casual stroke to the second loosening-up ball by Tuckett in the first over of the day, first slip taking an easy catch. Inspired by this unexpected success Tuckett bowled splendidly, and Smith provided excellent support with accurate-length leg-breaks. Against this attack, backed up by first-rate fielding, in which Melville at cover excelled, eight England wickets tumbled for 54 before lunch, and the last five produced no more than ten runs. For his unbroken spell of 80 minutes, Tuckett returned an analysis of 14–7–16–4. His length and direction rarely erred and he surprised his opponents by his speed through the air and off the ground. A particular feature of their out-cricket was the manner in which all the South Africans bowled to their well-placed fields. Mann, for instance, began his Test career with eight successive maiden overs to such punishing batsmen as Compton and Edrich, and he gave away only ten runs in 20 overs.

In the follow-on England received another big blow through Hutton's second cheap dismissal. Tuckett sent his off stump catapulting out of its socket, but Washbrook and Edrich put on 96 before Edrich hit over a full toss. Melville and his men pursued "tight" tactics against Washbrook, who gave a catch at the wicket at 133 in attempting to cut a ball well outside his off stump. When Dawson took a fine low return catch off Dollery, so making four men out for 170, everything looked set for a South African victory. At this point Yardley joined Compton. Before the close they added 108 in 100 minutes, but even so England, with six wickets to fall at the beginning of the last day, needed 47 to make South Africa bat again.

Yardley [the England captain] called for an hour's concentrated net practice from the remaining batsmen before play in the morning. He and Compton immediately displayed refreshing confidence, but Yardley added only six to his overnight 45 before being unaccountably dropped at first slip by Mitchell off Tuckett. Compton played one of the best innings of his career for his side, and Yardley provided the Yorkshire grit and ability which helped turn the tables. They made 237 together before Compton fell to a catch in the slips. He batted four hours and three-quarters without relaxing vigilance and without noticeable error. At no time did he offer the hitherto dominating attack the slightest hope, and his 163 out of 291 included 19 fours. On Compton's dismissal the odds still heavily favoured South Africa, but Yardley found another good partner in Evans, and runs came swiftly till Yardley fell to a slip catch off the new ball when needing one for his first Test century. Evans went on hitting powerfully and cleanly, and his 74, obtained in 75 minutes, contained 14 fours. More accurate bowling than that of Mann, who sent down 80 overs in the match for 104 runs on a batsman's wicket, could scarcely be imagined. Mitchell's misfortune in dropping Yardley was the turning-point in the game; otherwise the South Africans gave nothing away. Left 140 minutes to get 227 to win, they made no real attempt at the task. – R. J. Hayter

South Africa 533 (A. Melville 189, A. D. Nourse 149, O. C. Dawson 48, T. A. Harris 60, A. M. B. Rowan 34 not out; A. V. Bedser three for 106, W. E. Hollies five for 123) **and 166** for one (A. Melville 104 not out, K. G. Viljoen 51 not out).
England 208 (W. J. Edrich 57, D. C. S. Compton 65; L. Tuckett five for 68, V. I. Smith three for 46) **and 551** (C. Washbrook 59, W. J. Edrich 50, D. C. S. Compton 163, N. W. D. Yardley 99, T. G. Evans 74, extras 30; V. I. Smith four for 143).

ENGLAND v SOUTH AFRICA
Second Test Match

At Lord's, June 21, 23, 24, 25, 1947. England won by ten wickets. From first to last this was a delightful match. South Africa put up a brave fight and were by no means as inferior as the result would suggest. Their bowlers again provided an object lesson in length, direction and bowling to a field, and, in spite of a trying ordeal, their fielding remained at a superlatively high standard of efficiency and keenness. Moreover, Melville, Mitchell and Nourse once more proved their worth as batsmen of contrasting characters. Yet these factors were outweighed by the advantage England gained in winning the toss, the greatness of Edrich and Compton, who established a new world record in Test matches with a third-wicket stand of 370, the shock bowling and slip catching of Edrich, and the consistently fine work of Wright on his first appearance of the season against the touring side.

Through their excellent performance in the First Test, the South Africans attracted big crowds to Lord's and the gates were closed half an hour before the start on the first day, when the attendance was officially given as 30,600. The thousands of people turned away missed extremely interesting cricket. Except for an occasional ball which lifted in the early stages, conditions favoured batsmen and England received a sound start from Hutton and Washbrook, who achieved their first objective of staying together for the 90 minutes before lunch. Hutton made only 14 scoring strokes – 12 singles, a four and a two – from the 121 balls delivered to him in an hour and 50 minutes before playing outside an off-break. By comparison Washbrook looked set for a big score until, with the new ball just in use and the total 96, he flashed at a rising ball outside the off stump. A conjuring catch at second slip, where Tuckett held the ball at the third attempt, ended his attractive display.

In view of the obviously long tail, no little responsibility rested on Edrich and Compton, and an enthralling struggle developed between them and a determined attack before the two Middlesex batsmen assumed mastery. Then followed a sparkling exhibition of fluent strokeplay. Compton used everything in his complete repertoire, including the brilliant leg-sweep off a slow bowler, and Edrich specially excelled in on-side play. He hooked Rowan for one glorious six and frequently brought off a powerful lofted pulled-drive. In three hours ten minutes to the close, the stand produced 216 runs, Edrich reaching his first Test century in England and Compton his second in successive Test innings against South Africa. Taking into account the slow start and the 25 minutes lost through rain, England's average scoring-rate was satisfactory. The day was marred by an unfortunate accident to Melville. Shortly before the close, a throw-in from the deep struck him over the right eye. Melville sank to the ground but, after attention, was able to resume, although during the weekend his eye turned black and became almost completely closed.

Compton and Edrich thrilled another 30,000 crowd on the second day. Both were supremely confident, and by swift and sure running took full value for every stroke. No relief, in fact, came to South Africa until 20 minutes after lunch, when Edrich at last relaxed his concentration and was bowled. He gave a difficult stumping chance when 47, but that was his only blemish. He hit a six and 26 fours in 189 out of 391 in five minutes under six hours.

The partnership beat by 51 the 319 made by Melville and Nourse in the Nottingham Test and fell only 12 short of the highest for England by any wicket – 382 by Hutton and Leyland against Australia at The Oval in 1938. Compton, dismissed at 515, obtained 20 boundaries in his 208 out of 419 in five hours 50 minutes. His first Test double-century brought his total to 436 in three Test innings against South Africa.

Barnett led the way in carefree hitting by the following batsmen, so that England after lunch obtained 111 in 65 minutes for six wickets before Yardley declared. Tuckett maintained pace and hostility to the end. In his last spell he dismissed five men for 20 in seven overs, and at all times looked a better fast bowler than anyone England possessed. – R. J. Hayter

England 554 for eight dec. (C. Washbrook 65, W. J. Edrich 189,
    D. C. S. Compton 208, C. J. Barnett 33; L. Tuckett five for 115) **and 26**
    for no wkt.
South Africa 327 (A. Melville 117, B. Mitchell 46, A. D. Nourse 61,
    O. C. Dawson 36, T. A. Harris 30; D. V. P. Wright five for 95) **and 252**
    (B. Mitchell 80, A. D. Nourse 58, O. C. Dawson 33, A. M. B. Rowan 38
    not out; W. J. Edrich three for 31, D. V. P Wright five for 80).

ENGLAND v SOUTH AFRICA
Third Test Match

At Manchester, July 5, 7, 8, 9, 1947. England won by seven wickets. Few Test matches can have contained as many as three innings of such merit as those by Nourse, Edrich and Compton, who all showed exceptional skill and courage in conditions suited to bowlers. Nourse's display on the last day nearly enabled South Africa to avoid defeat, but the full value of his batting might have been more obvious if England's second-innings task had been 100 runs greater, since the ball was rearing and turning almost viciously towards the end.

For the greater part of the match the weather was unpleasant; on no day more so than Saturday, when a bitterly cold north-westerly wind straight down the pitch frequently lifted off the bails, and on one occasion reached such velocity that it blew down a sightscreen. Criticism of South Africa's batting in these circumstances might seem unjustified, but a rather ordinary English attack was flattered by an average scoring-rate of 46 runs an hour on an easy-paced wicket. The batting struggles which came later probably gave South Africa cause for regret at their ability to score only 278 for six wickets in the full day's play.

In view of heavy rain during the night and the probability of the pitch becoming difficult, South Africa on the second day obviously regarded time spent at the wicket just as valuable as runs scored, and their last four wickets held out for 115 minutes while adding 61. Viljoen soon received a painful blow on the instep and was rapped three times on the thumb, but, though limping, he defended stubbornly till a spectacular left-hand slip catch, high and wide, by Compton off Edrich brought about his departure when seven short of the century. In 15 overs Edrich dismissed three of the last four batsmen for 30 runs.

Sun and wind during lunch hastened the turf's drying, and Washbrook immediately began to attack the fast bowlers, taking three fours in an over from Tuckett, before the ball started to lift from a good length. Such deliveries accounted for England's opening pair, which brought Edrich and Compton together again with two men out for 48, the pitch difficult, and the bowlers eager. They wore down the fast attack, dealt severely with the slow bowlers, and looked quite at ease when Tuckett and Plimsoll returned. By this time the batsmen were so much on top that they took 38 from the first three overs with the new ball. Three times in this spell Edrich made huge pull-drives for six off Plimsoll. Compton passed 50 in 80 minutes, and an hour later reached his third successive Test century against South Africa. In three hours ten minutes the stand put on 228 before Compton was taken at short leg. His chanceless innings, full of delightful and impudent strokes, contained 17 fours.

Rain limited play to three hours on the third day. In that time England progressed much nearer victory. From the start the ball began to fly, and several times Edrich was hit on the arms, hands and thighs. But he added 50 to his overnight score before he played outside a fast ball which hit his leg stump. Edrich's 191 out of 375 was made in five hours 20 minutes, and included three sixes and 22 fours. He gave one chance, to mid-off when 101, but otherwise made no mistake in an admirable display of skill and determination.

The last day was notable for a gallant exhibition by Nourse, which compared favourably with any innings played during the season. Batting was a difficult task on a pitch which took spin and from which the ball went through at varying heights. Some of Compton's deliveries rose shoulder high, but fortunately for South Africa he did not strike his best bowling form. As Nourse and Viljoen produced 121 in 95 minutes, South Africa looked almost certain to save the game, but such a transformation occurred that the last seven wickets fell in an hour for 50.

For being left to get only 129 in a possible two hours and a half, England owed much to Edrich. To the end of the second South African innings he was on the field all the time except for half an hour. Besides making his highest score in Test cricket, he sent down 57 overs of considerable speed for eight wickets. Apart from him and Wright, who was handicapped by a poisoned foot, England's bowlers looked ordinary. – R. J. Hayter

South Africa 339 (D. V. Dyer 62, B. Mitchell 80, K. G. Viljoen 93; W. J. Edrich four for 95) **and 267** (A. Melville 59, A. D. Nourse 115, K. G. Viljoen 32; W. J. Edrich four for 77, D. V. P. Wright three for 32).
England 478 (W. J. Edrich 191, D. C. S. Compton 115, N. W. D. Yardley 41; L. Tuckett four for 148, J. B. Plimsoll three for 128) **and 130** for three (C. Washbrook 40, D. C. S. Compton 6).

TRAVEL NOTES

1912

In the third game of the 1911 Cheltenham Festival, Gloucestershire proved successful by 79 runs. As a matter of record it should be stated that, owing to the railway strike, the Northampton cricketers journeyed to Cheltenham by motor cars.

1948

Queensland created history by flying on their Southern tour; never before had a complete Sheffield Shield team travelled in this manner.

LEICESTERSHIRE v MIDDLESEX

At Leicester, July 12, 14, 15, 1947. Middlesex won by ten wickets. A more thrilling finish would be difficult to imagine. At lunch time on the last day Leicestershire led by 17 runs with six men to be dismissed, and only 80 minutes remained for play. But Middlesex got down the remaining wickets for 48 runs in 35 minutes, and so required 66 to win in 25 minutes. Edrich and Compton hit off the runs in seven overs with four minutes to spare, a fitting climax to a splendid match in which 1,405 runs were scored, 663 on the second day. Put in to bat by Edrich, captaining Middlesex for the first time, Leicestershire lost five wickets for 114 before Jackson and Riddington added 107. After losing Brown, struck on the eye by a rising ball, Middlesex scored at an amazing rate. Robertson and Edrich put on 159, and Edrich and Compton added 277 in 130 minutes. Edrich batted four and three-quarter hours and hit four sixes and 26 fours. Compton, who obtained 21 fours, reached 100 in as many minutes. In 140 minutes between lunch and tea Middlesex scored 310. Needing 328 to avoid an innings defeat, Leicestershire fought back well, but everything was dwarfed by the dramatic last hour and a quarter.

Leicestershire 309 (L. G. Berry 53, M. Tompkin 33, V. E. Jackson 117, A. Riddington 63; J. M. Sims six for 135) **and 393** (L. G. Berry 154, F. T. Prentice 31, M. Tompkin 76, G. Lester 40, extras 34; D. C. S. Compton five for 108).

Middlesex 637 for four dec. (J. D. Robertson 75, W. J. Edrich 257, D. C. S. Compton 151, A. W. Thompson 89 not out) **and 66** for no wkt (W. J. Edrich 29 not out, D. C. S. Compton 33 not out).

MIDDLESEX v ESSEX

At Lord's, July 19, 21, 22, 1947. Middlesex won by 102 runs. Notwithstanding the batting triumphs of Brown, Robertson, Edrich and Compton, the most heartening feature for Middlesex was the successful first appearance of Bedford, a seventeen-year-old Woodhouse Grammar School boy, who took six wickets for 134 in a match of 1,388 runs. He revealed more than average ability as a leg-break and googly bowler. Following aggressive innings by Brown, Robertson and Edrich, the fourth-wicket stand of Compton and Robins produced 150 in 70 minutes. Compton's 129 out of 198 in two hours contained a six and 14 fours. Essex were handicapped when Bailey split a hand in fielding and, after the insertion of six stitches, could not bowl again in the game. Middlesex made 389 in four hours ten minutes and dismissed three men before the end of the first day, but sound displays by Dodds, Horsfall, Ray Smith and Insole enabled Essex to get within 39 of their opponents. Then Middlesex hammered 356 in 170 minutes before Robins declared a second time, Edrich becoming the first man to reach a 2,000 aggregate for the season. Set to get 396 to win, Essex lost eight men for 161, but Insole and Wade delayed the end with a ninth-wicket stand of 83, and Bailey helped Wade add 49 for the last wicket.

Middlesex 389 for seven dec. (S. M. Brown 74, J. D. Robertson 39, W. J. Edrich 44, D. C. S. Compton 129, R. W. V. Robins 53; R. Smith four for 151) **and 356** for five dec. (S. M. Brown 76, J. D. Robertson 100, W. J. Edrich 83, D. C. S. Compton 48).

Essex 350 (T. C. Dodds 66, R. Horsfall 69, R. Smith 61, D. J. Insole 70; P. I. Bedford four for 81) **and 293** (F. H. Vigar 40, R. Horsfall 33, D. J. Insole 63, T. H. Wade 74 not out; J. A. Young three for 40).

NORTHAMPTONSHIRE v MIDDLESEX

At Northampton, July 23, 24, 25, 1947. Middlesex won by eight wickets. They claimed the extra half-hour on the second day, but failed to knock off 67 in 25 minutes, and the match continued for 25 minutes on Friday. Edrich made 267 not out – the highest score of his career, batting five and a quarter hours and hitting three sixes and 24 fours. It was his second successive double-century at Northampton. Compton helped him in a third-wicket stand of 211, and Mann and Edrich put on 155. Northamptonshire collapsed before the left-hand off-breaks and googlies of Compton, only Bennett, in his first Championship match, shaping confidently. The best stand came from the last pair, Fiddling and Clark, who put on 44. Following on 262 behind, Northamptonshire did better, Brookes batting two and a half hours. Northamptonshire's Barron, struck on the right ear by a fast rising ball, retired in the first innings and did not bat again.

Middlesex 464 for five dec. (W. J. Edrich 267 not out, D. C. S. Compton 110, F. G. Mann 54) **and 67** for two (D. C. S. Compton 13 not out).

Northamptonshire 202 (A. C. L. Bennett 50, A. W. Childs-Clarke 32; D. C. S. Compton six for 78) **and 328** (D. Brookes 107, A. C. L. Bennett 44, A. L. Cox 41, V. Broderick 31; J. M. Sims three for 116, D. C. S. Compton three for 100).

SUSSEX v MIDDLESEX

At Hove, August 2, 4, 5, 1947. Middlesex won by nine wickets. They pursued match-winning tactics with great success. Robertson and Brown gave them the customary flying start, and with Edrich, Compton and Mann also scoring briskly, runs came at an average rate of 85 an hour. Edrich hit ten boundaries in his stand of 131 in 85 minutes with Robertson, who gave three chances in the slips off Nye, and Compton's tenth hundred of the summer contained 13 fours. Although 40 minutes were lost through rain, Robins declared on the first day, and Compton's "chinamen" played a big part in the fall of three Sussex batsmen for 21 in the last half-hour. Sussex lost five wickets, all to Sims, after following on 206 behind on Monday, but Bartlett and C. Oakes halted Middlesex's progress with grand displays of clean and powerful strokes. Their sixth-wicket stand yielded 138 in 95 minutes, and Bartlett, who showed much of his pre-war form in an innings of two hours and a quarter, went on batting splendidly till dismissed by a spectacular one-hand slip catch by Denis Compton off Edrich. Two interruptions by rain on the last day caused Middlesex more anxiety, but Brown took 17 from Nye's first over and Robertson and Edrich knocked off the remaining 87 in 45 minutes.

Middlesex 401 for four dec. (J. D. Robertson 106, S. M. Brown 40, W. J. Edrich 76, D. C. S. Compton 100 not out, F. G. Mann 53 not out; J. H. Cornford three for 79) **and 111** for one (J. D. Robertson 43 not out, W. J. Edrich 54 not out).

Sussex 195 (J. G. Langridge 40, H. T. Bartlett 44, P. A. D. Carey 31;

D. C. S. Compton four for 90) **and 316** (J. G. Langridge 42, C. Oakes 89,
H. T. Bartlett 95; J. M. Sims six for 83).

KENT v MIDDLESEX

At Canterbury, August 6, 7, 8, 1947. Drawn. Fagg batted four
hours and a quarter and hit 17 fours in his second consecutive
three-figure innings. Timing his strokes perfectly, he always got a
large share of the runs before being fifth out at 299. Strained
muscles under the right shoulder compelled Edrich to retire just
before the close, and he did not bowl again, but when Middlesex
followed on despite a great display by Compton, who hit 13 fours
during three hours and a quarter at the crease, Edrich and Robertson pulled the game round by adding 193. Robins and
Thompson made 90 in 48 minutes, and the captain set Kent to get
232 in two hours. In the effort to win four wickets fell for 30.
Valentine and Pawson put on 95 in 37 minutes, but when the
former left at 132 Todd and Dovey relied on defence, a remarkable match ending quietly after much excitement. On Thursday
13,079 people paid, and on the five days of the Canterbury
Festival there were 46,756 spectators – double good averages of
pre-war years – apart from large attendances of members and
their guests.

Kent 423 for eight dec. (A. E. Fagg 184, L. E. G. Ames 55, H. A. Pawson
67; J. A. Young four for 87) **and 181** for six (B. H. Valentine 56,
H. A. Pawson 44, L. J. Todd 30 not out; J. A. Young four for 26).
Middlesex 225 (S. M. Brown 31, D. C. S. Compton 106; D. V. P. Wright six
for 87) **and 429** for eight dec. (J. D. Robertson 140, W. J. Edrich 130,
D. C. S. Compton 4, R. W. V. Robins 68, A. W. Thompson 49;
N. W. Harding four for 61).

SURREY v MIDDLESEX

At The Oval, August 9, 11, 12, 1947. Middlesex won by an
innings and 11 runs after giving a display worthy of potential
champions. Denis Compton achieved the best all-round performance of his career by hitting 137 not out and taking 12
wickets for 174 runs. The only regret on the opening day, when

Middlesex scored their 537, was that Brown should be bowled for 98 after helping Robertson in an opening stand of 211. Both men batted faultlessly, paving the way for Edrich and Compton to add 287 in two and three-quarter hours without being separated. The Surrey bowling was never loose, and Compton was content with nine fours compared with 18 by Edrich. Torn tendons in the right arm, damaged when bowling in the previous match, prevented Edrich fielding on the second day when before tea Surrey scored freely. Then came a collapse before the slow left-arm unorthodox over-the-wicket bowling of Compton which brought Middlesex victory before lunch on the third day. Both wicket-keepers, Leslie Compton and McIntyre, bowled. Altogether 54,000, of whom 47,000 paid, saw this match. The gates were closed by three o'clock on Saturday when 30,000 were present.

Middlesex 537 for two dec. (S. M. Brown 98, J. D. Robertson 127, W. J. Edrich 157 not out, D. C. S. Compton 137 not out).

Surrey 334 (D. G. W. Fletcher 42, H. S. Squires 98, E. R. T. Holmes 61, A. J. McIntyre 51; J. M. Sims three for 100, D. C. S. Compton six for 94) **and 192** (L. B. Fishlock 44, T. H. Barling 44; D. C. S. Compton six for 80).

MIDDLESEX v KENT

At Lord's, August 13, 14, 15, 1947. Kent won by 75 runs. They triumphed five minutes from the end of extra time after one of the most exciting struggles of the season. Kent scored so freely when holding a first-innings lead of 72 that they were able to set Middlesex the task of getting 397 to win at more than 90 an hour. When four wickets fell for 135, an easy victory for Kent seemed in sight, particularly as Wright was bowling in superb form. Then Compton found a good partner in Mann, and in 97 minutes the score raced along by 161 before Wright broke the threatening stand. During the partnership, most of the Kent fieldsmen were placed on the boundary. Compton hit 19 fours in his 13th century of the season, his seventh in seven successive games for Middlesex and one of his finest innings. Upon Compton's dismissal, when he attempted another big hit, Kent again set an attacking field for Wright and Davies, who accounted for the last five wickets in 37 minutes for 25 runs. In each innings Wright kept a remarkably accurate length and troubled most of the batsmen with variations of leg-breaks and googlies, which brought him 11 wickets for 194 runs. Robertson hit his fifth century in successive matches for Middlesex in the first innings, when Edrich was their next highest scorer with 28. All through, Kent batted much more consistently.

Kent 301 (L. J. Todd 62, A. E. Fagg 66, B. H. Valentine 61, D. V. P. Wright 36; J. M. Sims four for 87) **and 324** for eight dec. (L. E. G. Ames 69, B. H. Valentine 92, G. F. Anson 51, T. G. Evans 56; J. A. Young four for 65).

Middlesex 229 (J. D. Robertson 110, D. C. S. Compton 16; D. V. P. Wright seven for 92) **and 321** (W. J. Edrich 31, D. C. S. Compton 168, F. G. Mann 57; D. V. P. Wright four for 102, J. G. W. Davies four for 58).

ENGLAND v SOUTH AFRICA
Fifth Test Match

At The Oval, August 16, 18, 19, 20, 1947. Drawn. After four days of fluctuating play in extreme heat, South Africa finished 28 runs short of victory with three wickets in hand. The position warranted a spirited effort by each side to achieve success, but batsmen and fieldsmen alike seemed worn out by prolonged exercise in scorching sunshine, and the last few overs suggested lethargy when normal keenness might have brought triumph to South Africa, or further proof of the superiority shown by England in the series. Perhaps the three wins to England after a drawn match created some feeling of indifference, but the rush for a souvenir stump gave some of the fieldsmen more impetus than the necessity of stopping the ball off many strokes that earned runs.

The pitch, although showing distinct signs of wear as each day advanced, responded satisfactorily to the medium-weight roller next morning and, on the authority of the umpires, it was faster and easier on the Wednesday than on any of the three previous playing days. Seldom did runs come at all fast. England occupied seven hours and three-quarters over their first innings. Hutton, fourth out at 178, hit only six fours during three hours and a half, but he always appeared confident. Of his first 15 runs, 13 were singles, largely because Melville placed men at a distance to prevent boundaries, and the ball moved so fast on the dry turf that often a two was impossible. Only Robertson, in his first Test match, and Copson, last man, fell cheaply, but the best stand was 98 by Compton and Hutton, both out at the same total. Of the bowlers, Mann excelled; his first 35 overs, of which 16 were maidens, yielded only 33 runs, with Washbrook and Hutton victims of his slow left-handed guile.

Mitchell, after seven hours and three-quarters in the field, became the central figure of the match by playing two innings which placed him on a level with Melville, who made two centuries in the Test at Nottingham, their higher innings being equal, 189. Mitchell had the additional merit of carrying his bat, so that he was off the field for only 15 minutes while the last two first-innings wickets fell on Monday.

By far the most attractive cricket of the match came when England batted a second time, leading by 125. Hutton and Washbrook fell when forcing the pace, and half the side were out for 180, but Compton, then 53 after an hour of his best and most versatile strokeplay, went on with such freedom that, when caught from an on-drive, he claimed 113 out of 178 put on during an hour and three-quarters; his drives, cuts and forcing strokes brought 15 fours. His 14th century of the season was brilliant in every way. Yardley was able to declare 450 ahead, England having scored 325 in three hours and a half.

The final stage belonged to Mitchell. At times dreariness itself, he scored only 36 in two hours and a half before lunch and occupied four hours 50 minutes reaching 102 out of 275. Nourse, missed when 30 at short slip off a sharp cut which Hutton could not hold with his left hand, showed his usual aggression in hitting a dozen fours while 184 runs came in two hours 25 minutes. This stand suggested the possibility that South Africa might win, but three wickets fell for 34 more runs before Mitchell completed his hundred.

The aggregate attendances on the four days numbered 77,317,

of whom 71,201 paid at the turnstiles, and the receipts totalled
£14,103. The largest crowd, 26,980, assembled on Monday, and
the terraces presented a dazzling scene with the sun blazing down
on the compact mass of people in the lightest permissible
summer attire. – Hubert Preston

England 427 (L. Hutton 83, C. Washbrook 32, D. C. S. Compton 53,
   N. W. D. Yardley 59, K. Cranston 45, T. G. Evans 45, C. Gladwin 51
   not out; N. B. F. Mann four for 93, A. M. B. Rowan three for 92) **and
   325** for six dec. (L. Hutton 36, C. Washbrook 43, J. D. Robertson 30,
   D. C. S. Compton 113, R. Howorth 45 not out, T. G. Evans 39 not out;
   A. M. B. Rowan three for 95).
South Africa 302 (B. Mitchell 120, A. Melville 39, O. C. Dawson 55,
   N. B. F. Mann 36; W. H. Copson three for 46, R. Howorth three for 64)
   and 423 for seven (B. Mitchell 189 not out, K. G. Viljoen 33,
   A. D. Nourse 97, L. Tuckett 40 not out, extras 30; R. Howorth three
   for 85).

MIDDLESEX v SURREY

At Lord's, August 23, 25, 26, 1947. Middlesex won by eight
wickets. Though 35 minutes were lost through bad light, Middlesex scored 462 runs on the first day, when a stand of 304 in
three hours and a quarter by Compton and Mann completely
redeemed a poor start. By an attractive mixture of orthodox and
unorthodox strokes Compton hit 23 fours, and Mann, after a
shaky beginning, showed capital form in his first century for
Middlesex, which included 13 boundaries. Yet Surrey threw away
their chances. Compton was missed at 22 and Mann twice in the
first over he received. On dry turf which responded to spin,
Robins made good use of his slow bowlers. Going on at 27, Bedford at once dismissed Fishlock, and he continued to cause considerable trouble. Surrey followed on 260 behind but, after losing
two men for 15, offered much better resistance. Fortunately for
Middlesex, they required only 50 to win, for twice Gover found a
spot in the good-length area from which extra-fast balls rose
abruptly and resulted in easy catches after striking Brown and
Edrich on the hand.

Middlesex 462 for seven dec. (J. D. Robertson 37, S. M. Brown 48,
D. C. S. Compton 178, F. G. Mann 106; A. R. Gover three for 99) **and
51** for two (D. C. S. Compton 19 not out).

Surrey 202 (J. F. Parker 30, E. A. Bedser 31, J. C. Laker 33 not out;
P. I. Bedford five for 53) **and 309** (L. B. Fishlock 48, J. F. Parker 75,
J. C. Laker 60, extras 37; J. A. Young three for 51, J. M. Sims three
for 59).

MIDDLESEX v LANCASHIRE

At Lord's, August 30, September 1, 2, 1947. Lancashire won by
64 runs. Denis Compton's feat of equalling Hobbs's record overshadowed the merit of Lancashire's performance. Spin and flight
beat Compton early in the first innings, but in the second he
overcame the knee trouble which caused him to retire on the
opening day for a manipulative operation in the pavilion, and he
hit his 16th century. Although confined to defence for long
periods against bowlers who rarely sent down a loose ball,
Compton batted without fault. The strain of the occasion kept
him almost half an hour in the 90s. Then, after nearly three hours
at the crease, he earned the acclamation of the crowd by sending
his score to 102 with a square-leg boundary off Pollard. Compton altogether defied Lancashire for three hours and 20 minutes
and hit 17 fours. Lancashire provided much excellent batting,
bowling and fielding, and Bedford of Middlesex took the eye for
clever variations against experienced opponents. Sixty thousand
people watched the cricket during the three days.

Lancashire 352 (C. Washbrook 67, W. Place 38, J. T. Ikin 73, G. A. Edrich
34, K. Cranston 63; D. C. S. Compton four for 75) **and 153**
(C. Washbrook 32, W. Place 40; J. A. Young three for 41, P. I. Bedford
five for 54).

Middlesex 134 (W. J. Edrich 55, D. C. S. Compton 17; J. T. Ikin five for
37, E. J. Price three for 34) **and 307** (D. C. S. Compton 139,
R. W. V. Robins 31, J. M. Sims 41; J. T. Ikin three for 71, E. J. Price four
for 166).

FATHER AND SON 1923

DERBYSHIRE V WARWICKSHIRE

Weak batting again brought about Derbyshire's defeat, Warwickshire
winning easily on the second afternoon by ten wickets. Warwickshire
lost four men for 84 on the Saturday but W. G. Quaife mastered the
bowling on Monday and was the one batsman in the match to be seen
to much advantage. At the wickets four and a half hours he did not
make a mistake until after completing his hundred. At one time the
two Quaifes were opposed by the two Bestwicks. For father and son
to be batting against bowlers similarly related was a remarkable incident – regarded as unique in county cricket.

SOUTH OF ENGLAND v SOUTH AFRICANS

At Hastings, September 3, 4, 5, 1947. South Africans won by
nine wickets. The splendid victory achieved by their superior
cricket over a powerful side was, from a public viewpoint, rather
overshadowed by the achievement of Denis Compton, who created cricket history in beating the 1925 record of J. B. Hobbs of
16 centuries in a season. Compton's 17th hundred of the summer, sixth against South Africans and 12th in 25 innings, naturally aroused unusual excitement. The South Africans made him
fight keenly for every run, and when he reached three figures the
game was held up for five minutes while crowd and players
showed their appreciation. His county colleagues, Robins and
Edrich, went on to the field to join in congratulations. Compton
dashed down the pitch to the first ball after the resumption and
was stumped. He made 101 out of 151 in 108 minutes, hit 13
fours and offered nothing like a chance. By making 30 in the
second innings he brought his season's aggregate against South
Africa in first-class matches to 1,187. Compton's superb display
followed bright batting by the South Africans. So as not to
waste time for an interval between innings on the third morning,
Robins declared at the overnight score, though South of England stood 169 behind with a wicket to fall. Melville countered
by enforcing the follow-on and, in spite of a second good
innings by Edrich, Rowan and Mann ensured a win for the

South Africans. Between them Rowan and Mann claimed all 19
South wickets.

South Africans 510 for eight dec. (B. Mitchell 145, K. G. Viljoen 50,
  O. C. Dawson 166 not out, G. M. Fullerton 46) **and 31** for one.
South of England 341 for nine dec. (J. D. Robertson 55, W. J. Edrich 64,
  D. C. S. Compton 101, H. T. Bartlett 46, R. W. V. Robins 33;
  N. B. F. Mann four for 97, A. M. B. Rowan five for 108) **and 199**
  (W. J. Edrich 54, D. C. S. Compton 30, B. H. Valentine 33;
  N. B. F. Mann five for 71, A. M. B. Rowan five for 83).

SOUTH OF ENGLAND v SIR PELHAM WARNER'S XI

At Hastings, September 6, 8, 9, 1947. Sir Pelham Warner's XI
won by 26 runs. Denis Compton's achievement in passing
Hayward's 1906 aggregate of 3,518 runs aroused particular interest in a sternly contested Festival match. His Middlesex colleagues, Edrich and Robertson, gave Warner's XI a fine start with
111 in 70 minutes. Edrich drove with great power and hit ten
fours. The left-arm slows of Broderick and Laker's off-breaks
troubled South batsmen on a wicket made difficult by overnight
rain but, whether attacking or defending, Compton was always
master. Apart from Robertson, few of Warner's XI could cope
with the spin of Goddard and Wright on the second evening and
South needed 292 to win in four hours and three-quarters on the
third day. Compton showed an understandable but, for him,
unusual anxiety before completing the 35 runs needed to beat
Hayward. In both innings, Warner's XI made him fight hard for
every run. He gave an easy chance to gully when 22, but that was
his only error in the match. His dismissal was the beginning of
the end.

Sir Pelham Warner's XI 306 (J. D. Robertson 34, W. J. Edrich 79,
  M. F. Tremlett 31, V. Broderick 42 not out; T. W. Goddard four for 102,
  D. V. P. Wright three for 66) **and 184** (J. D. Robertson 65;
  T. W. Goddard five for 53, D. V. P. Wright four for 64).
South of England 199 (D. C. S. Compton 87 not out; V. Broderick five for
  73) **and 265** (H. A. Pawson 36, D. C. S. Compton 86, R. W. V. Robins
  45; J. C. Laker six for 109).

MIDDLESEX (CHAMPION COUNTY) v REST OF ENGLAND

At The Oval, September 13, 15, 16, 17, 1947. Middlesex won by nine wickets. For only the third time were the Champion County successful over Rest of England. Yorkshire were winners in 1905 and 1935, the last occasion on which the game took place. The match provided further personal triumphs for Compton and Edrich, who concluded their remarkable season in superb style. Compton, despite a heavily strapped knee which restricted his freedom, played his highest innings in England and was only three short of the 249 he made for Holkar against Bombay in the Indian championship final of 1944/45. Edrich followed Compton in beating Hayward's record aggregate. Middlesex began by losing three wickets for 53, but Compton and Edrich added 138 before Compton retired through a recurrence of his knee trouble. He resumed on Monday and in all he and Edrich put on 210 and made 426 between them out of the Middlesex total of 543. Compton hit 30 fours, Edrich a six and 21 fours. The Rest lost Washbrook first ball and Place also failed to score. Steady batting by Emmett and a bright display from Evans failed to save the follow-on. Only 50 minutes' play was necessary on the last day.

Middlesex 543 for nine dec. (W. J. Edrich 180, F. G. Mann 33,
D. C. S. Compton 246, R. W. V. Robins 33; T. W. Goddard four for 179)
and 21 for one.

Rest of England 246 (R. Howorth 30, G. M. Emmett 89, T. G. Evans 70;
L. H. Gray four for 47, D. C. S. Compton four for 57) **and 317**
(C. Washbrook 61, G. M. Emmett 43, N. W. D. Yardley 71, extras 31;
L. H. Gray three for 36).

POSTSCRIPT 1950

by R. J. Hayter

MCC TEAM IN SOUTH AFRICA, 1948/49

Although not at his brilliant best in the Tests, Compton played a number of spectacular innings, particularly when making 300 in 181 minutes at Benoni. His 1,781 runs and eight centuries established records for a season of first-class cricket in South Africa and he attracted large crowds wherever he went.

DENIS COMPTON IN 1947 (aged 29)

Runs in	Tests	Champ.	Others	Total	v SA	100s
May	–	363	469	832	303	3
June	436	157	–	593	436	2
July	151	484	11	646	151	4
August	166	1,029	–	1,195	166	7
September	–	–	550	550	131	2
	753	2,033	1,030	3,816	1,187	18

Bowling	Tests			Champ/Others			Total		
	O	R	W	O	R	W	O	R	W
May	–			38	111	4	38	111	4
June	58	98	4	67	159	11	125	257	15
July	30	104	1	100.2	357	16	130.2	461	17
August	15	61	0	253.2	862	28	268.2	923	28
September	–			74	301	9	74	301	9
	103	263	5	532.4	1,790	68	635.4	2,053	73

W. J. EDRICH IN 1947 (aged 31)

Runs in	Tests	Champ.	Others	Total	v SA	100s
May	–	558	200	758	200	4
June	296	257	–	553	296	2
July	256	707	84	1,047	256	3
August	–	735	–	735	–	2
September	–	–	446	446	118	1
	552	2,257	730	3,539	870	12

Bowling	Tests			Champ/Others			Total		
	O	R	W	O	R	W	O	R	W
May	–			191.1	519	33	191.1	519	33
June	46	117	4	84	200	6	130	317	10
July	88.5	253	12	97	287	8	185.5	540	20
August	–			55.5	137	4	55.5	137	4
September	–			–			–		
	134.5	370	16	428	1,143	51	562.5	1,513	67

WEATHER REPORT 1872

The 85th season of the MCC was one of storms, showers, sunshine, good wickets, splendid batting, great scoring and one-sided matches. A thunderstorm interrupted the progress of the opening match at Lord's; torrents of rain and hailstones of large size fell during the violent storm that stopped play in the MCC and Ground v Cambridge University match on the old ground; frequent and heavy showers of rain made a mud pond of the wickets, and prevented completion of that – so far – capitally contested match between the Gentlemen and Players of England; and the continuous heavy rainfall from morn to past midday that put cricket on one side for a whole day in Willshire's match will not readily be forgotten by the very many friends of the Kent bowler who felt interested in the success of the cricket battle between the Benedicts and Bachelors of England. June was nippingly cold, and July was wet and windy, but there are two sides to all tales told, and if the greater portion of the three months up at Lord's in 1871 was unseasonably stormy and showery (and it *was* so), sunshine at other times beamed brilliantly on the famous old turf.

THE BOOK GROUP

Dave Podmore sounded like a figure of fun when I first heard him on the radio. But there may be more to the England fringe player than meets the eye. Looking for something on Terence Rattigan when putting this chapter together, I noticed *Wisden*'s schools cricket in 1930 was written by one Austin Podmore; he had, in fact, been covering the schools for *Wisden* since the 1929 Almanack "and was engaged on the work for the present issue", says *Wisden* 1938, "when overtaken by illness". Typical Podmore, that is, being overtaken by illness.

Back in the nineteenth century, according to *Wisden* 1934, another Podmore, George, had several trial games for Oxford, but failed to get his blue. In 1871 he was presented with a bat for taking most wickets for XVIII of Eastbourne against the United South of England XI captained by W. G. Grace. A true Podmore if ever there was one, even if not a true blue Pod. So it's little wonder Dave Podmore has been just a nod from England selection on his day. The lad has form; it's in his jeans. Which, of course, will come as no surprise to readers of his 1996 memoirs, *Pod Almighty*, reviewed in *Wisden* 1997 by Sebastian Faulks (of *Birdsong* fame).

The way famous writers keep cropping up in *Wisden* is one of its fascinations, even if they weren't always famous at the time, except among their contemporaries as cricketers. The novels, poems and plays came later. In the case of Alec Waugh, brother of Evelyn, his first novel did not come late enough for Sherborne School, whose XI he captained in 1915. That same year he was asked to leave "for having the bad luck to be found out", as he himself put it. He used his unexpected leisure, prior to entering the Army, to write a sensational novel about the things that public school boys got up to when they weren't netting. Schools banned it, boys were beaten for reading it; almost 70 years on, his *Wisden* obituary couldn't bring itself to mention that he headed Sherborne's batting averages. Yorkshire wicket-keeper Richard Blakey (Rastrick Grammar School) obviously knew the score when he called his 1999 book *Taking It From Behind*. Poor Evelyn, meanwhile, had to go to Lancing instead of Sherborne on account of the scandal.

Jonathan Rice uncovered family links of a more wide-ranging kind when researching his article "Never a Famous Cricketer" for *Wisden* 2001. "Joseph Wells, the father of H. G., was a professional cricketer who took four wickets in four balls for Kent against Sussex in 1862. Among his quartet of victims was Spencer Austen-Leigh, the great-nephew of Jane Austen, so providing the only known cricketing connection between *Pride and Prejudice* and *The War of the Worlds*." But then there are also the cricketing connections between the "Musée des Beaux Arts", *The French Lieutenant's Woman*, Meryl Streep and the Sundance Kid, as the following pages disclose.

MY MAN JEEVES 1976

Wodehouse, Sir Pelham Grenville, the famous novelist, who died in hospital on Long Island on February 14, 1975 at the age of 93, had been a member of the Dulwich College XI in 1899 and 1900. He was godfather of M. G. Griffith, the late captain of Sussex.

by W. J. Ford, 1901

I fancy that Dulwich had a pretty useful side: they beat Brighton, Tonbridge and Bedford Grammar School easily, fell a prey to St Paul's by 101 runs, but saved the game against MCC and CCC Oxford, thanks to Sherlock's good defence. Averages are not big, but when we remember the clinging clay of the Dulwich ground after wet, this is not so surprising.

P. G. Wodehouse	Innings	Not outs	Runs	Highest	Average
1900	10	2	48	12	6.00
	Overs	Maidens	Runs	Wickets	Average
1900	28	3	114	7	16.28

1914

However, for Foster's ill-success, there was some compensation, Warwickshire finding an absolute prize in Percy Jeeves. This young cricketer – a Yorkshireman by birth – had been allowed by courtesy to play against the Australians in 1912, but it was not until last summer that he was qualified for county matches. His first season in the eleven was nothing short of a triumph. He came out first in bowling with 106 wickets, and scored 765 runs with an average of 20. This all-round record suggests tremendous possibilities in the near future. Jeeves is a good, punishing bat, but it is as a bowler that the Warwickshire people expect most of him. On the fast side of medium pace he has a very easy action, and when fresh he makes the ball come off the ground with plenty of life. Unaccustomed to three-day matches, he was, perhaps, asked to do a little too much, bowling 780 overs. He said himself, at the end of the season, that while he was struggling to get his hundred wickets he fully appreciated the difference between county cricket and ordinary club matches. Whatever may be in store for him, he was, beyond all question, one of the best of the cricketers discovered in 1913.

NOTE: P. G. Wodehouse saw Jeeves play for Warwickshire in 1913 and subsequently immortalised him by taking his name for his masterful literary butler.

Deaths in the War, 1917

Percy Jeeves (Royal Warwickshire Regiment) was killed on July 22, England losing a cricketer of whom very high hopes had been entertained ... He was chosen [in 1914] for Players against Gentlemen at The Oval, and by his fine bowling helped the Players to win the match, sending down in the Gentlemen's second innings 15 overs for 44 runs and four wickets. Mr P. F. Warner was greatly impressed and predicted that Jeeves would be an England bowler in the near future. Within a month war had been declared.

THE SIGN OF FOUR 1931

Doyle, Sir Arthur Conan, MD (Edin.), the well-known author, born at Edinburgh on May 22, 1859, died at Crowborough, Sussex, on July 7, 1930, aged 71. Although never a famous cricketer, he could hit hard and bowl slows with a puzzling flight. For MCC v Cambridgeshire at Lord's, in 1899, he took seven wickets for 61 runs, and on the same ground two years later carried out his bat for 32 against Leicestershire, who had Woodcock, Geeson and King to bowl for them. In *The Times* of October 27, 1915, he was the author of an article on "The Greatest of Cricketers. An Appreciation of Dr Grace." (It is said that Shacklock, the former Nottinghamshire player, inspired him with the Christian name of his famous character, Sherlock Holmes, and that of the latter's brother Mycroft was suggested by the Derbyshire cricketers.)

1894
NOTTINGHAMSHIRE v SOMERSET

Beyond everything else the feature of the game was the sensational bowling on the third morning of Shacklock, who took four wickets in four balls. With the second ball of an over he bowled Spurway; the third, Newton played on to the wicket, and the fourth and fifth bowled Trask and Gibbs.

WHEN WE WERE VERY YOUNG
WESTMINSTER SCHOOL, 1900, 1901

A. A. Milne	Innings	Not outs	Runs	Highest	Average
1899	14	0	110	19	7.85
1900	15	1	184	44	13.14
	Overs	Maidens	Runs	Wickets	Average
1899	58.4	18	200	7	28.57
1900	140	31	447	21	21.28

THE LOOM OF YOUTH 1982

Waugh, Alec, brother of Evelyn, died in Florida on September 3, 1981, aged 83. A great lover of cricket, he was "Bobby Southcott" in A. G. Macdonnell's *England, their England*, and for 50 years seldom missed a Test match at Lord's.

SHERBORNE SCHOOL 1915, 1916

A. R. Waugh	Innings	Not outs	Runs	Highest	Average
1914	9	1	186	65	20.66
1915	13	2	389	96	35.36

by Stephen Moss, 2000

Michael Davie and Simon Davie's excellent anthology, *The Faber Book of Cricket*, did unearth one piece of cricket prose by an unquestionably great writer, Evelyn Waugh, though he was only twenty when he wrote it. It was published in the Oxford student magazine *Cherwell* and recounts a disastrous day when his cricket-mad brother Alec drafted him into a college side to play a village team in Hertfordshire. It is everything that the traditional, lyrical view of village cricket is not. "When I returned home, I reasoned thus with myself," wrote Waugh. "Today I have wearied myself utterly; I have seen nothing and no one of any interest; I have suffered discomfort of every sense and limb; I have suffered acute pain in my great toe; I have walked several miles; I have stood about for several hours; I have drunken several pints of indifferently good beer; I have spent nearly two pounds . . . But my brother maintained that it had been a great day. Village cricket, he said, was always like that."

FRENCH WITHOUT TEARS 1978

Rattigan, Sir Terence Mervyn, CBE, the famous play-writer, who died in Bermuda on November 30, 1977, aged 66, was, like his father and his uncle, in the Harrow XI. He won his place in 1929 as an opening bat, but next year, though he played in the XI, was not in the side at Lord's. He was an elegant strokeplayer, but unsound.

by A. Podmore, 1930

Rome became the mainstay of the batting; Rothschild and Rattigan, with beautiful off-side strokes, made a good opening pair.

T. M. Rattigan	*Innings*	*Not outs*	*Runs*	*Highest*	*Average*
1929	12	0	345	100	28.75
1930	11	0	176	48	16.00

STRANGERS AND BROTHERS 1981

Lord Snow of Leicester (Charles Percy Snow) was captain of Newton's Grammar School, Leicester, and Leicester University College. He played for Leicester Town and, as a Fellow, for Christ's College, Cambridge, at a time when they were captained by his undergraduate brother, Philip. He eschewed in batting everything but the cut and leg-glance and was a useful top-spin bowler. In 1964 C. P. Snow was appointed the House of Lord's ministerial spokesman for Technology. Internationally celebrated as scientist and author, some of his 50 books and innumerable essays include brief cricket scenes and fictitious characters with cricketers' names. His study of G. H. Hardy in *The Saturday Book* (1948) is a classic cricket vignette. Using the nom de plume XX he contributed Cambridge notes to *The Cricketer* in the 1930s.

THE SOLDIER 1916
Deaths in 1915

Sub-Lieut Rupert C. Brooke (Royal Naval Division), born at Rugby on August 3, 1887, died at Lemnos of sunstroke on April 23. In 1906 he was in the Rugby XI, and although he was unsuccessful in the Marlborough match he headed the school's bowling average with a record of 19 wickets for 14.05 runs each. He had gained considerable reputation as a poet.

RUGBY SCHOOL, 1907

R. C. Brooke	*Innings*	*Not outs*	*Runs*	*Highest*	*Average*
1906	8	2	42	16	7.00
	Overs	*Maidens*	*Runs*	*Wickets*	*Average*
1906	65	4	267	19	14.05

OUT OF AFRICA 1933

Finch-Hatton, Hon. Denys George, was killed while flying in East Africa on May 14, 1931. He played in the Eton XIs of 1905 and 1906, scoring 41 not out against Winchester in the first year and 37 in the second. He was also a useful bowler.

1906

The fielding of the Eton XI was very fair, Gold, Finch-Hatton and Astor being the best.

Hon. D. G. Finch-Hatton	Innings	Not outs	Runs	Highest	Average
1905	10	3	177	60*	25.28
1906	13	2	198	44	18.00
	Overs	Maidens	Runs	Wickets	Average
1905	41	6	140	4	35.00
1906	89	12	336	11	30.54

NOTE: In the film *Out of Africa*, based on Danish author Karen Blixen's memoirs of life on a Kenyan coffee plantation, the role of Denys Finch-Hatton is played by Robert Redford. Although Redford had previously starred as a baseball player in *The Natural*, it is unlikely this contributed to his playing a former Eton cricketer. Karen Blixen was played by Meryl Streep.

THE MAGUS 2001

John Fowles, author of *The French Lieutenant's Woman* (for which Harold Pinter wrote the screenplay), appeared for Bedford School from 1942 to 1944 as a swing and "cutting" bowler, and had a trial for Essex; it is possibly not insignificant that he lines up in the 1943 *Wisden* alongside Auden, Bacon and Fletcher. Future academics and critics may be interested in Fowles's belief that "the gate-key to all Pinter's work is his intense and evident love of cricket".

1944

The Bedford School bowling fell below the level hoped for, and of six school matches three were lost and one drawn. Neither J. A. L. Auden, the captain, nor J. A. Bacon reached his form of 1942, though J. R. Fowles maintained consistency and claimed many victims with a ball that swung away late.

NOTE: Auden was a cousin of the poet, W. H. Auden.

J. R. Fowles	*Innings*	*Not outs*	*Runs*	*Highest*	*Average*
1943	7	1	76	19*	12.66
1944	8	4	88	21*	22.00
	Overs	*Maidens*	*Runs*	*Wickets*	*Average*
1942	116.4	11	332	15	22.13
1943	153	25	434	34	12.76
1944	138	20	377	26	14.50

SINISTER STREET 1973

Wisden is privileged to have received the last article by Sir Compton Mackenzie. It arrived a week before he died in Edinburgh on November 10 [1972], aged eighty-nine. In the last few years of his life Sir Compton was almost blind and only last summer he had a spell in hospital which left him with periodic fatigue. During his life he wrote about 100 books. His work included novels, biographies, histories, travel books, essays, stories for children, besides numerous broadcasts and television appearances.

Shillings for WG: Looking Back Eighty Years
by Sir Compton Mackenzie

Cricket is a pastime I have always enjoyed. I do not suggest that I was ever a good cricketer. I suffered, in my opinion, from the handicap of being a left-handed bowler and a right-handed batsman. I could bowl without disgracing myself, but as a batsman I was hopeless ... In 1939 when war with Germany was obviously drawing nearer, the second National Government invited various people to speak round the country to step up recruiting. I was invited to address the City of Bradford with Herbert Sutcliffe as my partner. I had been warned by Auckland Geddes that Bradford could be as difficult an audience as Manchester had been for him the previous week when it kept chanting "Tripe! Tripe!" When I stepped forward on the platform of the Alhambra on that Sunday evening, I said I hoped the citizens of

Bradford would not suppose that I was a representative of the National Government. "What I think of the National Government could not be said on any platform or in any pulpit on a Sunday evening." When I sat down Herbie Sutcliffe turned to me and said:

"Oh my, how I wish I could speak like you."

"You don't wish nearly as much that you could speak like me as I wish I could bat like you," I replied.

ENDGAME 1926
NORTHAMPTONSHIRE v DUBLIN UNIVERSITY

At Northampton, Saturday, Monday, July 18, 20, 1925. Quite outclassed, Dublin University lost by an innings and 56 runs.

Dublin University

Mr J. P. Pigot b Wright	0	–c Fitzroy b Wright	50
Mr T. A. McVeagh c Bellamy b Wright	32	–b Wooster	17
Mr M. Sugden b Norris	36	–b Wooster	17
Mr J. R. Peacocke b Wright	11	–c Fitzroy b Wooster	10
Mr A. W. Kelly b Wright	0	–b Wooster	7
Mr C. E. McCausland c Bellamy b Wright	21	–c Wright b Norris	20
Mr J. R. Wills b Wooster	28	–b Wooster	0
Mr S. Beckett b Towell	18	–c Brown b Wright	12
Mr W. J. McMahon b Norris	18	–not out	1
Mr S. T. Radcliffe lbw b Murdin	9	–lbw b Wright	3
Mr M. Hoffman not out	6	–b Norris	0
B 11, l-b 7	18	B 5, l-b 1	6
	197		143

Northamptonshire 396 (Mr W. W. Timms 71, Mr W. C. Brown 31, N. Bowell 48, Mr E. F. Towell 59, Mr P. A. Wright 83; Sugden three for 98, Beckett 8–2–17–0, Kelly three for 29).

NOTE: Samuel Beckett also played in this fixture in 1926 when, opening the batting, he scored four and one; in the single Northamptonshire innings his bowling figures were 15–0–47–0. In 1969 he became the first first-class cricketer to receive the Nobel Prize for Literature.

THE AMERICAN BASE BALL PLAYERS IN ENGLAND

1875

Twenty-two base ball players from America visited England at the back end of the cricket season, 1874, "their mission" – it was semi-officially stated – "being to give the English a practical insight into the workings of base ball". The Twenty-two comprised 11 members of the Boston (*red stockings*), and 11 of the Philadelphia Athletes (*blue stockings*), the two leading base ball clubs in the United States, where the game holds the same high and popular national position cricket does in England.

The visitors' stay in this country was limited to one month. They quickly got to work, making their first appearance in flannel on an English ground the 30th of July, at Edgehill, the ground of the Liverpool Cricket Club. They were a finely framed, powerful set of men, and, although "Base ball" did not take the popular fancy here, the splendid long-distance throwing and truly magnificent out-fielding of the Americans at once won the full and heartily expressed admiration of Englishmen, who frankly acknowledged the Americans' superiority to the generality of English fielders.

Nine Bostons v Nine Athletics played, with varying success, base ball matches on the Liverpool Club's cricket ground at Edgehill; on the Manchester Club's ground at Old Trafford; on the Marylebone Club's ground, "Lord's"; on Prince's ground, at

Belgravia; on the Richmond Club's ground in the Old Deer Park, Richmond; at the Crystal Palace, Sydenham; on the Surrey County Club's ground, "The Oval"; on the Yorkshire County ground, Sheffield; and at Dublin.

THE AMERICANS AT CRICKET

At several of the above grounds the Americans supplemented their base ball exhibitions with cricket matches. Not one of the English teams pitted against the strangers embodied the strength of the club they represented – indeed, some of them were very weak teams – and the Americans, having one or two good bowlers, several plucky hard-hitters and a team of good fielders, had the best of every match they played. The following is a summary of the results of the cricket matches.

At Lord's, August 3, 4. Drawn. Gentlemen of MCC XII 105; Americans XVIII 107.

At Prince's, August 6, 7. Americans XVIII won by an innings and 50 runs. Prince's Club and Ground XI 21 and 39; Americans XVIII 110.

At Richmond, August 8. Drawn. Richmond Club XIII 108; Americans XX 45 for six.

At The Oval, August 13, 14. Drawn. Americans XVIII 100 and 111; Surrey Club and Ground 27 and 2 for four.

At Sheffield, August 15, 17. Americans XVIII won by an innings and 42 runs. Sheffield Town XII 43 and 45; Americans XVIII 130.

At Dublin, August 22, 24, 25. Americans XIX won by 86 runs. Americans XIX 71 and 94; Ireland XII 47 and 32.

The Americans left Ireland for America on Wednesday the 26th of August.

OBITUARY 1938

Eligon, Mr Donald, died at Port-of-Spain, Trinidad, on June 4, 1937 aged twenty-eight. After playing for Shannon Cricket Club he joined the Trinidad inter-colonial team in 1934 and quickly became one of the outstanding bowlers in West Indies. His death was due to blood poisoning caused by a nail in his cricket boot.

ABC OF WORLD CRICKET

ANTARCTICA 1986

What was almost certainly the most southerly game of cricket ever played, and the coldest, took place in Antarctica, 700 kilometres from the South Pole, on January 11, 1985, between two teams drawn from the 60 scientists, lawyers, environmentalists and administrators engaged in an international workshop being held at the Beardmore South Camp and concerned with the Antarctic Treaty. New Zealand's representative on the Treaty, Christopher Beeby, captained the Gondwanaland Occasionals with players from Australia, New Zealand and South Africa. A British delegate to the conference, Arthur Watts, captained the Beardmore Casuals, a basically British team. The stumps were improvised, the pitch, such as it was, had been rolled by a Hercules transport aircraft, and the "midnight sun" allowed play to continue until 11.00 p.m. The Occasionals (129) beat the Casuals (102) by 27 runs.

BAHRAIN 2000
by Guy Parker

Cricket in Bahrain has been described as the hardest – perhaps even the worst – in the world. It is a reputation the cricket authorities on this desert island find easy to live down to. The standard of play is not the issue. Indeed, Bahrain won a four-nation six-a-side tournament involving Sri Lanka, India and Bangladesh at the Isa Town football stadium in November 1999. Luminaries such as Vinod Kambli, Robin Singh, Sanjay Manjrekar, Roshan

Mahanama, Kumara Dharmasena and the entire Bangladesh World Cup squad were swept off the park by Bahrain's wham-bam cricket. Instead, the reputation has more to do with local conditions. The cricketers who brave the appalling outfields (made up of stony, bumpy desert), the cracked concrete strips – which are inadequately covered with tatty coir mats and patched with canvas – and the derisory umpiring are forced to develop hard-edged tactics to win the 25-over matches. Winning is para-mount. Some sides would rather walk off the field than lose. Field placing is simple: eight or nine men are often placed on the boundary, with the emphasis on making the batsmen work for their runs in the heat. Sixes (the favourite shot) are greeted with car horns from the partisan spectators. Totals of 200-plus are chased with contrasting emotions of elation and despair which reach a violent crescendo. The top teams import professionals from the subcontinent. Failure can mean prompt repatriation – tough when you get only one chance a week.

COLOMBIA 1997
by Anthony Letts

Cricket is not endemic in the High Andes. Indeed, it is so alien to local culture that Colombian Customs reputedly impounded a priceless shipment of bats and balls from Venezuela some years ago as "dangerous, possibly subversive material". Bogota is a challenge for the bowler. At 8,300 feet above sea level, anyone trying to bowl medium-fast soon runs out of puff, and the ball will not swing much in the thin, dry air. A spinner gets a little more help from our new Astroturf than from the old matting we had until 1994, and the batsman does not have an easy time. The field is kikuyu grass: the ball will not skim the surface, and must be hit dangerously high to reach the boundary. Cricket's popular-ity in Colombia has ebbed and flowed depending on the numbers of expatriates. It was first regularly played by Shell employees in the mid-1950s. Since then English schoolmasters, Scottish accountants and Pakistani bankers have come and gone, and now oil – this time BP – again provides most of the players.

DENMARK 1990
by Peter S. Hargreaves

The 1989 season ranked as probably Denmark's best to date at top level, with the only defeats out of ten matches against other countries being two by Allan Border's Australian tourists, and a narrow one by Canada in The Netherlands. This last was immediately avenged by two excellent victories over that country. However, it was particularly the Dutch who suffered at Denmark's hands during the summer, with a first loss ever on Dutch soil to their Scandinavian rivals, another in England at the International Youth Tournament, and a third in Jutland at the first official European Women's Tournament. In May and July, matches were played for the first time against both West Germany and Italy in Denmark, and while the farcical results caused some comment, the wish to encourage these new associations was an honest enough one.

ESTONIA 2001
by Philip Marsdale

Like most good ideas and institutions, the Estonian Cricket Club (*Esti Kriketi Klubi*) was born in a pub, in this case The Lost Continent in Tallinn. The first club email from the chairman, Kristian Garancis, said "Practice will be on Sunday 1300hrs providing no snow". That was in 1998, and from there we developed. The first pitch was an outdoor basketball court, with one old bat and a tennis ball. We progressed to a very bumpy soccer pitch in a lovely setting surrounded by forest (and topless lady sunbathers), but under threat from scheduled soccer matches. Later that same year the club moved to the Hippodrome, the trotting track, where the management have been excellent hosts – and most flexible, as we built an all-weather pitch in the middle of the racecourse.

FRANCE 1998
by Simon Hewitt

Richie Benaud, who has French ancestry and a home near Nice, delighted Gallic cricket in October by agreeing to become honorary patron of France Cricket – the new ruling body of the game in France – and offering to advise on coaching and development. The Benaud *oui-oui* came soon after a two-day, 700-mile inspection by ICC chief executive David Richards and Jørgen Holmen, chairman of the Associate Members, in connection with French hopes for promotion from Affiliate to Associate status in 1998. Five new grounds were built in 1997. The unluckiest was Robin Marlar's ground (complete with turf wicket) at Mollans-sur-Ouveze, Provence, which was wrecked by wild boar, who dug their snouts into the turf and almost ploughed it up. "Hampshire Hogs on tour, I expect," said Marlar.

KEEPING COUNT 1938

Going to Magdalene College, Cambridge, William Roe received his blue in 1883 from C. T. Studd but, though on the winning side, he did not get a run and the Oxford wickets were shared by his captain and C. Aubrey Smith. He was famous already for the highest score then on record, having made 415 not out when, on invitation, he completed the Emmanuel Long Vacation Club eleven in a game against Caius Long Vacation Club in 1881. W. N. Roe got these runs out of 708 for four wickets in five hours. This was in reply to a score of 100 and Caius gave up the match rather than continue on the third day. So close was his concentration on the game that he counted all his runs and on this occasion he challenged the scorer with having given him one less than his total!

THE GAMBIA 1994

The *Daily Observer*, published in the Gambian capital, Banjul, carried an interview with the national coach J. B. Jarra, 75, described as "The Gambia's greatest cricket bowler of all time" and known as "Teacher". Jarra, a leg-spin and googly bowler, was selected for the national team in 1955, when The Gambia was still a British colony, after an expatriate gave up his place in the team to him. Jarra said he remained dedicated to promoting the game among young Gambians because he loved it and did not wish to see it fade away.

HUNGARY 1994

In May, the *Hungarian Times* reported the formation of the Magyar Cricket Club, which intended to play three other teams of expatriates, with kit provided by the British Embassy, on a matting wicket at Obudai Island. Two months later, however, it was reported that the kit had been stolen.

ITALY 1946

When the end of hostilities in Europe appeared in sight, the thoughts of all cricketers serving in the Italian war theatre turned to the game for which few of them for so long had found either the time or opportunity. Some of the more ardent enthusiasts decided to embark on a programme of ground preparation to be completed in time for the forthcoming season. The story of their work is one of successful perseverance over difficulties. Firm, flat meadows did not exist. The problem was to find flat surfaces of any kind. Appeals to various departments of the Services brought willing and excellent assistance, and in a comparatively short time grounds of first-class order sprang up all over the country. That at Bari, in its perfect Adriatic setting, was particularly good. The plain earth outfield of this large enclosure responded so well to treatment from the "Bulldozer" and heavy roller that it soon became a true surface. Matting was stretched over the concrete wicket, sightscreens and score boxes were erected, the arena roped off, seating accommodation provided for hundreds of people, refreshment tents and marquees were put up, scorecards – with the fall of the last wicket – given away and loudspeakers provided a running commentary all through the game. At Eboli, the RATD ground offered much the same amenities. Those at Caserta, Capua, Rome, Naples, Civvetavecchia and Leghorn also reflected considerable credit on the men who prepared them. In one game at Civvetavecchia on July 21, the temperature reached 110 degrees in the shade.

JAPAN 1997
by Trevor Bayley

Enthusiasm for cricket is high in Japan and the Gunma Cup, a two-day competition for Japanese men, enjoyed great popularity in its third year. Tokyo Bay CC won the cup for the second time. During the competition one of their players, Hiroki Minami, fell foul of a local rule which deducts five runs for a shot on to the nearby tennis court and was dismissed with a score of minus three. There are very few grounds we can use and if an innocent tennis player were injured it would cause serious problems.

KENYA 1997
KENYA v WEST INDIES

At Pune, February 29, 1996. Kenya won by 73 runs. Kenya's victory was hailed as one of the biggest upsets in cricket history. It was the more extraordinary for being the work of their bowlers, rather than their highly rated batting. Captain Maurice Odumbe thought his team was done for when he lost the toss; once they were all out for 166, he was certain of it. But his amateur attack dismissed West Indies for 93, their lowest World Cup total and their second worst in any one-day international. Kenya had struggled to 81 for six after Walsh removed their top three. The last four, however, added 85, thanks to Hitesh Modi and seventeen-year-old Thomas Odoyo, and survived into the final over, though the highest scorer was extras, with 35. Part-time wicket-keeper Jimmy Adams equalled the World Cup record of five dismissals. West Indies' nightmare began with Richardson being bowled leg stump by Rajab Ali. Three balls later Campbell was also bowled, by Suji. The collapse became critical when Lara was caught behind by Tariq Iqbal, whose stout figure and village-standard juggling had hitherto caused much mirth. Only Chanderpaul and Harper reached double figures and both fell to the off-spin of Maurice Odumbe, whose figures of three for 15 in ten overs mirrored those of his more famous counterpart, Harper. The last wicket went the same way as the first – Cuffy was bowled by Rajab Ali, who fell into his team-mates' arms. As the Kenyans ran an exuberant victory lap, cheered on by local spectators, West Indies realised that, level on points with Kenya and Zimbabwe, they could no longer be certain of reaching the quarter-finals.

Man of the Match: M. Odumbe.

LUXEMBOURG 2000
by Adrian Wykes

An exceptionally warm and dry summer in the Grand Duchy saw the inauguration of a national league. Over 80 players took part in ten matches, as the Optimists pipped the Communities to the title. Black Stuff, Euratom and the Maidens completed the line-up, and new teams have applied to join in 2000. Just as importantly, the first-ever conversation at the wicket in Letze-buergesch – a dialect that has much in common with Flemish and German – took place between two Black Stuff batsmen, even though the club is theoretically drawn from the Irish community. Cricket formally appeared at the European School for the first time, and evening cricket continued to attract keen interest. Among teams to play this year were the social (Britannia Pub, Hash Harriers, the George and Dragon), the financial (Flemings, the Court of Auditors) and the apparently extra-terrestrial (Astra Satellites). Court of Auditors boasted eight nationalities on one occasion, a genuine reflection of this cosmopolitan society. But the best witness to this was the claim of a Danish translator at the European Parliament to be the grandson of Ellis Achong, the Trinidadian originator of the "chinaman".

MALAYSIA 1994
by Charlie Chelliah

The decision to include cricket in the 1998 Commonwealth Games in Kuala Lumpur means the sport now has backing from the government, which is obliged to ensure that the sport has the best possible facilities for the Games. Cricket in Malaysia has a sizeable following but cannot be compared to soccer and bad-minton. These sports have created millionaires here and parents would like to guide their children towards them rather than cricket, where they will only end up with a tan and no money.

However, the Ministry of Education has included cricket as a curriculum sport and new eight-a-side formats have been introduced into schools to encourage involvement.

OBITUARY 1938

Sheepshanks, Mr Ernest Richard, was killed on December 31, 1937 while acting as special correspondent to Reuter's with the insurgent forces in Spain. Born on March 22, 1910, he met his tragic end when 27. Very prominent in every respect at Eton, he was president of "Pop", captain of cricket, and a member of the association football and fives teams. At Cambridge he took part in the Freshmen's match in 1929 and the Seniors' matches of 1930 and 1931, but did not play for the University. In 1929 he appeared in the Yorkshire eleven.

NEPAL 1993
by Jai Kumar Shah

In Nepal, cricket is second only to soccer in popularity. A festival of daily matches in Kathmandu in early 1992 was watched by crowds of up to 4,000, with 8,000 watching the final. In 1989 at least 15,000 people in Biratnagar, south of Everest in the Eastern Region, watched two teams from India, Patna and Benares, in the final of an invitation tournament. More than 25 teams are now competing in Kathmandu alone and eight of them competed for the Rameshwore Memorial Shield in April. This was won by Kathmandu Khel Mandal. Their player Sri Nivas Rana was named as Man of the Series and he was awarded a television set, courtesy of Khetri Sausages.

OMAN 2004
by Madhu Sampat

Cricket in Oman only really became organised in 1979, but officials are proud of the indigenous participation. There are about 110 Omani nationals (most of them Arabs) playing amongst the 60 teams that compete in eight divisions. Teams are obliged to include one Omani, or otherwise field ten players, and the Omani must bat in the top five. Raha and Muscat are generally Oman's leading clubs, faring well in the United Arab Emirates' main domestic competitions, the Ramadan Floodlit tournament and the Bukhatir League.

PAPUA NEW GUINEA 1994
by Wayne Satchell

For the first time in the history of the Port Moresby competition the title was shared in 1993. In the 50-over A-grade grand final, Steamships Mobil and Elcom both bowled each other out for 201 and so became Joint Premiers. A new development was the Mobil Country Cup, which brought 32 teams into Port Moresby for a week-long competition. However, there were complaints that not much work was done in town during the week because of the interest that was generated. Cricket in Papua New Guinea dates back to the arrival of missionaries along the Papuan coast in the nineteenth century. The Board is anxious to maximise the junior cricket programme, known as Liklik Cricket.

QATAR 1999
by Mike Coward

The elite cricketers of India and Pakistan staged two unofficial matches for their expatriate supporters in the Qatari capital of Doha in August 1998. Mohammad Azharuddin's Indian XI won the first match against Rashid Latif's Pakistanis by 16 runs at the Al Arabi Stadium, but lost the return at the Al Wakra Stadium by 141 runs. As with an earlier game in nearby Dubai, the matches were played on artificial surfaces on soccer fields. The Qatari games attracted crowds of 5,000 and were beamed live to the subcontinent. Further matches between the rivals are planned for Muscat and, possibly, Kuwait.

RUSSIA 1994

In July, an English touring team, the Explorers, played what was reported to be the first formal match in Moscow since the Bolshevik Revolution. Their opponents were the MCC: the newly formed Moscow Cricket Club. Owing to a misunderstanding, the pitch was originally laid out for a croquet match. Broom-handles had to be used in place of stumps: the man bringing some of the kit was stopped at Heathrow because he had forgotten to get a visa.

SOUTH KOREA 1995
by John A. Kaminsky

Cricket revived in Korea in the late 1980s through the expatriate Indian community. It is played by six teams of nine-a-side (representing Australia, India, New Zealand, British Embassy, International All Stars and the Rest of the World) over 15 overs on a small, irregular-shaped soccer field controlled by the US military in the UN compound. We bowl only from one end, on a wicket that consists of bare ground, covered by one layer of rubberised matting overlaid by felt carpet; despite the small ground, bowlers tend to have the upper hand – shooters and fliers are par for the course. The scoring rules are modified but complex, taking into account the back wall (four if hit on the full), the willow tree (six) and the embankment with the black-berries. The regular competition is played twice a year, spring and autumn.

by Olivier de Braekeleer, 1998

After the cricketers lost a battle with Korean Customs over excessive import duties on equipment, two of the six new stumps broke during the first game. In the autumn, the final of the Gillette Kimchi Cup had to be postponed because the playing surface of rubber mat and felt carpet had disappeared, together with the shed where they had been stored after the semi-finals. Little did we know that the US military authorities had marked the shed for demolition – nor that the contractor would not realise the vital importance of the equipment. Cricketers are resourceful in emergency, though: a new mat and felt were acquired locally, enabling the Pakistan team to beat the Rest of the World.

TRISTAN DA CUNHA 1930
MCC Annual Report

In the hope that the inhabitants of Tristan da Cunha may be interested, sets of cricket stumps, bats, balls, etc have been forwarded to that lonely island.

by Peter S. Hargreaves, 1997

News travels slowly from this South Atlantic island, but the first match for ten years took place there in January 1995 through the initiative of a local official, Alan Waters. The coir matting once used as a surface had long since disappeared, and it was not safe to play with a cricket ball on the concrete, so a rounders ball was used. Some of the older islanders could still handle a bat but were no longer sufficiently co-ordinated to take catches. British missionaries originally helped the game thrive: among the Victorian pioneers was Edwin Dodgson, Lewis Carroll's brother. The game was also played regularly in the 1950s when the matting was laid at a spot called Hottentot Fence, but that era ended with the volcanic eruption of 1961 which forced the island to be evacuated.

USA 1994
by Gerald Howat

Some 700 clubs, with an average membership of between 20 and 30, currently play in the United States, an increase of about a quarter in the last four years. Most play limited-overs cricket on matting wickets. Outfields can be slow, especially in states where legislation requires grass in public places to be at least two and a half inches long to avoid liability insurance claims for injury.

VANUATU 1996
by Mark Stafford

There are 400 cricketers and 12 league teams in Vanuatu, the nation in the South-West Pacific that was formerly the Anglo-French New Hebrides. Eight of the teams play in the capital, Port Vila, and four in Luganville, the major town in the north of the island group. The length of games depends on when everyone turns up. We schedule starting times, but invariably "island time" takes over. The game has been played here throughout the century, and there is no novelty effect for local people; this is illustrated by the fact that people take the shortest route across the ground while play is in progress. In Luganville the games are often played in a small park on the main street; shopkeepers on the other side put up their cyclone shutters to protect their windows from the big-hitters.

WALES 1928
MCC v WALES

At Lord's, Wednesday, Thursday, Friday, June 1, 2, 3, 1927. Sidney Barnes, now resident in Wales, assisted the Principality in this match, which MCC won by seven wickets. Although beaten in this way the Welshmen emerged from the struggle with some credit as, after failing so badly in the first innings that they had to follow on 288 in arrear, they played up so well that they set MCC 108 to make to win, and staved off defeat until nearly six o'clock on the third day. In achieving this much, the visitors owed nearly everything to Bell, who carried his bat right through the second innings and scored 209. Barnes, aged fifty-four, bowled with much skill in the early stages of the game and was repeatedly unlucky in missing the stumps after beating the bat.

XANADU 2000
by Stephen Moss

The – for want of a better phrase – tweedy English view has dominated the literary representation of cricket in the past: romantic, lyrical, infused with a sense of love and loss. It has produced works of passion, elegance and beauty, yet at the beginning of a new century the tradition appears played out. The convoluted, self-conscious style of the Cardus school is unwieldy for modern readers; we want our prose in black and white, not purple. Its anglocentricity is absurd for a game where the balance of power now lies on the Indian subcontinent and in Australia. The commemoration of the past is dangerous for a sport which must quickly find a role for the future. Cricket writing, like cricket as a whole, must remake itself.

YORKSHIRE 2002
by Roy Hattersley

Perhaps, even in the early 1990s, Yorkshire were still suffering from the repercussions of "the Boycott affair". Whatever the merits of the argument – Boycott versus the committee – the damage that the conflict did to the county was immense. In 1978, members were asked to vote on what some thought were rival propositions: endorse sacking Boycott as captain or ask the committee to resign. I voted "yes" to both, hoping that a clearout would put the damaging disputes behind us.

ZAMBIA 1968

The growth of cricket in various parts of the world was emphasised when Zambia made their first overseas tour last summer. They were represented by Zambia Eagles, a multi-racial team of youngsters who left Lusaka on June 22 and in four weeks played 18 matches against schools and clubs in England and Northern Ireland [won 9, lost 4, drew 5]. The team comprised eight Europeans, five Asians and one Zambian. When they arrived they had a short practice at The Oval and their first match against Westminster School was ruined by rain. At first the batsmen experienced difficulty in timing their strokes, but the tail hit effectively and later Derek Brockwell and Trevor Lake made some excellent scores. Among the pace bowlers, Bernard Horton was the most successful. Philippe Edmonds and John Barwis were more effective with spin and generally the fielding provided a good lesson for the English schools.

BOWLERS ON SONG

"By and large," Sussex captain Robin Marlar wrote in 1959, "cricket is governed by a self-perpetuating oligarchy of willow-wielders! On almost every committee and at most conferences, batters comfortably outnumber the game's honest toilers." Marlar, it should be said, was more than mere honest toiler. Here's *Wisden* on the 1953 University Match. "At once the rest of the Oxford batsmen were non-plussed by Marlar, who played on their unwillingness to come out and kill the spin, and in half an hour the whole side was out for the addition of 15 runs. Marlar, in five overs of deadly bowling, took four wickets for five runs." He has served on his fair share of committees, and it's unlikely that much has happened since 1959 to make him revise his opinion of them.

That was the year when, after disastrously wet summers in 1956 and 1958, English county cricket experimented with full covering of pitches, both overnight and in the event of play being abandoned for the day. By the laws of Sod and Murphy, of course, 1959 proved a fine summer, the gates were good and soon enough the experiment was sidelined. The powers that be even rejected the 1964 Australian team's request for full covering whenever play wasn't in progress, pointing out in their reply that rain-affected pitches could provide interesting cricket. As shown in some of the following match reports, they could certainly provide bowlers with impressive hauls of wickets. However, commercial realities forced English cricket to think again, and in 1980 the counties voted to try full covering once more in the Championship. Not everyone was in full agreement.

"I cannot forebear," wrote incoming editor John Woodcock in *Wisden* 1981, "from lamenting even a temporary loss of a part of the very heritage of English cricket – a drying pitch and a sizzling sun." Bowlers joined in the lamentations, especially spin bowlers, who were the biggest losers when the "sticky dog" was muzzled. But batsmen smiled and nodded appreciatively towards the committee-room when they walked out to bat on the more predictable pitches that covering brought. As for the spectators – the same spectators in whose interest full covering was originally introduced – those remaining slid lower down their deck-chairs and slumbered.

A. P. "TICH" FREEMAN 1929

Winning 12 and losing only one of their first 20 matches, Kent made a bold bid for the Championship until the month of July was well advanced, but then came such a striking change in the fortunes of the side that three games in succession ended in defeat. The team finished second in the competition, with a slightly better record than either Notts or Yorkshire, but after those three disasters they naturally were never again really in the running for first honours. Still, if going down badly upon four occasions and on another missing a splendid chance, Kent enjoyed many days of pronounced success in 1928 and finished up with a record of two more wins and one fewer loss than in 1927.

In making this advance, Kent owed most to Freeman, who, putting a rare amount of spin on the ball and flighting it cleverly, bowled with so much skill that he went from one triumph to another. It is not possible here to set out his achievements in full, but among his outstanding performances may be noted: 12 for 154 against Essex at Leyton, 11 for 90 against Gloucestershire, 12 for 196 against Derbyshire, 10 for 88 against Warwickshire, 13 for 168 against Northamptonshire, 14 for 181 against Essex at Canterbury, and 15 for 224 against Leicestershire, while in the second innings of the match against the West Indies he secured nine of the ten wickets for 104 runs.

He took 216 wickets at a cost of 17 runs apiece in Championship matches, 246 in all Kent contests, and altogether 304 in first-class fixtures for 18 runs each. Not only did he in securing more than 200 wickets beat his own record, but he went on to surpass that of Tom Richardson, whose 290 wickets had stood since 1895 as the biggest aggregate ever obtained in first-class matches in a season. In the nature of things, no such extraordinary success as that of Freeman can be expected another year, so Kent will still need some fresh bowling and, in default of a real recovery of form on Wright's part, the attack threatens to be of indifferent quality.

NOTE: *Wisden*'s caution was misplaced. Alfred Percy Freeman went on to take 1,122 wickets in the four consecutive seasons from 1928 to 1931, and in eight consecutive seasons (1928–1935) he took 2,090 wickets. In each of those seasons he finished with more than 200 wickets. Just 5ft 2in tall, he bowled leg-breaks and googlies; his career aggregate of 3,776 wickets between 1914 and 1936, average 18.42, is second only to that of Wilfred Rhodes in the all-time list of first-class wicket-takers.

JIM LAKER
Notes by the Editor, *Wisden*, 1957

Whatever deeds the England batsmen accomplished against Australia, all were utterly dwarfed by Laker and his off-spin. It is said that records are made to be beaten, but I never expect to see again one bowler take 19 wickets in any match, let alone all ten twice in the same season against the Australians. And will Laker's 46 wickets in an England-Australia rubber ever be surpassed?

ENGLAND v AUSTRALIA
Fourth Test Match

At Manchester, July 26, 27, 28, 30, 31, 1956. England won by an innings and 170 runs, with just over an hour to spare, and so retained the Ashes. This memorable game will always be known as "Laker's Match" because of the remarkable performance by the Surrey off-break bowler in taking nine wickets for 37 runs in the first innings and ten wickets for 53 in the second. Laker broke all the important bowling records in the history of cricket. His achievements were:

1. Nineteen wickets in a match, the most in any first-class game. The previous best was 17, achieved 20 times. The most in a Test match was 17 for 159 by S. F. Barnes for England against South Africa at Johannesburg in 1913/14.

2. Ten wickets in an innings for the first time in Test cricket. The previous best for England against Australia was eight for 35 by G. Lohmann of Surrey in 1886/87; for England in any Test innings, nine for 28 by G. Lohmann against South Africa in 1895/96.

3. Ten wickets in an innings twice in one season for the first time. Laker previously took ten for 88 for Surrey, also against the Australians at The Oval in May.

4. Thirty-nine wickets in four Test matches, equalling the record of A. V. Bedser as the highest number in an England-Australia series, with one match to play.

5. Fifty-one wickets in five matches against the Australians to date in the season.

Apart from Laker's personal records, other noteworthy points about the match were:

1. It was the first definite result in a Test match between England and Australia at Manchester since 1905.

2. For the first time since 1905 England won two matches in a home series against Australia.

3. For the first time since five Test matches were played in a series regularly from 1897/98, England held the Ashes for three series.

Those are bare facts, interesting in themselves, but they fail to capture the drama of one of the most exciting and controversial matches for a long time. The excitement came towards the last day, first when England were trying hard to make up the time lost by rain to gain the victory which would settle the destination of the Ashes, and later as Laker drew nearer and nearer his ten wickets in the innings. The controversy arose over the preparation of the pitch, and for days cricketers, officials, critics and the general cricketing public could talk of little else.

England establish a platform

The England selectors sprang a surprise when they named Rev. D. S. Sheppard among the twelve from whom the team would be chosen. Sheppard, who had given up regular cricket to take up Holy Orders, had played only four innings for Sussex during the season when selected. One of these was 97 against the Australians at Hove. His previous Test appearance was two years earlier when he captained England against Pakistan. Like nearly every move the selection committee made during the season, this one proved fully justified.

May won the toss for the third time in the series and he gave England a big advantage. The pitch was completely useless to fast and fast-medium bowlers, and Richardson and Cowdrey, as at Nottingham, gave delightful displays. Cowdrey, strong in driving, was first to leave, but Richardson did not survive much longer, batting three hours 40 minutes for 104, his first Test century. Sheppard and May continued the mastery of the Australian attack, but towards tea time puffs of dust became noticeable when the ball landed, and it seemed that the pitch was breaking up unusually early. Johnson and Benaud, the Australian spin bowlers, were unable to exploit the conditions and England finished the first day with a total of 307 for three. A curiosity was that the first five England batsmen were all amateurs, something that had last happened against Australia in 1899 when C. B. Fry, A. C. MacLaren, K. S. Ranjitsinhji, C. L. Townsend and F. S. Jackson were the men concerned.

Mutterings about the pitch could be heard that evening, but they rose to full fury next day. The Australians still could not get the ball to bite as much as they ought to have done and England went gaily on before being all out for the highest total against Australia since 1948. Sheppard, 59 overnight, completed a chanceless century and gave not the lightest suggestion of lack of match practice. Evans, revelling in the situation, hit lustily and scored 47 out of 62 in 29 minutes. England made their 459 runs in 491 minutes, an unusually rapid rate for Test cricket in recent years.

The Australians crumble

Australia began their reply just after half-past two and before play ended on the second day they had lost 11 wickets. McDonald and Burke began steadily with a stand of 48, but they had to fight hard against the spin of Laker and Lock, who were brought on early. Laker did not start his devastating work until switched to the Stretford End, from where he took each of his 19 wickets. McDonald and Harvey fell at the same total, and after tea the last eight wickets went in 35 minutes for 22 runs. Lock took his only wicket with the first ball after the interval and Laker did the rest, his after-tea spell being seven wickets for eight runs in 22 balls. While admitting that Laker spun his off-breaks appreciably, the Australian batsmen gave a sorry display and appeared to give up too easily.

Following on 375 behind, Australia were unfortunate to lose McDonald, who retired with a knee injury after scoring 11. Harvey replaced him and was out first ball, hitting a full toss into the hands of short mid-on. Harvey failed to score in either innings. Australia finished the day with one wicket down for 51 and the controversial storm broke that night. Accusations were made that the pitch had been prepared specially for England's spin bowlers and these were denied by the Lancashire authorities. The Australians were said to be extremely bitter over the conditions of the pitch, but their captain, Johnson, declined to comment on the subject. The arguments continued over the weekend, and not until Laker's wonderful bowling on the last day overshadowed everything did they abate.

Rain plays a hand

The weather changed completely on Saturday, when rain allowed only three-quarters of an hour's cricket. In that brief period Australia added six runs and lost the wicket of Burke. Sunday was an atrocious day and Monday was almost as bad. In two spells of 45 minutes and 15 minutes, Australia took their score to 84 without further loss. Conditions were terrible for cricket, a fierce wind making batting and bowling extremely difficult. Lignum bails were used and were most successful, not once being blown off.

England looked like being robbed of victory by the weather, but it improved considerably on the last day and play began only ten minutes late. The soaking the pitch received left it slow and easy paced and, by fighting, determined cricket, McDonald and Craig remained together until lunch when the score was 112 for two with four hours left.

Shortly before the interval the sun appeared and almost immediately the ball began to spin quickly. Afterwards Laker began another devastating spell, sending back Craig, Mackay, Miller and Archer in nine overs for three runs. Benaud stayed with McDonald for an hour and a quarter to tea when, with an hour and 55 minutes left, England needed to capture four wickets. Occasionally Laker changed ends, but only when he returned to the Stretford End did he continue his success. After tea the ball spun quicker than at any time in the match and Australia's last hope vanished when McDonald fell to the second ball. His 89, made in five hours 37 minutes, showed that the bowling could be played by determined concentration and he deserved the highest praise for his great effort.

Making history

The tension mounted as Laker captured his eighth and ninth wickets. There was never a question of giving Laker his tenth wicket, for England's only thought was victory. Lock repeatedly beat the bat, but it was not his match and at 27 minutes past five a great cheer went up as Laker successfully appealed to the umpire, Lee, for lbw against Maddocks. The match was over and Laker had taken all ten wickets.

He earned his triumph by remarkable control of length and spin and it is doubtful whether he bowled more than six bad-length balls throughout the match. As Johnson said afterwards: "When the controversy and the side issues of the match are forgotten, Laker's wonderful bowling will remain." That night the rain returned, and the following day not a ball could be bowled in any of the first-class matches, so it can be seen how close was England's time margin, and how the greatest bowling feat of all time nearly did not happen. – Leslie Smith

England 459 (P. E. Richardson 104, M. C. Cowdrey 80, Rev. D. S. Sheppard 113, P. B. H. May 43, T. G. Evans 47, J. C. Laker 3; I. W. Johnson four for 151).

Australia

C. C. McDonald c Lock b Laker	32	– c Oakman b Laker	89
J. W. Burke c Cowdrey b Lock	22	– c Lock b Laker	33
R. N. Harvey b Laker	0	– c Cowdrey b Laker	0
I. D. Craig lbw b Laker	8	– lbw b Laker	38
K. R. Miller c Oakman b Laker	6	– b Laker	0
K. D. Mackay c Oakman b Laker	0	– c Oakman b Laker	0
R. G. Archer st Evans b Laker	6	– c Oakman b Laker	0
R. Benaud c Statham b Laker	0	– b Laker	18
R. R. Lindwall not out	6	– c Lock b Laker	8
†L. V. Maddocks b Laker	4	– lbw Laker	2
*I. W. Johnson b Laker	0	– not out	1
		B 12, l-b 4	16
	84		205

1/48 2/48 3/62 4/62 5/62 6/73   1/28 2/55 3/114 4/124 5/130
7/73 8/78 9/84   6/130 7/181 8/198 9/203

Bowling: *First Innings* – J. B. Statham 6–3–6–0; T. E. Bailey 4–3–4–0; J. C. Laker 16.4–4–37–9; G. A. R. Lock 14–3–37–1. *Second Innings* – J. B. Statham 16–9–15–0; T. E. Bailey 20–8–31–0; J. C. Laker 51.2–23–53–10; G. A. R. Lock 55–30–69–0; A. S. M. Oakman 8–3–21–0.

DIVINE RETRIBUTION 1906
ESSEX V SURREY

On Essex going in a second time, McGahey and Turner scored 95 together, and Gillingham and Reeves 112 in just over an hour. Gillingham was brilliantly caught by Inns, the Essex cricketer [acting as substitute fielder for Surrey], who died suddenly about a fortnight later.

Rev. F. H. Gillingham c Strudwick b Lees . . 3 – c sub b Hobbs . . 95

OBITUARY, 1906

J. H. Inns, who was born at Writtle, near Chelmsford, on March 30, 1877, died at Leyton on June 14 [1905]. He was a good wicket-keeper, and was stated to be one of the finest fieldsmen in England.

ANIL KUMBLE 2000
by Qamar Ahmed

In January 1999, Pakistan arrived for their first Test series with neighbours India for nine years, and the first on Indian soil since 1986/87. Three previous attempts to organise a Pakistani tour of India in the 1990s had been aborted because of threats of disruption by right-wing Hindu fundamentalists. In 1998, both countries had tested nuclear weapons, adding a new dimension to their traditional tension. The Shiv Sena party, led by maverick politician Bal Thackeray, were the most prominent opponents of the visit. Early in January, activists dug up the Test pitch in Delhi, forcing the Indian Board to move the First Test to Chennai.

INDIA v PAKISTAN
Second Test Match

At Delhi, February 4, 5, 6, 7, 1999. India won by 212 runs, their first victory over Pakistan since 1979/80, to draw the series. But the headlines belonged to leg-spinner Anil Kumble. He claimed all ten wickets in Pakistan's second innings, becoming only the second man in history to take ten in a Test innings, following English off-spinner Jim Laker in 1956. Kumble's match figures of 14 for 149 were the third best by an Indian in Tests. Richard Stokes, a fifty-three-year-old English businessman, had as a schoolboy seen Laker take some of his ten wickets at Old Trafford in 1956, and he arrived at Feroz Shah Kotla – on his birthday – just in time to see Kumble repeat the feat.

Kumble had bowled six overs without taking a wicket on the fourth morning, mostly from the Football Stand End. Pakistan had little hope of winning after being set a formidable target of 420, but needed only a draw to take the series and had seemed well placed at 101 without loss. After lunch, Kumble operated from the Pavilion End: he bowled 20.3 overs and claimed ten for 47, aided by some brilliant fielding and a substandard pitch – hastily repaired after the fundamentalists' vandalism a month earlier. Pakistan were all out for 207.

Kumble started the slide when Shahid Afridi was given out caught behind dabbing outside off stump. Afridi lingered in protest at the decision by home umpire Jayaprakash, whose performance was much condemned by Pakistani observers. With his next ball, Kumble had Ijaz Ahmed lbw as he stretched forward. Inzamam-ul-Haq averted the hat-trick, but played on off an inside edge minutes later. Yousuf Youhana, pushing forward, was lbw; Moin Khan was caught low down in the slips; and Saeed Anwar, who had defended for two and a half hours, was caught bat and pad at short leg. Pakistan had slumped to 128 for six, and Kumble had taken six for 15 in 44 balls. "That was the moment when I thought all ten could be mine," he said afterwards.

But he had to wait until after tea for No. 7, as Salim Malik and Wasim Akram held firm in a stand of 58. Then Kumble resumed the demolition. He bowled Malik, trying to pull; Mushtaq Ahmed was caught at gully off an awkward bounce; and the next ball hit Saqlain Mushtaq on the toe and trapped him lbw. That ended Kumble's 26th over, with one wicket remaining. Azharuddin privately instructed Srinath to bowl a wayward line in his next over. Wasim, who had resisted for an hour and a half, then kept out the hat-trick ball, and the next one, but top-edged Kumble's third ball to Laxman at short leg.

Kumble was carried back to the pavilion on his colleagues' shoulders as the crowd rejoiced. "My first reaction is that we have won," he said. "No one dreams of taking ten wickets in an innings, because you can't. The pitch was of variable bounce, and cutting and pulling was not easy. All I had to do was pitch in the right area, mix up my pace and spin, and trap the batsmen. The first wicket was the hardest to get – the openers were cruising."

India 252 (S. Ramesh 60, V. V. S. Laxman 35, R. Dravid 33, M. Azharuddin 67, A. Kumble 0; Saqlain Mushtaq five for 94) **and 339** (S. Ramesh 96, S. C. Ganguly 62 not out, A. Kumble 15, J. Srinath 49, extras 31; Wasim Akram three for 43, Saqlain Mushtaq five for 122).

Pakistan 172 (Shahid Afridi 32, Salim Malik 31; Harbhajan Singh three for 30, A. Kumble 24.3–6–75–4) **and 207** (Saeed Anwar 69, Shahid Afridi 41, Wasim Akram 37; A. Kumble 26.3–9–74–10).

MARTIN BICKNELL 2001
by David Llewellyn

Bicknell scored 500 runs for the first time, giving him credence as an all-rounder, and while his 60 wickets at 17.53 were apparently not enough to catch the eye of the England selectors, they went a long way to securing the Championship for Surrey. He had a memorable game against Leicestershire on his home ground, Woodbridge Road, Guildford, claiming the best match return by an England bowler – 16 for 119 – since Jim Laker's 19 for 90 against Australia in 1956. In recent years, his flawless seam bowling has been singularly neglected by his country.

SURREY v LEICESTERSHIRE

At Guildford, July 19, 20, 21, 2000. Surrey won by ten wickets. Bicknell, on his home ground, turned the game on its head with the best match return in England since 1956 – and the best by a fast bowler since 1952. But the bare figures, 16 for 119, scarcely capture the drama of his superb seam and swing bowling on a near-perfect pitch. With hundreds from Smith and Ward – both demonstrating what could be achieved with discipline and concentration – matched by seven first-innings wickets for

MOST WICKETS IN A MATCH IN ENGLAND SINCE 1945

19–90	J. C. Laker	England v Australia at Manchester	1956
16–83	B. Dooland	Nottinghamshire v Essex at Nottingham	1954
16–83	G. A. R. Lock	Surrey v Kent at Blackheath	1956
16–84	C. Gladwin	Derbyshire v Worcestershire at Stourbridge	1952
16–112	J. H. Wardle	Yorkshire v Sussex at Hull	1954
16–119	**M. P. Bicknell**	**Surrey v Leicestershire at Guildford**	**2000**
16–137	R. A. L. Massie	Australia v England at Lord's	1972
16–215	T. P. B. Smith	Essex v Middlesex at Colchester	1947
16–220	M. Muralitharan	Sri Lanka v England at The Oval	1998
16–225	J. E. Walsh	Leicestershire v Oxford University at Oxford	1953

Bicknell and six for Ormond, Leicestershire held a slim 30-run advantage when they batted again in the last hour of the second day. By the close, the game was as good as settled. Bicknell had captured five for 24 in seven overs, the first two, Maddy and Sutcliffe, with deliveries that would have bowled the best. Next morning, Wells and DeFreitas threw the bat at everything until, in his fourth over, Bicknell began a spell of four for four in 16 balls that brought him Championship-best figures of nine for 47 and made him the first to 50 first-class wickets in the season. Leicestershire's first-innings 318 was the highest total Surrey had conceded to date; in the second, 87 was the lowest. Ward followed the third hundred of his career with an unbeaten 61 as Surrey wrapped up victory by mid-afternoon.

Leicestershire 318 (I. J. Sutcliffe 37, B. F. Smith 102, D. Williamson 47, extras 53; M. P. Bicknell 28.1–5–72–7). *Second Innings –*

D. L. Maddy b Bicknell	0
I. J. Sutcliffe b Bicknell	7
B. F. Smith lbw b Greenidge	8
D. I. Stevens c Butcher b Bicknell	14
N. D. Burns lbw b Bicknell	0
A. Habib c Butcher b Bicknell	2
V. J. Wells c Brown b Bicknell	17
P. A. J. DeFreitas c Butcher b Bicknell	24
D. Williamson not out	1
A. Kumble c B. C. Hollioake b Bicknell	5
J. Ormond b Bicknell	0
L-b 3, w 2, n-b 4	9
	87

1/0 2/7 3/31 4/31 5/33 6/33 7/80 8/81 9/87
Bowling: M. P. Bicknell 12.5–3–47–9; C. G. Greenidge 11–6–35–1; Saqlain Mushtaq 1–0–2–0.

Surrey 288 (I. J. Ward 107, N. Shahid 47, A. D. Brown 34, M. P. Bicknell 0, extras 41; J. Ormond six for 87, A. Kumble three for 68) **and 119** for no wkt (M. A. Butcher 47 not out, I. J. Ward 61 not out).

HEDLEY VERITY 1933

Verity had splendid records for several matches, getting nine wickets for 41 against Somerset, 11 for 86 against Northants and 11 for 67 against Derbyshire, but these performances were completely overshadowed by his wonderful triumph in the second innings of Notts at Leeds, where for the second time in two years he accomplished the great feat of taking all ten wickets in an innings. Not only did Verity secure all ten wickets – seven for three runs with the last 16 balls he sent down – but he obtained the whole ten wickets at a cost of only ten runs. In so doing, Verity accomplished what was probably an unprecedented achievement for, if in connection with the earlier instances of all ten wickets in an innings the cost is not known, no case, since bowling analyses have been kept, can be found of all ten wickets being obtained at such a low cost. Verity has acquired a faculty of making the ball "lift" and this development brought him lots of wickets, largely through batsmen giving catches in the slips or to the fieldsmen standing close in.

YORKSHIRE v NOTTINGHAMSHIRE

At Leeds, Saturday, Monday, Tuesday, July 9, 11, 12, 1932. Verity in this match took – for the second time in his career – all ten wickets in an innings. Prior to lunch on the last day Notts scored 38 without loss but, on resuming, their ten wickets went down for 29 runs. Verity not only performed the hat-trick in sending back Walker, Harris and Gunn, but got rid of Arthur Staples and Larwood with the last two balls of his next over and then, disposing of Voce and Sam Staples with the third and fourth balls of his following over, brought the innings to a close. This splendid bowling feat Sutcliffe and Holmes followed up by hitting off in about an hour and a half the 139 runs required for victory. Thus, Yorkshire gained a glorious win by ten wickets although, when on Monday afternoon a thunderstorm burst over the ground, they had stood 71 behind with only one wicket to fall.

Nottinghamshire 234 (W. Walker 36, C. B. Harris 35, G. V. Gunn 31,
B. Lilley 46 not out, H. Larwood 48; H. Verity two for 64, M. Leyland
four for 14). *Second Innings –*

W. W. Keeton c Macaulay b Verity	21
F. W. Shipston c Wood b Verity	21
W. Walker c Macaulay b Verity	11
A. W. Carr c Barber b Verity	0
A. Staples c Macaulay b Verity	7
C. B. Harris c Holmes b Verity	0
G. V. Gunn lbw b Verity	0
B. Lilley not out	3
H. Larwood c Sutcliffe b Verity	0
W. Voce c Holmes b Verity	0
S. J. Staples st Wood b Verity	0
B 3, n-b 1	4
	67

Bowling: W. E. Bowes 5–0–19–0; G. G. Macaulay 23–9–34–0;
    H. Verity 19.4–16–10–10.

Yorkshire 163 for nine dec. (P. Holmes 65, W. Barber 34; H. Larwood
five for 73) **and 139** for no wkt (P. Holmes 77 not out, H. Sutcliffe 54
not out).

AHAD KHAN 1966
by Ghulam Mustafa Khan

In North Zone, Services, ably supported by Nayyar Husain (189
runs, avge 46.25 and 19 wickets, avge 10.73), won their matches,
and Railways' Ahad Khan was their leading wicket-taker including nine for seven against D. I. Khan. This match was a remarkable one. Against a weak team Railways made 415 for two on the
first day, 825 for six on the second day, and declared at 910 for six
on the third morning. D. I. Khan were bowled out for 32 and 27.
Jervez Akhtar made 337 not out, and in all four batsmen scored
centuries. Ahad took 29 wickets (avge 8.76) in the tournament.

At Lahore, December 2, 3, 4, 1964. Railways won by an innings and 851
    runs.

Railways 910 for six dec. (Pervez Akhtar 337 not out, Javed Baber 200,
    Ijaz Husain 124, Mohammad Sharif 106 not out).

Dera Ismail Khan 32 (Ahad Khan seven for 14) **and 27** (Ahad Khan nine for 7).

SOMETHING TO SING ABOUT 1912

YORKSHIRE v NORTHAMPTONSHIRE

Rain stopping play soon after lunch on Friday and preventing any cricket at all on Saturday, so little progress was made with this match that, with less than an innings completed on each side, the game furnished the solitary instance during the whole summer of a Championship contest yielding no points to either side ... During the interval on Thursday – Coronation Day – the large company present joined in singing the National Anthem.

COLIN BLYTHE 1908

Kent's bowling just as much as in 1906 depended on Blythe and Fielder. It was no fault of theirs that Kent lost so many matches, as Blythe took 141 wickets and Fielder 151, both having an average of under 17 runs a wicket. Never very robust, Blythe had to stand out of two or three county matches through illness, and on one occasion he was kept away by a Test match.

NOTE: Blythe, who suffered from epilepsy, was reckoned by *Wisden* 1918 to be "one of five left-handed slow bowlers of the first rank produced by England in the last 40 years, the other four being Peate, Peel, Briggs and Rhodes". He was killed in France in November 1917 while serving with the Kent Fortress Engineers.

NORTHAMPTONSHIRE v KENT

At Northampton, Thursday, Friday, Saturday, May, 30, 31, June 1, 1907. Kent were seen at quite the best in this match, and forced a victory in brilliant style. Rain restricted cricket on the opening day to three hours and prevented anything being done on the Friday, but, despite this serious loss of time, Kent had won at half-past four on the Saturday afternoon by an innings and 155 runs. This was mainly the work of Blythe who, bowling superbly, took all ten wickets in Northamptonshire's first innings and had a record for the match of 17 wickets for 48 runs. By consistently good batting Kent, in the time available on the first afternoon, scored 212 runs for the loss of four wickets, and on the Saturday morning the batsmen hit out in fearless style. Then, on going in, Northamptonshire gave a deplorable display. Against Blythe's bowling, seven wickets fell for four runs, two of them extras, but Vials, after being missed, hit pluckily and the innings extended beyond the luncheon interval. In the end, however, the total only reached 60, and following on 194 behind Northamptonshire were dismissed in an hour and a quarter for 39. Kent only just won in time, for no sooner had the players left the field than rain fell heavily.

Kent 254 (H. T. W. Hardinge 73, J. Seymour 37, K. L. Hutchings 52, C. Blythe 6; W. East five for 77, L. T. Driffield four for 50).

Northamptonshire

W. A. Buswell st Huish b Blythe .	0	– c Woolley b Blythe.	7
M. Cox st Huish b Blythe.	0	– st Huish b Blythe.	12
C. J. T. Pool c Fielder b Blythe . .	0	– st Huish b Blythe.	5
W. H. Kingston lbw b Blythe . . .	2	– lbw b Blythe	0
G. J. Thompson b Blythe	0	– c Hardinge b Blythe	1
W. East c Huish b Blythe	0	– c Huish b Fairservice.	0
E. M. Crosse c Fairservice b Blythe	0	– c Hardinge b Blythe	2
A. R. Thompson c Seymour b Blythe	10	– c Humphreys b Blythe.	7
G. A. T. Vials not out	33	– b Fairservice	1
W. Wells c Humphreys b Blythe .	0	– b Humphreys	0
L. T. Driffield b Blythe	12	– not out	1
B 1, l-b 2.	3	B 3.	3
	60		39

Bowling: *First Innings* – C. Blythe 16–7–30–10; W. J. Fairservice 12–5–17–0; A. Fielder 3–0–10–0. *Second Innings* – C. Blythe 15.1–7–18–7; W. J. Fairservice 9–3–15–2; E. Humphreys 6–3–3–1.

GEORGE DENNETT 1913

Of Gloucestershire's play last season there is no need to say much. Everything else was dwarfed by Dennett's remarkable bowling. Except from Parker, Dennett received no substantial support, but nevertheless in county matches he took 118 wickets at exactly 16 runs apiece. For the first time in his career he secured 16 wickets in one game, but his most startling piece of work was done against Kent at Dover. Going on for the second time when Kent's score stood at 100, he took six wickets in 20 balls without a run being hit from him. Playing always for a weak side, Dennett has never secured quite the position to which he was entitled. Had it been his good fortune to play cricket in Gloucestershire's great days, he would have been far more famous. The bad weather was, of course, all in his favour last year, but he was obviously in his best form.

KENT v GLOUCESTERSHIRE

At Dover, Thursday, Friday, Saturday, August 22, 23, 24, 1912. A most sensational day's cricket took place on Thursday, 30 wickets going down for an aggregate of 268 runs. As a result of this remarkable work, Kent were left with an innings to play and 57 runs to make to win. On Friday, however, with the wicket practically under water, not a ball could be bowled, and the conditions being equally hopeless on Saturday the match had to be abandoned as a draw. The sun shining after a rainy night, S. H. Day sent Gloucestershire in to bat. The visitors scored 40 before their third wicket fell, but then collapsed altogether against Blythe and Carr. A marvellous bowling achievement on the part of Dennett stood out as the great feature of the extra-ordinary day's play. Kent, thanks to Humphreys and Jennings, had 100 on the board with four men out when Dennett resumed, and in 20 balls took the last six wickets without having a single run hit from him, the Kent batsmen, whether they attempted to hit or merely to defend, being helpless against his left-hand slows. The match held out promise of being finished off on Thursday, Carr in the second innings of Gloucestershire taking the first seven wickets at a cost of eight runs, 25 runs meanwhile coming from Blythe. In this way the visitors had seven men out before the arrears of 39 were cleared off. Late in the afternoon, however, Brownlee, Barnett and Parker played with plenty of resolution.

Gloucestershire 67 (C. Blythe five for 27, D. W. Carr five for 38) **and 95**
(C. Blythe two for 54, D. W. Carr eight for 36).

Kent 106 (E. Humphreys 40, D. W. Jennings 32; E. G. Dennett seven for
54).

CHAMINDA VAAS 2003
SRI LANKA v ZIMBABWE

At Sinhalese Sports Club, Colombo, December 8, 2001. Sri
Lanka won by nine wickets. Toss: Sri Lanka. Vaas became the
first bowler to claim eight wickets in a one-day international –
five days after taking 14 Test wickets on the same ground against
West Indies. As in the Test, his success was based on controlled,
each-way swing on a true pitch. He dismissed Ebrahim with his
first ball and took Sri Lanka's first limited-overs hat-trick in
his sixth over – starting with Carlisle, the only Zimbabwean to
reach double figures, and followed by Wishart and Taibu, both
to vicious in-swingers. Vaas was on course for all ten until
Muralitharan, who had held the previous one-day record – seven for
30 against India in 2000/01 – picked up the last two. Zimbabwe
were routed for 38, the lowest total in limited-overs internationals,
five less than Pakistan's 43 against West Indies at Cape Town in
1992/93. That match had also produced the previous lowest
aggregate in a completed one-day international – 88 for 13
wickets – and at 32.2 overs had been the shortest international
uninterrupted by bad weather; this game shattered both records.
The crowd had witnessed a mere 78 runs for 11 wickets in 20
overs: Sri Lanka needed just 26 balls as they zoomed to victory
before noon.

Zimbabwe

D. D. Ebrahim lbw b Vaas	0
G. W. Flower b Vaas	1
*S. V. Carlisle c Perera b Vaas	16
†A. Flower c Sangakkara b Vaas	0
C. B. Wishart lbw b Vaas	6
D. A. Marillier not out	4
T. Taibu lbw b Vaas	0
H. H. Streak lbw b Vaas	0
M. L. Nkala c Sangakkara b Vaas	1

T. J. Friend b Muralitharan 4
H. K. Olonga c Jayawardene b Muralitharan 0
   L-b 1, w 1, n-b 4. 6
   (15.4 overs)   38

1/0 2/11 3/11 4/27 5/27 6/27 7/29 8/32 9/38
Bowling: W. P. U. J. C. Vaas 8–3–19–8; D. N. T. Zoysa 7–2–17–0;
M. Muralitharan 0.4–0–1–2.

Sri Lanka 40 for one (4.2 overs).

BALL OF THE CENTURY
1933

A very slow bowler, William Fuller-Maitland added to a fine command of length and skill in "flighting" the ball – what *Scores and Biographies* described as a "great curve", getting many wickets – a fine leg-break and, at times, according to a famous old enthusiast, a phenomenal one. This admirer of Fuller-Maitland remembered that in the University match of 1867 J. S. E. Hood was bowled by a ball which came right round his legs. The ball pitched so wide that Hood left it alone, only, much to his chagrin, to find himself bowled. The enthusiast used to say that in the course of half a century, he had seen only three other balls which did so much. According to the same authority, Fuller-Maitland was the best slow bowler that had ever appeared in the University match except A. G. Steel, as that great cricketer was in 1878.

by Greg Baum, 2000

There are three elements to Shane Warne's greatness – skill, novelty and drama – and all were manifest in the one great delivery that made his name, at Old Trafford in 1993. The delivery was exceptionally skilful. It began its flight innocently so as to lull Mike Gatting, drifted to leg, pitched in the batsman's blind spot, then rounded on him fiercely and bent back off stump. It was at once pinpoint in its accuracy and prodigious in its spin, qualities that had always been thought to be irreconcilable. Later in the summer, John Woodcock would write that it was doubtful if there had ever been a bowler who could aim the ball as precisely and turn it as far as Warne. This is a sentiment that has echoed down the seasons.

The delivery was something different. West Indies and their battery of pace bowlers had set the agenda for 20 years; spin, particularly wrist-spin, had become nearly defunct, but suddenly here it was again in more irresistible form than ever before. Most of all, the Gatting ball was not just early in his spell, but his very first delivery – in the match, in the series, in Ashes cricket. That gave the ball a sense of theatre, and Warne a name for showmanship that has grown at each new threshold of his startling career, and at its peak made him nearly mystical. In the modern era, only Ian Botham could compare.

HAY FEVER 1933

Going up to Oxford after four years in the Harrow XI, Mr William Fuller-Maitland, as a freshman in 1864, obtained a place in the University team. In that same season he appeared for the Gentlemen against the Players at The Oval and in the following summer he assisted the Gentlemen at Lord's. Indeed for some six years he was a fairly regular participant in the great match of the season but, after the summer of 1869, when he once again figured in the Gentlemen's team at The Oval, the cricket field saw him no more. Thus his career was almost as brief as it was brilliant. In answer to an enquiry early last year as to the cause of his retirement from the game when, with his fame solidly established, he was at the height of his powers, Mr Fuller-Maitland wrote: "One reason was that I always suffered badly from hay fever in the months of June and July. Another reason – that I had a great wish to see as much of the world as I could. In my travels I spent three years in America, India and Spain and had no hay fever at all. When three years more were over, I went into Parliament."

SKITTLED OUT

Second Royal Surrey Militia's game against Shillinglee in August 1855 was not first-class but, being a first-class embarrassment for the Militia, it found a place in the first-ever *Wisden* under the category of "Extraordinary Matches". Why? Because all 11 batsmen failed to score in their first innings.

Yet, as Basil Easterbrook reveals in his *Wisden* 1971 article, "The Dreaded Cypher", the Militia almost missed out on a place in history when their No. 10 batsman "hit one to cover-point and set off like an Olympic sprinter going for the tape. Major Ridley [0 not out] rent the pastoral scene with a stentorian voice of command – 'Go back, Sergeant.' Sgt Ayling, pulled up all standing, fell base over apex and was run out by 15 yards. There were those who accused the gallant Major of moral cowardice, but I see him as a man with a sense of history. There is something aesthetically perfect about that scorecard – no catches, no stumpings, no lbws and no runs." The Militia might have wished there had been no scorecard at all.

The lowest total in first-class cricket is 12, as the table on the next page shows. *Wisden* 2004 lists 27 innings under 20, some of which are described among the lowest county totals that follow. Some, but not all: there's still room for debasement, even if present-day pitches, full covering and the decline in spin bowling on the county circuit suggest that all except Durham may have hit rock-bottom.

Patriotism, or maybe national shame, has prevented me from getting into lowest Test totals. Suffice to say, *Wisden* lists them every year in the Test Records section, and *Wisden* 1956 provides a full account of the record lowest score, 26, along with the gruesome scorecard in which only one batsman reached double figures and five others have the dreaded cipher against their name.

LOWEST INNINGS TOTALS

12†	Oxford University v MCC and Ground at Oxford	1877
12	Northamptonshire v Gloucestershire at Gloucester	1907
13	Auckland v Canterbury at Auckland	1877/78
13	Nottinghamshire v Yorkshire at Nottingham	1901
14	Surrey v Essex at Chelmsford	1983
15	MCC v Surrey at Lord's	1839
15†	Victoria v MCC at Melbourne	1903/04
15†	Northamptonshire v Yorkshire at Northampton	1908
15	Hampshire v Warwickshire at Birmingham	1922

†*Denotes that one batsman was absent.*

Wisden, 2004

The abbreviated scores that accompany the following match reports contain an italic note when half the side did not score. There are no match reports or bowling figures for the Kent and Middlesex games because, as mentioned in an earlier chapter, the Almanack did not give these details until 1870.

DERBYSHIRE (16) 1880
NOTTINGHAMSHIRE v DERBYSHIRE

At Nottingham, July 10, 11, 1879. Morley's marvellous bowling in both innings prevented Derbyshire standing much chance against their rivals. Although in the early part of the day the wickets were dead, they improved towards noon and Daft, who had won the toss, decided on batting. Selby shone far more brilliantly than any of his fellows. Going in first wicket down, he was the seventh to leave, having been batting three hours for his well played 53. All the Notts men scored, with a solitary exception.

Derbyshire commenced in a disastrous manner and continued so to the end. Before a run had been scored, Rigley and Cook were both caught at cover-point; Mr Smith returned the ball at three, Platts was stumped at four, and at 11 Mr Wallroth was caught at long-field. Now came a complete collapse. At 16 the last four wickets fell for nothing: Osborne was clean bowled, Hay was caught at cover-point, Mycroft at wicket, and the Rev. E. Forman clean bowled. Of course the visitors followed on and at the close of the day had lost two wickets for nothing. On Friday the weather was better. The only double-figure score made for Derbyshire was by Foster. Of the remainder little need be said, as in the double innings they obtained only 60 runs and were thus defeated by an innings and 99 runs.

Nottinghamshire 159 (J. Selby 53; W. Mycroft four for 71, J. Platts four for 45).

Derbyshire 16 (T. Foster 7, *seven batsmen did not score*; A. Shaw 11–7–9–3, F. Morley 10.2–7–7–7) **and 44** (T. Foster 19, *six batsmen did not score*; A. Shaw 24–14–16–5, F. Morley 23–11–28–5).

DURHAM (67) 1997
MIDDLESEX v DURHAM

At Lord's, May 9, 10, 11, 13, 1996. Middlesex won by 306 runs. David Follett, in his third Championship match, claimed eight for 22, the best figures at Lord's for 20 years, to dismiss Durham for 67, the county's lowest total in their five first-class seasons. He bowled with hostility and accuracy: two middle stumps went cartwheeling and his two lbws included Roseberry with his first delivery of the innings. On the opening day, when 16 wickets fell, another Middlesex seamer, Fay, playing his second first-class game because of Nash's bad back, had taken three in his second over, helping to make up for his team's poor batting. But Roseberry, returning to Lord's for the first time since leaving Middlesex, and Scott enabled Durham to take an 18-run lead. When the home side resumed, however, Weekes and Gatting shared the only three-figure stand of the match, and Gatting reached his 90th hundred, completing his set of centuries against the other 17 first-class counties. Durham's target was 374; thanks to Follett, they fell more than 300 short.

Middlesex 191 (M. W. Gatting 74, K. R. Brown 32; M. M. Betts three for 78, M. J. Foster four for 21) **and 391** (P. N. Weekes 73, M. W. Gatting 171, R. L. Johnson 35; M. M. Betts four for 101).

Durham 209 (M. A. Roseberry 43, J. A. Daley 34, C. W. Scott 59; A. R. C. Fraser three for 47, R. A. Fay three for 33) **and 67** (S. L. Campbell 23; A. R. C. Fraser 10–3–20–1, R. A. Fay 8–2–12–0, D. Follett 12.2–3–22–8, P. C. R. Tufnell 6–1–8–1).

ESSEX (30) 1902
ESSEX v YORKSHIRE

At Leyton, Thursday, Friday, August 15, 16, 1901. The season at Leyton closed with a genuine sensation, a match of very small scores ending just after 12 o'clock on the second day in a victory for Yorkshire by an innings and 33 runs. As rain had fallen heavily overnight, the bowlers were expected to do well, but for what actually happened no one could have been in the least prepared. Essex promptly lost the game, for on winning the toss and going in at a quarter to one – the state of the ground having prevented an earlier start – they were out in as nearly as possible an hour for a total of 30. Four wickets fell for one run, and the only chance of retrieving this disastrous start disappeared when Lucas was run out. Bowling at a great pace, and swerving in an extraordinary way, Hirst was in the opinion of the Essex batsmen quite unplayable. He took seven wickets – six of them bowled down – and only 12 runs were hit from him. Later in the day, in the second innings of Essex, he was just as deadly, taking five wickets

---

UP COUNTRY WITH THE ALMANACK 1926

A great cricket enthusiast, Major Edwards went to big matches in any part of the country whenever possible, and had a large circle of intimate friends among county cricketers. He spent a considerable time in Africa, and years ago found solace during solitary days up country reading *Wisden*, to which he frequently contributed. During the war he was gassed badly, and in a later expedition to Southern Russia he lost all his baggage except his set of *Wisden*, which accompanied him on all his travels. Major Edwards never tired of retailing stories of first-class cricketers.

out of six, but there his wonderful success ended, the three
wickets that fell the next morning being obtained by Rhodes. The
Yorkshiremen found Walter Mead extremely difficult on the
damaged pitch, and only Taylor, Tunnicliffe and Frank Mitchell
could do anything against him. In a match in which the bowlers
had things so entirely their own way, it was a great feat on Taylor's part to score 44, and apart from a couple of lucky snicks he
played very finely.

Essex 30 (C. P. McGahey 11; G. H. Hirst 8.1–3–12–7, W. Rhodes
8–0–17–2) **and 41** (W. Reeves 12; G. H. Hirst 10–6–17–5, W. Rhodes
10–2–20–4).
Yorkshire 104 (T. L. Taylor 44; W. Mead six for 40, W. Reeves three for 36).

GLAMORGAN (22) 1925
LANCASHIRE v GLAMORGAN

At Liverpool, Wednesday, Thursday, Friday, May 14, 15, 16,
1924. Phenomenal bowling by Parkin enabled Lancashire to win
comfortably by 128 runs, notwithstanding a bad batting failure
on the Thursday morning. The saturated turf on the Aigburth
ground prevented play on Wednesday, despite fine weather, and
batsmen could do nothing on the drying pitch next day until
Makepeace and Hallows opened Lancashire's second innings
with the one stand of the match, 107 runs coming before Hallows
left. That admirable partnership on a pitch that remained very
soft gave Lancashire an advantage which the bowlers followed up
with deadly effect. Both sides had been dismissed in two hours
and 20 minutes in the first innings, Spencer, right-hand medium
pace, proving most effective for Glamorgan, while Parkin got rid
of five men before a run was scored off him. Altogether in the
match Parkin took ten wickets for 36 runs, R. Tyldesley with
seven for 53 giving valuable help.

Lancashire 49 (A. Rhodes 10; J. Mercer 12–3–27–3, T. Arnott 3–2–5–0,
H. Spencer 10.1–5–9–5, F. P. Ryan 2–2–0–2) **and 208** for eight dec.
(J. W. H. Makepeace 41, C. Hallows 49, G. Duckworth 34; D. Davies
four for 43).

Glamorgan 22 (W. Bates 11, *six batsmen did not score*; C. H. Parkin
   8–5–6–6, R. K. Tyldesley 7.3–1–16–4) **and 107** (J. Mercer 45 not out;
   C. H. Parkin four for 30, R. K. Tyldesley three for 37).

GLOUCESTERSHIRE (17) 1897
AUSTRALIANS v GLOUCESTERSHIRE

At Cheltenham, Thursday, Friday, Saturday, August 20, 21, 22,
1896. In this, the second match of the Cheltenham week, the
Australians beat Gloucestershire by an innings and 54 runs. The
game was a memorable one, Gloucestershire in their second
innings being dismissed for 17 – the smallest score ever made by
an English team against Australian bowlers. The wicket, drying
after drenching rain, was excessively difficult, but for all that
Trumble and McKibbin bowled in marvellous form. It will be
seen that Trumble took six wickets for eight runs and McKibbin
four for seven. Though so badly beaten at the finish, Gloucestershire did very well up to a certain point, scoring 133 and getting
six Australian wickets down for 54. Then, however, Gregory's
splendid batting, and some mistakes in the field by the county,
turned the fortunes of the game. On the second day the weather
was so bad that only three overs could be bowled. In scoring his
71, Gregory was at the wickets an hour and 50 minutes, the way
in which he overcame the difficulties of the pitch being beyond
praise. Townsend bowled finely and with better support in the
field would have had an astonishing record. Even as it was, he
took eight wickets for just under ten runs each. At one point
he got rid of four batsmen in three overs.

Gloucestershire 133 (G. L. Jessop 30; H. Trumble two for 68,
   T. R. McKibbin six for 48) **and 17** (W. G. Grace 9, *six batsmen did
   not score*; H. Trumble 10–6–8–6, T. R. McKibbin 9.1–7–7–4).
Australians 204 (S. E. Gregory 71 not out; C. L. Townsend eight for 79).

The Australians in England by Sydney H. Pardon
There is one thing left to be said and that unfortunately is not of
a pleasant nature. Up to last season one of the special virtues of
Australian bowling was its unimpeachable fairness. Despite the
evil example set by many English throwers, team after team came

over to this country without a bowler to whose delivery exception could be taken, but unhappily things are no longer as they once were. We have not the least hesitation in saying that a fast bowler with the action of Jones, or a slow bowler with a delivery so open to question as McKibbin, would have found no place in the earliest elevens that came to England.

Jones's bowling is, to our mind, radically unfair, as we cannot conceive a ball being bowled fairly at the pace of an express train with a bent arm. The faults of our own bowlers with regard to throwing have been so many and grievous that we are extremely glad Jones was allowed to go through the season unchallenged, but now that the tour is a thing of the past it is only a duty to speak plainly on the matter. We do so with the more confidence as we know that our opinion is shared by a great many of the best English players.

As was only natural in the case of a slow bowler, McKibbin's action was less talked about, but there can be little doubt that he continually threw when putting on his off-break. It is no new matter for McKibbin's delivery to be called in question, as we believe Blackham once went to the length of saying that he would probably be no-balled if he ever went to England. Now that the evil effects of our own laxity with regard to unfair bowling have spread to Australia, it is to be hoped that the MCC will at last be moved to action in the matter.

HAMPSHIRE (15) 1923
WARWICKSHIRE v HAMPSHIRE

At Birmingham, Wednesday, Thursday, Friday, June 14, 15, 16, 1922. This was the sensational match of the whole season, at Birmingham or anywhere else, Hampshire actually winning by 155 runs after being out for a total of 15. That their astounding failure in the first innings was just one of the accidents of cricket, and not due in any way to the condition of the ground, was proved by their getting 521 when they followed on. The victory, taken as a whole, must surely be without precedent in first-class cricket. Hampshire looked in a hopeless position when the sixth wicket in their second innings went down at 186, but Shirley helped Brown to put on 85 runs, and then, with Livsey in after McIntyre had failed, the score was carried to 451. Brown batted splendidly for four hours and three-quarters and Livsey made his first hundred without a mistake.

Warwickshire 223 (F. R. Santall 84, Hon. F. S. G. Calthorpe 70; J. A. Newman four for 70, G. S. Boyes four for 56) **and 158** (E. J. Smith 41, W. G. Quaife 40 not out, Hon. F. S. G. Calthorpe 30; A. S. Kennedy four for 47, J. A. Newman five for 53).

Hampshire 15 (C. P. Mead 6 not out, *eight batsmen did not score*; H. Howell 4.5–2–7–6, Hon. F. S. G. Calthorpe 4–3–4–4) **and 521** (A. Bowell 45, Hon. L. H. Tennyson 45, G. Brown 172, W. R. Shirley 30, W. H. Livsey 110 not out; H. Howell three for 156, Hon. F. S. G. Calthorpe two for 97, W. G. Quaife three for 154).

KENT (18) 1868
KENT v SUSSEX

At Gravesend, June 6, 7, 1867. Sussex won by an innings and 40 runs.

Kent 98 (J. Southerton 7 wkts, James Lillywhite 3 wkts) **and 18** (W. S. Norton 6, *one man absent, five batsmen did not score*; J. Southerton 6 wkts, James Lillywhite 3 wkts).

Sussex 156 (H. Killick 37, G. Wells 31; R. Lipscomb 6 wkts).

LANCASHIRE (25) 1872
LANCASHIRE v DERBYSHIRE

At Old Trafford, May 26, 27, 1871. This was the first match played by the Derbyshire CC, whose eleven easily won their maiden match. Hickton (Derbyshire born) played for his native county, and A. Smith (Lancashire born, but resident in Derbyshire nearly all his life) played for *his* native shire. Mr Appleby was playing in the Gentlemen of the North v the Gentlemen of the South match at Lillie Bridge, consequently Lancashire lost the aid of their best bowler. The first innings of Lancashire was a curiosity, being played out in about one hour, for 25 runs, from (less one ball) 25 [four-ball] overs. The wickets in that very brief county innings fell as follows:

1	2 and 3	4, 5 and 6	7	8	9 and 10
2	4	5	15	19	25

In their second innings the Lancashire men were more fortunate. Coward's 36 was a fine display of defence that included 20 singles; he also made a splendid on-drive for four from Platts, this four being the only hit scored from the 23 balls bowled by Platts. Mr Hillkirk's 17 included the only five hit in the match, a beautiful straight drive from Hickton. Mr Hillkirk also made a four and a three in his rapidly scored 17. Whatmough's 28 not out was a creditable performance. Reynolds bowled 13 round-arm overs for 14 runs, but all the five wickets booked to his name were due to his slows. The Lancashire men fielded well. For Derbyshire, Mr Sowter's 47 not out was an excellent display of steady batting that included 25 singles. Burnham (Notts born) played capital cricket in his 31; he made three fours – two drives, the other a fine cut. Burnham also long-stopped well. Gregory clean bowled five of the six wickets due to him in Lancashire's first innings. Platts obtained the last three wickets of Lancashire just in time to win the match for his shire as, in less than ten minutes after, heavy rain fell and continued to fall for the remainder of that day. Derbyshire won by an innings and 11 runs.

Lancashire 25 (A. Smith 11 not out; D. Gregory 12.3–7–9–6, W. Hickton 12–5–16–4) **and 111** (C. Coward 36; D. Gregory three for 46, W. Hickton three for 58, J. Platts three for 4).

Derbyshire 147 (J. W. Burnham 31, U. Sowter 47 not out; F. R. Reynolds five for 54).

NAME CHECK 1975

Uel Addison Titley appeared for the XI while at Rugby, but did not get his colours. He went up to Cambridge and for some years wrote on cricket for *The Times*, but was better known as the rugby correspondent for that newspaper. His unusual first name was given by his father, Samuel Titley, who said: "Everybody calls me Sam. The boy can have the other half."

LEICESTERSHIRE (25) 1913
LEICESTERSHIRE v KENT

At Leicester, Thursday, Friday, June 6, 7, 1912. An astonishing performance by Blythe enabled Kent to gain a very easy victory by eight wickets. So completely at the mercy of the famous left-hander were the home batsmen that the match might have been concluded in the three and a half hours during which play lasted on the opening day had not an injury compelled the deadly bowler's retirement. A tremendous return from Mounteney hit Blythe on the leg, the ball going to mid-off where Humphreys held the catch. Knight and Whitehead then improved matters, but recovery was impossible after the disastrous first innings and, though the pitch was not nearly as treacherous on the Friday, Kent were caused no trouble, except by King. Quite unplayable at the start of the match, Blythe bowled with almost equal effect in the second innings, and came out with the wonderful analysis of 15 wickets for 45 runs. In view of the state of the game, King's achievement almost equalled Blythe's. Of the 32 wickets that fell, left-handed bowlers claimed all but four. Hubble, in scoring 46 out of 54, played a fine forcing game under difficult conditions.

Leicestershire 25 (A. E. Knight 7, A. Lord 7; C. Blythe 7.5–3–9–7, F. E. Woolley 7–2–15–3) and 155 (A. E. Knight 42, J. H. King 49; C. Blythe 21.1–3–36–8).

Kent 110 (J. C. Hubble 46; J. H. King 18.3–6–26–8) and 72 for two (F. E. Woolley 37 not out).

MIDDLESEX (20) 1865
MCC AND GROUND v MIDDLESEX

At Lord's, July 25, 26, 1864. MCC and Ground won by five wickets.

Middlesex 20 (I. D. Walker 7; J. Grundy 5 wkts, G. Wootton 5 wkts) and 154 (T. Hearne 33, A. W. Daniel 52; J. Grundy 5 wkts, G. Wootton 4 wkts).

MCC and Ground 113 (J. Grundy 33; R. D. Walker 3 wkts, T. Hearne 6 wkts) and 63 for five (V. E. Walker 3 wkts).

ECLIPSED 2000

<small>WORCESTERSHIRE V SRI LANKA A</small>

In this match "non-arrival of kit stopped play" – and then the solar eclipse did. The kit disaster cost the whole first day. The Sri Lankans had flown back from Copenhagen a day earlier. However, their original flight had been forced to turn back because of technical trouble and, although the players caught a later flight, their bags did not. A courier was supposed to be bringing them to Worcester next morning, but he got caught in pre-eclipse traffic and did not arrive until 5 p.m., an hour after play was called off. The match finally began at 11.45 next morning, after the solar eclipse, which darkened all Britain; it was only partial over Worcester, but cricket was clearly going to be impossible. More conventionally, rain interrupted Worcestershire's first innings.

NORTHAMPTONSHIRE (12) 1908
GLOUCESTERSHIRE v NORTHAMPTONSHIRE

At Gloucester, Monday, Tuesday, Wednesday, June 10, 11, 12, 1907. In this game a fresh record was made by Dennett and Jessop in dismissing Northamptonshire for 12 runs. This is the smallest total for a first-class inter-county match, the previous lowest being 13 by Notts against Yorkshire at Trent Bridge in 1901. Play on the first day was restricted to 50 minutes, Gloucestershire losing four wickets for 20 runs, and, despite some hitting by Jessop, being all out next day for 60. The first innings of Northamptonshire lasted only 40 minutes, Dennett, who made the ball turn in a remarkable manner, being practically unplayable. Dennett accomplished the hat-trick in dismissing Hawtin, Beasley and Buswell with successive balls, and should have had four wickets in as many balls, Wrathall dropping a catch offered by East. In Gloucestershire's second innings, Jessop and Mackenzie were the only batsmen to overcome the difficulties of the wicket, but Northamptonshire were set 136 to get to win. At their second attempt the visitors again failed before Dennett, who in the course of the day took 15 wickets for 21 runs. Northamptonshire finished up on the second day in practically a hopeless position, wanting 97 runs to win with only three wickets left, but rain came to their rescue. Not a ball could be bowled on the Wednesday, the game having to be abandoned as a draw.

Gloucestershire 60 (G. L. Jessop 22; G. J. Thompson five for 29, W. East five for 26) **and 88** (G. L. Jessop 24; G. J. Thompson three for 43, W. East seven for 36).

Northamptonshire 12 (E. M. Crosse 4, C. J. T. Pool 4, *six batsmen did not score*; G. Dennett 6–1–9–8, G. L. Jessop 5.3–4–3–2) **and 40** for seven (M. Cox 12; G. Dennett 15–8–12–7).

NOTTINGHAMSHIRE (13) 1902
NOTTINGHAMSHIRE v YORKSHIRE

At Nottingham, Thursday, Friday, June 20, 21, 1901. This match furnished the sensation of the season at Trent Bridge, the Notts eleven finding Rhodes and Haigh unplayable on a sticky wicket and being got rid of for 13 – the lowest total ever obtained in county cricket and, with one exception, the lowest on record in first-class matches. One wicket fell for a single run on the Thursday evening, and on the following day, when owing to the state of the pitch cricket did not begin till ten minutes to one, the innings was finished off in 54 minutes, the batsmen being absolutely helpless. Counting the few minutes' play overnight, the innings lasted as nearly as possible an hour. A. O. Jones made a leg hit for four, and Carlin a two, the other seven runs being all singles. The innings was so extraordinary in character that it may be of interest to give the fall of the wickets:

$\frac{1}{1}$	$\frac{2}{3}$	$\frac{3}{3}$	$\frac{4}{4}$	$\frac{5}{8}$	$\frac{6}{8}$	$\frac{7}{10}$	$\frac{8}{10}$	$\frac{9}{12}$	$\frac{10}{13}$

When Notts followed on, A. O. Jones and Iremonger scored 82 in an hour before the first wicket fell, but after that Hirst bowled in form just as wonderful as that of Rhodes and Haigh in the first innings, and soon after six o'clock the match came to an end, Yorkshire winning by an innings and 18 runs. Shrewsbury started playing in the match but split his hand so badly in fielding a ball at point that he had to retire before play had been in progress an hour, his place in the Notts team, thanks to Lord Hawke's courtesy, being taken by Harrison. Denton's batting for York-shire was exceptionally good.

Yorkshire 204 (J. Tunnicliffe 31, D. Denton 73; J. R. Gunn five for 49).

Nottinghamshire 13 (A. O. Jones 4; G. H. Hirst 1–0–1–0, W. Rhodes
7.5–4–4–6, S. Haigh 7–2–8–4) **and 173** (A. O. Jones 47, J. Iremonger
55 not out, J. R. Gunn 35; G. H. Hirst six for 26, W. Rhodes one for 53,
S. Haigh one for 53, E. Wainwright two for 28).

SOMERSET (25) 1948
GLOUCESTERSHIRE v SOMERSET

At Bristol, August 2, 4, 1947. Gloucestershire won by 316 runs.
Gloucestershire lost five wickets for 117 before Neale and Wilson
by steady batting effected an improvement. Apart from Law-rence, who hit a six and five fours, the Somerset batsmen found
Goddard's off-breaks too much for them and narrowly avoided
the follow-on. Hazell kept Gloucestershire struggling on the
Bank Holiday, when 12,000 people attended, but Somerset, set
342 to get, failed completely and were out for the smallest total
of the season. Lambert and Barnett began the collapse, which
Goddard, making the ball turn and lift, completed by taking five
wickets in seven deliveries, including the hat-trick.

Gloucestershire 244 (W. L. Neale 63, A. E. Wilson 61, extras 35;
H. L. Hazell three for 53, G. R. Langdale three for 31) **and 195** for nine
dec. (W. L. Neale 45, G. M. Emmett 39; H. L. Hazell five for 62).

Somerset 98 (J. Lawrence 34; C. J. Barnett three for 24, T. W. Goddard
seven for 61) **and 25** (F. S. Lee 17, *six batsmen did not score*;
C. J. Barnett 5–2–10–2, G. E. Lambert 3–1–10–2, T. W. Goddard
3–1–4–5, C. Cook 1.4–1–1–1).

SURREY (14) 1984
ESSEX v SURREY

At Chelmsford, May 28, 30, 31, 1983. Drawn. On the second
afternoon Surrey were skittled out for the lowest score in their
history, their first innings lasting a mere 14.3 overs. Philip and
Foster, making the ball swing in the humid atmosphere, were
their tormentors and only a boundary from Clarke, the sole one

of the innings, spared them the humiliation of recording the low-est-ever first-class score. Five wickets fell with the total on eight. The next day a fine century from Knight, well supported by Clinton, enabled Surrey to win back some self-respect. After a barren opening day because of rain, Fletcher showed that there was nothing wrong with the pitch with a century full of grace and elegance after Knight had gambled on putting the home side in to bat.

Essex 287 (K. W. R. Fletcher 110, K. S. McEwan 45; P. I. Pocock three for 49).

Surrey 14 (G. S. Clinton 6, *seven batsmen did not score*; N. Phillip 7.3–4–4–6, N. A. Foster 7–3–10–4) **and 185** for two (G. S. Clinton 61 not out, R. D. V. Knight 101 not out).

SUSSEX (19) 1874
SUSSEX v NOTTINGHAMSHIRE

At Brighton, August 14, 15, 1873. 231 overs (less one ball) and 231 runs were all the scorers had to book in this remarkably small county contest. The feature of this little cricket go was an innings of 19 played by the ten Sussex men [Henry Phillips had not arrived in time, having missed the train, but he did keep wicket and bat in Sussex's second innings]; their innings was commenced at 12.35 and concluded at 1.20, therefore was of exactly three-quarters of an hour's duration. One man made nine runs by two threes and three singles; another man took his bat out for eight, made by two twos and four singles; two others scored one run each, but the rest of the crew were ciphered. There were just 20 [four-ball] overs and two balls bowled in that small affair, wherein the wickets were summarily tumbled down as follows:

$\frac{1}{5}$	$\frac{2}{8}$	$\frac{3, 4 \text{ and } 5}{10}$	$\frac{6 \text{ and } 7}{11}$	$\frac{8}{12}$	$\frac{9}{19}$

Sussex's second innings contained five times as many runs. Mr G. Cotterill made 17; Killick knocked off 20; and James Lillywhite secured Sussex from a one-innings defeat by a carefully played 34 not out. In Notts' innings, William Oscroft was highest scorer with 23; four others made double figures; but little Phillips was "up to his work"; he had four wickets; and the innings ended for 101. The 15 runs required by Notts to win were quickly knocked off by Wyld, who made the whole 15, and Notts won by ten wickets. (A singular bit of retributive cricket was played a fortnight later on, when nearly the same Notts eleven, who here got the Sussex men out for 19 runs, were themselves got out by 16 of Derbyshire for an innings of 14 runs!)

Sussex 19 (F. F. J. Greenfield 9, *one man absent, five batsmen did not score*; A. Shaw 10.2–5–8–6, F. Morley 10–5–11–3) **and 96** (J. Lillywhite 34 not out; A. Shaw 50–29–38–6, F. Morley 44–26–49–4).
Nottinghamshire 101 (J. Lillywhite 54–27–56–7) **and 15** for no wkt.

WARWICKSHIRE (16) 1914
KENT v WARWICKSHIRE

At Tonbridge, Thursday, Friday, Saturday, June 19, 20, 21, 1913. The resumption of fixtures between Kent and Warwickshire after a lapse of 14 years yielded the most remarkable day's play during the whole of the season. Kent found themselves in a very awkward position on Saturday morning for, with the pitch in a terribly treacherous condition, they were 158 runs behind with their four best batsmen out. The six outstanding wickets falling in three-quarters of an hour for 28 runs, Warwickshire were left with a lead which looked certain to decide the match in their favour. Blythe and Woolley, however, making the most of the conditions, actually dismissed Warwickshire in 45 minutes for 16, the two famous left-handers being quite unplayable, but after this startling achievement it was impossible to believe Kent would be capable of hitting off 147 runs. Before lunch Humphreys and Seymour were disposed of for 16 – 18 wickets so far having fallen in the day for 60 runs. Afterwards, however, Woolley hit away with such dazzling brilliancy that, under conditions which still placed batsmen at a marked disadvantage, he scored 76 in 80 minutes, Kent gaining a truly memorable victory by six wickets.

Warwickshire 262 (C. Charlesworth 47, W. G. Quaife 31, C. S. Baker 59, P. Jeeves 30, S. Santall 31; F. E. Woolley five for 44) **and 16** (J. H. Parsons 5; C. Blythe 5.2–1–8–5, F. E. Woolley 5–1–8–5).

Kent 132 (F. R. Foster six for 62, P. Jeeves four for 27) **and 147** for four (F. E. Woolley 76 not out).

WORCESTERSHIRE (24) 1904
YORKSHIRE v WORCESTERSHIRE

At Huddersfield, Thursday, Friday, Saturday, July 16, 17, 18, 1903. Although not a ball could be bowled on the Thursday, and play was limited on Friday to an hour and three-quarters, and on Saturday to two hours, Yorkshire narrowly missed a sensational victory, Worcestershire, when the game had to be abandoned as a draw, being still 25 runs behind with only four wickets to go down. Worcestershire, it was thought, would profit by batting first, but the wicket proved extremely difficult and their innings was finished off by Rhodes and Hirst for 24 – the lowest score in a first-class match all season. Rhodes, who divided the wickets with Hirst, had only four singles scored off him. Further rain then delayed progress with the game until a quarter to six when, with the wicket so sloppy that the Worcestershire bowlers could scarcely stand, Yorkshire made a capital start, Brown and Tunnicliffe putting on 43 and Denton, in company with Tunnicliffe, raising the total to 76 without further loss. There came another heavy fall of rain during Friday night and, with neither wind nor sun, the wicket was not fit for cricket until half-past four. Hawke at once declared Yorkshire's innings closed and, on Worcestershire going in, Rhodes and Hirst got down four wickets in half an hour for eight runs. Arnold then found a useful partner in Isaac, these two staying together for three-quarters of an hour. Forty minutes from time, however, the visitors had only four wickets to go down, but Arnold and Pearson kept up their wickets during this period.

Worcestershire 24 (W. S. Caldwell 11; G. H. Hirst 9.3–3–18–5, W. Rhodes 9–6–4–5) **and 27** for six (G. H. Hirst 20–10–16–3, W. Rhodes 21–16–8–3).

Yorkshire 76 for one dec. (J. Tunnicliffe 38 not out).

YORKSHIRE (23) 1966
YORKSHIRE v HAMPSHIRE

At Middlesbrough, May 19, 20, 1965. Hampshire won by ten wickets. The game was a disaster for Yorkshire who, in the second innings, were dismissed for 23, the lowest total in their history. The pitch was lively throughout. On the first day 22 wickets fell for 253. Trueman, with a hurricane innings of 55 off 22 balls in 29 minutes, saved Yorkshire from complete collapse. Shackleton, although hit by Trueman for 26 off one over, still took six for 64. Only Marshall did much for Hampshire, who led by four. Before the close Yorkshire lost two second-innings wickets for seven runs, and next morning they were demoralised by the fast bowling of White who, in one spell, took five wickets without cost and altogether claimed six for ten. Hampshire needed only 20 to inflict on Yorkshire the first defeat at Middlesbrough. Yorkshire's previous lowest total was 26 against Surrey at The Oval in 1909.

Yorkshire 121 (F. S. Trueman 55; D. Shackleton six for 64, R. M. Cottam four for 45) **and 23** (D. Wilson 7 not out; D. Shackleton 9–5–7–2, D. W. White 10–7–10–6, R. M. Cottam 1.4–0–2–2).
Hampshire 125 (R. E. Marshall 51; R. A. Hutton three for 33) **and 20** for no wkt.

MY LORDS! 1982

In 1922, his last year at Harrow, and again in 1923, Leonard Crawley had headed the Worcestershire batting averages, in 1923 actually averaging 86, but Lord Harris discovered that neither he nor the leading Worcestershire professional batsman, Fox, was properly qualified and MCC declared both ineligible for the county. This led to a famous scene in the Long Room at Lord's between Lord Deerhurst, the Worcestershire president, and Lord Harris, with J. W. H. T. Douglas, unseen it is thought by the protagonists, mimicking the actions of a boxing referee in the background.

WHAM! BAM!

For those with the leisure or the inclination to watch cricket intimately, to read about it and analyse its subtleties, the game offers a fascination few others can match. So many varied factors, physical and psychological, are brought into play as bowler and batsman spar for superiority. Spectators are drawn forward in their seats, their concentration so intense that the proverbial pin might drop and the sound echo round the ground.

But what gets cricket grounds really going is a bit of rough; the unleashing of violence when a batsman smashes the bowling to all corners – or any corner as long as the ball gets there in the shortest possible time, preferably by the aerial route. Wham! Bam! brings crowds to their feet, even if only metaphorically in some quarters. This is cricket, after all.

We relish the clean, swift swing of the bat as it rushes to meet the ball; we thrill to the resounding whack with which the ball is dispatched and we buzz in anticipation of an encore. The artistry of the on-drive and the elegance of the cover drive are set to one side. Anarchy rules, anything might happen, and without inhibition we voice our approval when another six soars over the boundary. We glance around, meet other shining eyes and laugh with them at this mayhem the batsman is wreaking. For where once we were spectators, not far removed from an audience, the man in the middle with the blazing bat has turned us all into roaring-boys. And don't we just love it.

BIG HITTING

Notes by the Editor, *Wisden*, 1946

Of the 11 matches, each of three days played last summer which the MCC ranked as first-class, that between England and Dominions at Lord's rivalled as an attraction those in which Australia took part, and we saw in M. P. Donnelly, the left-handed New Zealander, who toured England in 1937, a batsman ready to join company with the best exponents of the game now that he will have regular first-class experience while at Oxford University. His fine strokeplay, notably to the off, provided some of the best cricket seen last season, and for arousing spectators to enthusiasm was exceeded only by gigantic hitting in which C. G. Pepper and Keith Miller emulated the giants of the past – not in the rate of scoring but in the carry of their big drives.

In that same Dominions match at Lord's, Miller on-drove a ball to the roof of the broadcasting box over the England dressing-room at a height said to exceed that of the record hit by Albert Trott which cleared the pavilion. That was one of seven sixes by Miller in a score of 185. Pepper hit six sixes while making 168 in two hours and a half at Scarborough against H. D. G. Leveson Gower's eleven. He revelled in straight drives, one of which off Hollies cleared the four-storied houses and landed the ball in Trafalgar Square. In this he rivalled the historic efforts of C. I. Thornton in 1886, when A. G. Steel was the bowler and Thornton's 107, made in 29 hits, included eight sixes, 12 fours, two twos and seven singles.

While these tremendous drives remain chronicled because earning six runs, one may doubt if the length of carry and height of any of them equalled that by G. J. Bonnor in the first England and Australia match at The Oval in 1880. Always associated with the superb catch which G. F. Grace made, this hit was described to me quite recently by Mr S. F. Charlton, an Old Cranleighan, who saw all the match. He wrote that Shaw, the bowler from the Vauxhall End, signalled with a gesture of his hand for G. F. Grace to look out, and the next ball with his guile in it brought about the catch near the sightscreen – most certainly an amazing piece of cricket. The youngest of the three Graces playing for

England just waited while the batsmen twice ran up and down the pitch before the ball fell into his safe hands.

NOTE: Two weeks after the Oval Test match, Fred Grace died of congestion of the lungs at the age of twenty-nine while travelling to a match at Winchester. "A brilliant field, a splendid batsman, at times a very successful bowler, and one of the most genial and popular men that ever appeared in the cricket field," *Wisden* 1881 mourned.

TED ALLETSON 1912
SUSSEX v NOTTINGHAMSHIRE

At Brighton, Thursday, Friday, Saturday, May 18, 19, 20, 1911. A phenomenal display of driving on the part of Edward Alletson rendered this match memorable. Alletson went in when Notts in their second innings, with seven men out, were only nine runs ahead. Before lunch he took 50 minutes to make 47, but on resuming hit away with such extraordinary power and freedom that he added 142 out of 152 for the last wicket in 40 minutes, actually scoring his last 89 runs in 15 minutes. Twice he sent the ball over the stand, and on six other occasions cleared the ring, while in one over from Killick that included two no-balls he hit three sixes and four fours – 34 runs in all. His glorious innings was made up by eight sixes, 23 fours, four threes, ten twos and 17 singles. Sussex, instead of gaining the easy victory which appeared assured before Alletson's tremendous hitting, had 237 to make in three hours and a quarter. Robert Relf and Vine scored 112 in 75 minutes, but six men were out for 148 and the eighth wicket fell ten minutes before time.

Nottinghamshire 238 (A. O. Jones 57, G. Gunn 90, J. R. Gunn 33; G. R. Cox three for 58, E. H. Killick five for 14) **and 412** (J. Iremonger 83, G. Gunn 66, E. B. Alletson 189; A. E. Relf three for 92, G. Leach three for 91, E. H. Killick one for 130).

Sussex 414 (R. R. Relf 42, J. Vine 77, R. B. Heygate 32, G. R. Cox 37, E. H. Killick 81, G. Leach 52, C. L. A. Smith 33 not out; W. Riley three for 102, A. O. Jones three for 69, G. M. Lee three for 45) **and 213 for eight** (R. R. Relf 71, J. Vine 54, G. Leach 31; W. Riley four for 82, J. R. Gunn three for 41).

GEORGE BONNOR 1885
SMOKERS v NON-SMOKERS

At Lord's, Monday, Tuesday, September 15, 16, 1884. This match was played for the benefit of the Cricketers' Fund Friendly Society, and, contrary to the anticipations of many, proved one of the most attractive contests of the season. It owed its origin to Mr V. E. Walker, whose desire was in the first place to promote the welfare of a very deserving charity, and in the second to see members of the redoubtable Australian team opposed to each other. Bonnor's remarkable hitting was of course the feature of the match. His 124 is the highest score he has made in England, and the manner in which he punished the bowling of Spofforth was perhaps the most extraordinary part of it. The great bowler had certainly never been hit with such astonishing freedom in this country before.

When he had made 44 Bonnor was missed by the wicket-keeper standing back. At lunch time he had made 63 and the total stood at 125 for two. On resumption of play runs came just as fast, and at 3.20 Bonnor completed his hundred with a big off-drive for six off Spofforth, which was followed by a couple of fours off the same bowler, the second pitching on to the roof of the pavilion. At last, with the score at 190, he was caught at slip off Peate, having scored 124 out of 156 put on while he was in, by one six, 16 fours, seven threes, ten twos and only 13 singles.

Non-Smokers 250 (G. J. Bonnor 124, R. G. Barlow 39; E. Peate six for 30) **and 15** for one.

Smokers 111 (W. G. Grace five for 29) **and 152** (W. Gunn 43 not out; R. G. Barlow five for 24, W. G. Grace three for 63, G. J. Bonnor one for 16).

NOTE: The Law relating to sixes was not changed until 1910. Up to that time the ball had to be hit out of the ground rather than simply over the boundary for a six; otherwise some of Bonnor's fours would have been sixes.

LORD-IN-WAITING 1932

BY LORD HAWKE

Brown and Tunnicliffe then proceeded to make 554 for the first wicket. I was No. 3 that day in Jackson's place. As they walked out to bat I put on my pads. I took them off for the lunch interval; I put them on again and took them off again for the tea interval. Again I put them on, and sat another couple of hours. Such is cricket!

IAN BOTHAM 1982

ENGLAND v AUSTRALIA

by John Thicknesse

At Manchester, August 13, 14, 15, 16, 17, 1981. England won by 103 runs, retaining the Ashes by going three-one up in the series. Like its two predecessors, the Fifth Test was a game of extraordinary fluctuations and drama, made wholly unforgettable by yet another *tour de force* by Man of the Match Botham, who, with the pendulum starting to swing Australia's way in England's second innings, launched an attack on Lillee and Alderman which, for its ferocious yet effortless power and dazzling cleanness of stroke, can surely never have been bettered in a Test match, even by the legendary Jessop.

Striding in to join Tavaré in front of 20,000 spectators on the Saturday afternoon when England, 101 ahead on first innings, had surrendered the initiative so totally that in 69 overs they had collapsed to 104 for five, Botham plundered 118 in 123 minutes. His innings included six sixes – a record for Anglo-Australian Tests – and 13 fours, all but one of which, an inside edge that narrowly missed the off stump on its way to fine leg, exploded off as near the middle of the bat as makes no odds. Of the 102 balls he faced (86 to reach the hundred), 53 were used up in reconnaissance in his first 28 runs (70 minutes). Then Alderman and Lillee took the second new ball and Botham erupted, smashing 66 off eight overs by tea with three sixes off Lillee, all hooked, and one off Alderman, a huge pull far back in the crowd to the left of the pavilion. He completed his hundred with a fifth six, a sweep, added the sixth with an immense and perfectly struck blow over the sightscreen, also off Bright, and was caught at the wicket a few moments later off twenty-two-year-old Mike Whitney.

Unkindly, it was to the greenhorn Whitney, running back from deep mid-off, that Botham, at 32, offered the first of two chances – nearer "quarter" than "half" – a high, swirling mis-hit over Alderman's head. The other came at 91 when Dyson, sprinting off the third-man boundary, then sliding forward on his knees and elbows, made a heroic effort to get his hands underneath a sliced square-cut off Lillee. Of the 149 Botham and Tavaré added for the sixth wicket – after a morning in which England had lost three for 29 off 28 overs – Tavaré's share was 28. But his seven-hour 78, embodying the third-slowest 50 in Test cricket (304 minutes) was the rock on which Knott and Emburey sustained the recovery as the last four wickets added 151.

England 231 (C. J. Tavaré 69, M. W. Gatting 32, I. T. Botham 0, P. J. W. Allott 52 not out; D. K. Lillee four for 55, T. M. Alderman four for 88) **and 404** (G. Boycott 37, C. J. Tavaré 78, I. T. Botham 118, A. P. E. Knott 59, J. E. Emburey 57; T. M. Alderman five for 109).

Australia 130 (M. F. Kent 52; R. G. D. Willis four for 63, I. T. Botham three for 28) **and 402** (K. J. Hughes 43, G. N. Yallop 114, A. R. Border 123 not out, R. W. Marsh 47; R. G. D. Willis three for 96, I. T. Botham two for 86).

ALLY BROWN 2003
SURREY v GLAMORGAN

At The Oval, June 19, 2002. Surrey won by nine runs. This sensational match left a trail of broken records in its wake. Thanks to a belter of a pitch and a 60-yard boundary under the gasometers, it was a batsman's – and statistician's – delight. At its heart was Ally Brown's brilliant, scarcely credible world-record 268, yet this was no one-man show. Perhaps most astonishing was that Glamorgan, not given a prayer by anyone after conceding 438, so nearly won. Robert Croft, acting-captain while Steve James tended his sick daughter, led a never-say-die fightback with a captain's innings that was also a phenomenal feat of pinch-hitting. He smacked Bicknell's first five balls for four as he sprinted to 50 in 22 balls. His hundred came up in 59 minutes off 56 balls, whereas Brown's first hundred had taken 98 minutes and 80 balls. Hemp, the game's third centurion, got there in 85 balls and kept the run-rate near the required 8.78; off the last ten overs, Glamorgan needed a just-about-feasible 103. Thomas made amends for haemorrhaging 12 runs an over by cracking an unbeaten 71 off only 41 balls. But wickets were falling at the other end, mainly to Hollioake who, with ten runs needed off two balls, bowled Cosker to complete a wonderful contest.

WORLD LIMITED-OVERS RECORDS SET DURING SURREY V GLAMORGAN

Individual score	**268** by A. D. Brown, beating 222 not out by R. G. Pollock for Eastern Province v Border at East London in 1974/75.
Total	**438–5** by Surrey, beating 413–4* (60 overs) by Somerset v Devon at Torquay in 1990.
Match aggregate	**867** by Surrey (438–5) and Glamorgan (429), beating 754 scored by India Seniors (392–6) and India B (362) at Chennai in 2000/01.
Runs conceded	**108** by S. D. Thomas (9–0–108–3), beating 107 by C. C. Lovell (12–0–107–2) for Cornwall v Warwickshire at St Austell in 1996.

* Superseded as second-highest limited-overs score by Glamorgan in this match; also beaten by Buckinghamshire (424–5) v Suffolk at Dinton in the first round of the 2003 C&G Trophy.

The honours, though, went to Brown for his second – and only the sixth ever – one-day double-hundred, following his 203 in a Sunday League game against Hampshire in 1997. His brutal innings contained 192 in boundaries, including 12 sixes, one short of Ian Botham's world record, and his 268 came off only 160 balls, at a strike-rate of 167. His pulling, especially, was perfection, but he also hit 22 fours and two sixes through or over the covers, driving off the back foot as well as the front. "I'm in the best form of my life," he said later. Asked to name his best shots, he chose "the sixes I hit when Darren Thomas pitched it short".

Ward made an admirable 97 off 95 balls with four sixes and helped add 286 for the first wicket but he, like everyone else, was eclipsed by Brown.

Surrey 438 for five (50 overs) (I. J. Ward 97, A. D. Brown 268, extras 30; S. D. Thomas three for 108).

Glamorgan 429 (49.5 overs) (R. D. B. Croft 119, D. L. Hemp 102, A. Dale 49, S. D. Thomas 71 not out; A. J. Hollioake five for 77).

PERCY FENDER 1921
NORTHAMPTONSHIRE v SURREY

At Northampton, Wednesday, Thursday, Friday, August 25, 26, 27, 1920. Though beaten by eight wickets in a match which produced 1,475 runs – a record in county cricket – the Northamptonshire players had good reason to be pleased with themselves. Scores of 306 and 430 against Surrey were immeasurably above their ordinary form. Surrey's huge total was the more remarkable

---

FASTEST HUNDREDS

Minutes

35	P. G. H. Fender (113*)	Surrey v Northamptonshire at Northampton	1920
40	G. L. Jessop (101)	Gloucestershire v Yorkshire at Harrogate	1897
40	Ahsan-ul-Haq (100*)	Muslims v Sikhs at Lahore	1923/24
42	G. L. Jessop (191)	Gentlemen of South v Players of South at Hastings	1907
43	A. H. Hornby (106)	Lancashire v Somerset at Manchester	1905
43	D. W. Hookes (107)	South Australia v Victoria at Adelaide	1982/83
44	R. N. S. Hobbs (100)	Essex v Australians at Chelmsford	1975

NOTES: The fastest recorded authentic hundred in terms of balls received was scored off 34 balls by D. W. Hookes (above).

Fast hundreds scored in contrived circumstances when runs were given from full tosses and long hops to expedite a declaration are not included.

Wisden, 2004

---

as Hobbs contributed only three runs to it. The hitting on the second afternoon was some of the fiercest of the season, Fender actually getting his hundred in 35 minutes. Peach and Ducat also played in dazzling style.

Northamptonshire 306 (A. P. R. Hawtin 34, C. N. Woolley 58, F. I. Walden 128; P. G. H. Fender three for 69) **and 430** (W. Adams 31, R. A. Haywood 96, C. N. Woolley 42, F. I. Walden 63, S. G. H. Humphrey 31, W. Wells 71, A. E. Thomas 30; J. W. Hitch three for 137, T. F. Shepherd three for 27, P. G. H. Fender two for 118).
Surrey 619 for five dec. (A. Sandham 92, C. T. A. Wilkinson 43, H. A. Peach 200 not out, A. Ducat 149, P. G. H. Fender 113 not out; C. N. Woolley three for 116) **and 120** for two (J. B. Hobbs 54, T. F. Shepherd 42 not out).

Notes by the Editor, *Wisden,* 1976

Percy Fender, who at the age of 80 still directs The London Wine Exchange, in a charming letter, gave his version to my enquiry during the autumn: "All I can tell you about that innings at Northampton is that when I went in to bat, I knew that Wilkinson (the Surrey captain) was wanting to declare, so I looked at the clock to see how long I had before tea (the second day) and it was then seven minutes past four o'clock. When we came in to tea at 4.30, I was 91. That is all I can say of my own knowledge; for the rest I have to rely upon what has been written by others. Boyington was the Surrey scorer then and I have always been told that he wrote against the name of each batsman the time when he went in to bat. The scorebook of the day, if still in existence, would confirm that if it is true.

"I only know that at tea Wilkinson told me to 'get on with it' as he would make his declaration as soon as I got my hundred. When Peach got his 200, I was 99, and the over was completed. I have always thought that there were two other points of considerable interest that day. First, that Peach and I must have made about 170 runs during the time we were at the wicket together, viz., 42 minutes, and secondly the fact that Northants made nearly 750 runs in their two innings added together, yet lost the match by eight wickets, all in three six-hour days."

NOTE: Research of the scorebook has shown that Fender scored his hundred from between 40 and 46 balls. His 113 not out came in an unbroken sixth-wicket partnership of 171 in 42 minutes with Peach.

ANDREW FLINTOFF
1994

Andrew Flintoff, fifteen, a pupil at Ribbleton Hall High School, Preston, hit 234 not out in only 20 overs with 20 sixes and 20 fours, for St Anne's against Fulwood and Broughton.

1999
LANCASHIRE v SURREY

At Manchester, June 18, 19, 20, 21, 1998. Lancashire won by six wickets. This will go down in history as Flintoff's match, or perhaps just Flintoff's over. In a battle between two of English cricket's highest-rated young players, he crashed 34 in an over from his former England Under-19 team-mate, Tudor. Since Tudor also bowled two no-balls, the over cost him 38, the most expensive in first-class history – excluding only the bizarre 77-run over at Christchurch in 1989/90, when Robert Vance was bowling deliberate no-balls to try and contrive a finish. It happened on Sunday afternoon, as Lancashire closed on their victory target of 250 in 53 overs. Flintoff hit 64444660; the first and fifth deliveries were no-balls. All the hits were on the leg side. Flintoff missed the last ball to lose his chance of passing Garry Sobers and Ravi Shastri's 36 off an over. He was out for 61 off 24 balls with Lancashire just short of victory. Yet Tudor had taken five for 43 in the first innings. "He was bowling very fast," said Surrey captain Adam Hollioake. "Anyone who says there is no young talent in English cricket should come and watch these two guys." It was a spectacular end to a match of fits and starts. The first day and most of the third were lost to rain, but 16 wickets fell on the second. Shahid hit a hundred off joke bowling to set up the finish. Crawley (who kept wicket because Hegg was injured) and Wood did the groundwork. Then Flintoff took wing.

Surrey 146 (M. P. Bicknell 41; Wasim Akram four for 42, P. J. Martin three for 35) **and 254** for one dec. (J. D. Ratcliffe 33, I. J. Ward 81 not out, N. Shahid 126 not out).

Lancashire 151 for seven dec. (P. C. McKeown 42, A. Flintoff
0, M. Watkinson 42; A. J. Tudor five for 43) **and 250** for four
(N. T. Wood 80 not out, J. P. Crawley 78, A. Flintoff 61).

NOTE: Under England and Wales Cricket Board (ECB) playing conditions,
two extras were scored for every no-ball, whether scored off or not.

GILBERT JESSOP 1975
by Rowland Ryder

At one end stocky Jessop stands,
The human catapult,
Who wrecks the roofs of distant towns,
When set in his assault.

Gilbert Laird Jessop played in cricket's golden age; more precisely from 1894 to 1914. Next to "W. G." the chief stars in the
galaxy of batsmen were Ranjitsinhji, Fry and Jessop. Fry to some
extent modelled himself on Ranjitsinhji; Jessop was a nonpareil.
He played his first innings for Gloucestershire on July 31, 1894 at
Old Trafford. Gloucestershire were bowled out for 99 but Jessop
hit Mold for four off his first ball, and scored 29 in less than no
time. "Well, we've found something this time," said the Doctor.
His diagnosis was correct.

1897 was the first of his great years. In the 'Varsity match,
which Cambridge won by 179 runs, he took six for 65 in
Oxford's first innings and made 42 in Cambridge's second. This
is how one of the Oxford bowlers, F. H. E. Cunliffe, described
Jessop's innings. "Jessop started by hitting Hartley's first ball
smash up against the wall of the pavilion, when it rebounded far
into the field of play; he followed this up by hitting everything
we gave him and for five or six overs we had a lively time. We
reckoned afterwards that he had only received 15 balls, but he
got 42 runs off them, and it was a relief to see him caught at
cover-point."

University fixtures completed, Jessop played during the last
half of the season for Gloucestershire. At Bristol he scored a
brilliant century against the Philadelphians, and at Edgbaston
when all seemed lost, against Warwickshire, he scored 126 out of

176 in 95 minutes and nearly won the match for Gloucestershire.
A few days later, against Yorkshire, in a fantastic display of hitting, he scored 101 out of 118 in 40 minutes and, despite the
terrific pace of his innings, gave no chance.

Wisden chose him as one of the Five Cricketers of the Year for
the 1898 issue and wrote of him, "We have never before produced
a batsman of quite the same stamp. We have had harder hitters,
but perhaps never one who could in 20 minutes or half an hour,
so entirely change the fortunes of the game." The section devoted
to Gloucestershire in the same issue makes the compelling asser-
tion that "until he was disposed of no one could say what was
likely to happen". All this when his career had barely started.

An innings for all time

It was on Wednesday, August 13, 1902, at Kennington Oval, in
the Fifth Test against Australia, that Jessop played what has been
described as the greatest innings in the history of cricket. England had been set 263 to win on a wicket that was helpful to the
Australian bowlers. The score was 48 for five, the game, it seemed,
as good as lost when Jessop went in to bat. For the space of an
hour and a quarter he proceeded to savage the Australian bowling. There were two streaky shots before he had made 30; after
that there was no holding him. Field adjustments were in vain,
for in this mood no one could set a field to him. When he was out,
he had scored 104 out of 139 in 75 minutes, and England went
on, amid a crescendo of excitement, to win by one wicket.
Describing his innings years afterwards, Jessop wrote that he was
chiefly pleased with the restraint he had shown when batting
against Trumble; it is interesting to conjecture what would have
been the views of Trumble himself on this matter.

Heart of a lion, timing of an angel

Jessop was no village slogger. He was a great batsman with
massive powers of concentration. He had the eyes of a hawk,
the heart of a lion and the timing of an angel. His genius lay
in the split-second thinking that enabled him to choose from
an armoury of strokes to deal with anything that Rhodes or

Trumble or Kotze or a hundred others could bowl. A gentle, friendly and amusing companion, he dominated the game when he was on the field; the better the bowler and the tougher the odds, the more he liked it. Peaked cap on head, sleeves rolled up, stocky, fearless and five feet seven, he faced the bowler, prepared for death or glory. And it was pretty often glory.

VIV RICHARDS 1987
WEST INDIES v ENGLAND
by John Thicknesse

At St John's, Antigua, April 11, 12, 13, 15, 16, 1986. West Indies won by 240 runs. Richards's 110 not out in West Indies' second innings, the fastest Test hundred ever in terms of balls received (56 to reach three figures, 58 in all), made the final Test historic on two counts. The other was West Indies' achievement in emulating Australia, previously the only country to win all five home Tests on more than one occasion.

Richards's display, making him the obvious candidate for the match award, would have been staggering at any level of cricket. What made it unforgettable for the 5,000 or so lucky enough to see it was that he scored it without blemish at a time when England's sole aim was to make run-scoring as difficult as possible to delay a declaration. Botham and Emburey never had fewer than six men on the boundary and sometimes nine, yet whatever length or line they bowled, Richards had a stroke for it. His control and touch were as much features of the innings as the tremendous power of his driving. As can be calculated from the following table, he was within range of his hundred six balls before completing it (with a leg-side four off Botham), while from the time he reached 83 off 46 balls there had been no doubt, assuming he stayed in, that he would trim several deliveries off J. M. Gregory's previous record of 67 for Australia against South Africa at Johannesburg in 1921/22. The full innings went:

```
··36126141 (24 off 10)    ·211·412·1 (36 off 20)    112·2111·· (45 off 30)
·1·1624441 (68 off 40)    12··664612 (96 off 50)    ··21·461 (110 off 58)
```

Plundered in 83 minutes out of 146 while he was at the wicket, it had to be, by any yardstick, among the most wonderful innings ever played.

West Indies 474 (D. L. Haynes 131, I. V. A. Richards 26, M. D. Marshall 76, R. A. Harper 60, M. A. Holding 73) **and 246** for two dec.
(D. L. Haynes 70, R. B. Richardson 31, I. V. A. Richards 110 not out).
England 310 (G. A. Gooch 51, W. N. Slack 52, D. I. Gower 90, extras 51; M. D. Marshall three for 64, J. Garner four for 67) **and 170**
(G. A. Gooch 51, extras 43; R. A. Harper three for 10).

SAEED ANWAR 1998
INDIA v PAKISTAN

At Chennai, May 21, 1997 (day/night). Pakistan won by 35 runs. Saeed Anwar broke the record for the highest individual innings in a one-day international by scoring 194, from 146 balls, with 22 fours and five sixes, three in succession in one over from Kumble, which went for 226664. He beat the previous record, Viv Richards's unbeaten 189 for West Indies v England at Old Trafford in 1984, by five, and might have reached a double-hundred had he not top-edged a sweep to be caught at fine leg in the 47th over. It was a remarkable exhibition of controlled aggression, even if he was helped by a runner, Shahid Afridi, for most of the innings (he was suffering from heat exhaustion and loss of fluid). India were left a target of 328. They began on a poor note when Inzamam-ul-Haq took an athletic catch to dismiss Tendulkar, but Dravid sustained them with his maiden hundred in limited-overs internationals – also briefly assisted by a runner, Tendulkar, until the fielding side objected. They soon fell behind, however, after he pushed a catch to mid-wicket, one of five wickets for Aqib Javed. Afterwards, Tendulkar said Anwar's innings was the best he had seen, and the former Test bowler Bishen Bedi said batting like that comes "once in a lifetime". Some observers – including TV commentator Glenn Turner – diluted their praise by noting that his runner made the innings much easier, given the extreme heat. Anwar himself said: "To beat India is something special. Only we know the pressure we were subjected to back home after our loss in the World Cup." In contrast to past bitterness in India–Pakistan matches, the 45,000 crowd gave him a standing ovation.

Pakistan 327 for five (50 overs) (Saeed Anwar 194, Ijaz Ahmed, sen. 39, Inzamam-ul-Haq 39 not out).

India 292 (49.2 overs) (S. C. Ganguly 33, R. Dravid 107, V. G. Kambli 65, R. R. Singh 35; Aqib Javed five for 61).

STRICTLY FOR THE BIRDS

1932

Playing for Alton in August 1921, Mr Bernhard W. Bentinck had the unusual experience of being bowled by a ball (delivered by H. E. Roberts, the Sussex professional) which was deflected on to the wicket through striking and killing a swallow.

1989

It was in 1936 that there occurred the "sparrow incident" with which Jahangir Khan's name has become associated. Playing for Cambridge against MCC at Lord's, he was bowling to T. N. Pearce, who had just played a defensive push when it was noticed that the bails had been dislodged. It was then that a dead sparrow was found beside the stumps. The unfortunate bird was stuffed and subsequently displayed in the Memorial Gallery at Lord's; but while legend has it that the sparrow was struck by the ball in flight, it is thought no one actually saw this happen.

2000

AUSTRALIA v INDIA, THE OVAL

Two pigeons met untimely deaths during India's innings. The first was shot down in mid-flight by Reiffel when he drilled the ball back from the outfield; the second, pecking the ground at short third man, was walloped by a thick edge from Jadeja's bat, leading to speculation that pigeons also had problems seeing the white ball in the gloom.

SHAHID AFRIDI 1998
PAKISTAN v SRI LANKA

At Nairobi, October 4, 1996. Pakistan won by 82 runs. Sensational batting by teenage leg-spinner Shahid Afridi swept Pakistan into the final. He was promoted to No. 3 – he had not batted in his previous international – and dashed to a hundred in 37 balls, 11 fewer than the limited-overs international record set by Jayasuriya against Pakistan in Singapore six months earlier. He was said to be 16 years 217 days old, but he looked older, and the ages of several established Pakistani players had recently been challenged. His brilliance was not in dispute. In all, he scored 102 from 40 balls, with 11 sixes (equalling Jayasuriya's record) and six fours, out of 126 for the second wicket. The full innings was 0610400600661166264400661411041606024100. He took 41 off the 11 balls he faced from Jayasuriya, whose ten overs went for 94, though he also managed three wickets. The ground was not especially small, and most of the sixes went into the car park, anyway. They would have been sixes almost anywhere. Nor were they slogs; it was an exhibition of wonderful clean hitting. After Afridi was out, Saeed Anwar scored a more sedate 115 from 120 balls and Pakistan galloped to 371, the second-highest total ever scored in a one-day international.

Pakistan 371 for nine (50 overs) (Saeed Anwar 115, Shahid Afridi 102, Salim Malik 43; S. T. Jayasuriya three for 94).

Sri Lanka 289 (49.5 overs) (P. A. de Silva 122, A. Ranatunga 52, H. D. P. K. Dharmasena 51; Waqar Younis five for 52, Saqlain Mushtaq four for 33).

RAVI SHASTRI 1986
by P. N. Sundaresan

The other personal performance of note was that of Ravi Shastri, who, in scoring 200 not out for Bombay against Baroda in the West Zone of the Ranji Trophy, hit six sixes in one over from the Baroda left-arm slow bowler, G. Tilak Raj, to equal the world record of G. S. Sobers. That gave him 12 sixes in his innings, an Indian record, and he hit one more to join C. G. Greenidge, G. W. Humpage and Majid Khan on 13. Only the former New Zealand captain, J. R. Reid, with 15, has hit more.* Shastri's double-hundred was also a world record, coming in 113 minutes off 123 balls.

At Bombay, January 8, 9, 10, 1985. Drawn.

Bombay 371 for four dec. (L. S. Rajput 66, G. A. Parkar 170 retired hurt,
S. S. Hattangadi 83) **and 457** for five dec. (L. S. Rajput 136,
S. M. Gavaskar 49, R. J. Shastri 200 not out).

Baroda 330 for eight dec. (S. Keshwala 100 not out, M. Amarnath 88,
G. Tilak Raj 55) **and 81** for seven (B. S. Sandhu four for 43).

* *Andrew Symonds hit 16 sixes for Gloucestershire v Glamorgan
in 1995.*

JIM SMITH 1939
GLOUCESTERSHIRE V MIDDLESEX

At Bristol, June 15, 16, 17, 1938. Middlesex won by an innings
and 42 runs. When everything else in this game is forgotten,
Smith's drastic punishment of the tired Gloucestershire bowling
on the second afternoon will be remembered. He scored 66 in 18
minutes – the first 50 coming in the record time of 11 minutes –
with eight sixes and two fours the most powerful of his strokes.
Smith hit Sinfield for three sixes in succession and obtained the
other five off Emmett. The Middlesex total, made possible by
splendid centuries by Edrich and Hulme, and an entertaining

FASTEST FIFTIES

Minutes

11	C. I. J. Smith (66)	Middlesex v Gloucestershire at Bristol	1938
13	Khalid Mahmood (56)	Gujranwala v Sargodha at Gujranwala	2000/01
14	S. J. Pegler (50)	South Africans v Tasmania at Launceston	1910/11
14	F. T. Mann (53)	Middlesex v Nottinghamshire at Lord's	1921
14	H. B. Cameron (56)	Transvaal v Orange Free State at Johannesburg	1934/35
14	C. I. J. Smith (52)	Middlesex v Kent at Maidstone	1935

NOTE: Fast fifties scored in contrived circumstances when runs were given from full
tosses and long hops to expedite a declaration are not included.

Wisden, 2004

display from Robins, was the highest they had ever made against Gloucestershire. Neale and B. O. Allen were the only Gloucestershire batsmen to show to advantage. Neale's defence in both innings was above reproach and Allen, by stylish driving and hard hitting to leg, on the last day made his first hundred of the summer in a vain effort to avert an innings defeat for his team. Allen and Neale were associated in a fourth-wicket stand of 161.

Gloucestershire 209 (C. J. Barnett 43, G. M. Emmett 41, W. L. Neale 54 not out; C. I. J. Smith one for 35, R. W. V. Robins three for 91) **and 322** (B. O. Allen 104, W. L. Neale 94, C. J. Scott 31; C. I. J. Smith two for 55, B. L. Muncer three for 44).

Middlesex 573 (W. J. Edrich 118, J. D. Robertson 43, D. C. S. Compton 45, J. H. A. Hulme 143, R. W. V. Robins 78, C. I. J. Smith 66; R. A. Sinfield six for 184).

GARRY SOBERS 1969
GLAMORGAN v NOTTINGHAMSHIRE

At Swansea, August 31, September 1, 2, 1968. Nottinghamshire won by 166 runs. This was the history-making match in which the incredible Garfield Sobers created a new world record by hitting six sixes in a six-ball over. Somehow one sensed that something extraordinary was going to happen when Sobers sauntered to the wicket. With over 300 runs on the board for the loss of only five wickets, he had the right sort of platform from which to launch a spectacular assault, and the manner in which he immediately settled down to score at a fast rate was ominous.

Then came the history-making over by the twenty-three-year-old Malcolm Nash. First crouched like a black panther eager to pounce, Sobers with lightning footwork got into position for a vicious straight drive or pull. As Tony Lewis, Glamorgan's captain, said afterwards, "It was not sheer slogging through strength, but scientific hitting with every movement working in harmony." Twice the ball was slashed out of the ground, and when the last six landed in the street outside it was not recovered until the next day. Then it was presented to Sobers and will have a permanent place in the Trent Bridge Cricket Museum.

MOST RUNS SCORED OFF AN OVER

(All instances refer to six-ball overs)

36	G. S. Sobers off M. A. Nash, Nottinghamshire v Glamorgan at Swansea (six sixes)	1968
36	R. J. Shastri off Tilak Raj, Bombay v Baroda at Bombay (six sixes)	1984/85
34	E. B. Alletson off E. H. Killick, Nottinghamshire v Sussex at Hove (46604446)†	1911
34	F. C. Hayes off M. A. Nash, Lancashire v Glamorgan at Swansea (646666)	1977
34	A. Flintoff off A. J. Tudor, Lancashire v Surrey at Manchester (64444660)†	1998
32	I. T. Botham off I. R. Snook, England XI v Central Districts at Palmerston North (466466)	1983/84
32	P. W. G. Parker off A. I. Kallicharran, Sussex v Warwickshire at Birmingham (466664)	1982
32	I. R. Redpath off N. Rosendorff, Australians v Orange Free State at Bloemfontein (666644)	1969/70
32	C. C. Smart off G. Hill, Glamorgan v Hampshire at Cardiff (664664)	1935
32	Khalid Mahmood off Naved Latif, Gujranwala v Sargodha at Gujranwala (666662)	2000/01

† *Includes two no-balls. Tudor's over to Flintoff cost 38 runs, the two no-balls counting for two extra runs each under ECB regulations.*

Wisden, 2004

All other events were overshadowed by Sobers's achievement, but the rest of the cricket was not without distinction. In the Nottinghamshire first innings Bolus hit a magnificent century in three hours 50 minutes, including six sixes and 15 fours. Glamorgan could not match such boldness, although Walker batted steadily for his second century of the season. With a first-innings lead of 140, Nottinghamshire then lost half their wickets for 70, but again Sobers accomplished the inevitable, scoring 72 out of 94 in nine minutes under two hours. Eventually Glamorgan had to get 280 to win in four hours, but good bowling by Taylor, who made the most of a damp patch caused by overnight rain, resulted in them being dismissed for 113.

Nottinghamshire 394 for five dec. (J. B. Bolus 140, R. A. White 73, G. Frost 50, G. S. Sobers 76 not out; M. A. Nash four for 100) **and 139** for six dec. (G. S. Sobers 72).

Glamorgan 254 (Majid Khan 41, P. M. Walker 104 not out, B. Lewis 38; G. S. Sobers two for 63, D. J. Halfyard three for 71) **and 113** (A. R. Lewis 52; M. N. Taylor five for 47, R. A. White four for 9).

ANDREW SYMONDS 1996
GLAMORGAN v GLOUCESTERSHIRE

At Abergavenny, August 23, 24, 25, 26, 1995. Drawn. At 11.55 on the third morning, Gloucestershire's twenty-year-old Anglo-Australian batsman Andrew Symonds hit the 16th six of his innings off Watkin just right of the sightscreen. It landed on a tennis court about 20 feet over the boundary and gave Symonds a world record, beating the 15 by John Reid for Wellington v Northern Districts in 1962/63. Symonds went on to hit four more sixes in the second innings, surpassing the world match record of 17, by Jim Stewart for Warwickshire v Lancashire in 1959. The 16 sixes came in an unbeaten 254 from only 206 balls; there were also 22 fours. Symonds became the youngest player to score a double-century for Gloucestershire and, though he was undoubt-edly helped by the short boundaries, it would have been a hugely effective innings on any ground in the world. Even without Symonds, this contest would have maintained the reputation of Pen-y-Pound for producing extraordinary county matches. Glamorgan collapsed from 145 for one to 203 for eight, before recovering to 334. Then Gloucestershire slumped to 79 for five before Symonds began his assault. They eventually led by 127 before Glamorgan hit back, beginning the final day in sight of records of their own – the third-wicket stand between Hemp and Maynard was then worth 302. However, Srinath broke the partnership four runs later and, working up remarkable pace from his gentle run, tore through the batting for career-best figures of nine for 76. That left Gloucestershire to score 345 in at least 77 overs. Symonds's four further sixes came in a score of 76 and at 204 for three Gloucestershire were favourites. But rain hit their chances and this switchback game had one final twist: Watkin and Thomas broke through and Gloucestershire finished defending desperately with last man Pike in for the concluding 20 balls.

Glamorgan 334 (H. Morris 67, D. L. Hemp 71, S. D. Thomas 78 not out, extras 50; J. Srinath four for 74, M. C. J. Ball four for 54) **and 471** (H. Morris 62, D. L. Hemp 157, M. P. Maynard 164, extras 37; J. Srinath nine for 76).

Gloucestershire 461 (A. J. Wright 31, M. A. Lynch 32, A. Symonds 254 not out, R. C. J. Williams 52, J. Srinath 39; S. L. Watkin three for 122, R. D. B. Croft three for 90) **and 293** for nine (M. W. Alleyne 64, A. Symonds 76, M. A. Lynch 56 not out; S. L. Watkin three for 51, S. D. Thomas five for 99).

CHARLES "BUNS" THORNTON 1930

In his day he was one of the biggest – if not the mightiest of all time – of hitters. Like many others of his day, Thornton always regarded cricket more as a game than as a serious business. Adventurous by nature, he felt that in cricket he could indulge this spirit to the full. Whenever he was captain he liked going in first. Individual in style, he jumped quickly to the ball in making his magnificent drives, and in this respect differed from the famous Australian hitters, Bonnor, McDonnell and Lyons, all of whom were fast-footed. In his brilliant career he put together many scores of a hundred in remarkable time, and the length of some of his drives was enormous.

It is on record, for instance, that in the North v South match at Canterbury in 1871, he hit a ball from W. M. Rose a strictly measured 152 yards, while at the practice nets at Hove the same year he sent it 168 yards 2 feet and 162 yards. Playing against Harrow at Lord's in 1868, he drove the ball over the old pavilion, and at The Oval he accomplished the same feat, while it is noted that at Canterbury he hit V. E. Walker out of the ground each ball of an over. The over then consisted of four balls. Hitting the ball out of the ground was a feat he always took a delight in accomplishing. On one occasion at Scarborough, off the bowling of A. G. Steel, he drove a ball over a four-storeyed house into the adjoining street, called Trafalgar Square.

To slow bowlers Thornton was a terror, and on James Southerton, in particular, he was generally very severe. He often threatened to hit Southerton out of The Oval, and at length succeeded. As the ball sailed over the fence Thornton dropped his bat, put his hands on his hips and laughed uproariously, saying, "I told you I would do it, Jim." Southerton shook his head, and replied, "Quite right, Mr Thornton, but I shall get you out." And get him out he did. As a matter of fact he hit Southerton twice over the pavilion, once over the scoring-box, and also for a two in a four-ball over; altogether he hit out of three sides of The Oval.

by Alfred Lubbock, 1909

G. L. Jessop is a fine hitter, gets his runs fast, and is amusing to watch, but I should not consider as an actual hitter he is anything to be compared to C. I. Thornton, and the latter was quite as fast a run-getter at times.

BREAKING GLASS

There must be potential here for a serious sociological study into cricket's class divide as mirrored by authority's attitude to players who make contact with silicon-based substances. That's glass to you and me, but if we're talking theses at promoted polys, we may as well parrot the jargon.

Singer/songwriter Nick Lowe said it for the man and woman in the deck-chairs with his 1978 top-ten tune, "I Love the Sound of Breaking Glass". Doubtless someone with a couple of GCSEs could swing some research on the frisson that spectators experience when a well-struck ball smashes a car window – preferably the batsman's – or the shattering of glass reverberates from the pavilion following a dismissal.

When it comes to the bat breaking glass, rather than the ball, cricket administrators invariably put fustigation before frisson. *Wisden* 2004 reports that Australian opener Matthew Hayden was fined $A2,200 after he "inadvertently smashed a glass panel on his stomp back to the dressing-room" during the 2003 Sydney Test against England. In the circumstances, England captain Nasser Hussain got off lightly with a severe reprimand when he broke the glass door of a Rawalpindi dressing-room fridge after being out lbw in a one-day international. Maybe match referee Barry Jarman reckoned Hussain would get enough stick from his team-mates for damaging their fridge – it was a warm night – so didn't bother wielding the big stick himself.

As for why the authorities take the attitude they do, Hilaire Belloc provides a clue in his *New Cautionary Tales*: "Like many of the Upper Class, He liked the Sound of Broken Glass." There we have it. Cricket, it's obvious, is administered by a lower class, most likely the middle one.

THE BOUNDER 1875
MCC AND GROUND v SOUTH OF ENGLAND

That Mr Thornton was in his old hard and fast form may be imagined from the fact that he drove one ball from Alfred Shaw so hard and so far, that it passed through an open door of the pavilion, "pitched in the centre of the pavilion room, and bounded out through a back window of that building".

ART BREAKING 1986

Against Hampshire at Canterbury in 1923 Kent soon after the start were 20 for three. Bryan was naturally and properly cautious and took two hours to reach 50: when he was out he had made 236 out of 345 in four and three-quarter hours. One tremendous drive swerved round the right-hand end of the screen, through an open window into the pavilion dining-room, struck the edge of the table, flew up into the picture of "Canterbury Week 1877", which still bears the scar, and was retrieved with a piece of glass embedded in it.

SHE SLIPPED, YER HONOUR 1950
MIDDLESEX v DERBYSHIRE

The equanimity of the Lord's pavilion was disturbed when Gladwin, after being run out by his partner, accidentally put his bat through the dressing-room window.

TEMPER, TEMPER 1994
MIDDLESEX v AUSTRALIANS

A crowd approaching 10,000 turned out to watch a game in which the cricket seemed to take second place to clashes of temperament. Not that the players directed their hostility towards the opposing team; the first display of temper occurred when Gatting kept a disgruntled Fraser out of the Middlesex attack until the 20th over. Fraser's first four overs cost 35 runs and his obvious annoyance when taken off led to a severe finger-wagging from his captain. But Gatting was even less pleased later in the day when he was run out – sent back, quite justifiably, by Roseberry. Still seething, he put his hand through a glass panel in the dressing-room door and was taken to hospital for stitches. The injury ruled him out of the one-day internationals. His opposite number, Border, also expressed his frustration when bowled by a full toss from Fraser, swiping at the stumps with his bat.

SMASH HIT 1997
MIDDLESEX v ESSEX

Earlier, a six by Pooley broke the window in the office of MCC's assistant secretary for cricket, John Jameson, some 30 feet up in the pavilion annexe.

PAINFUL 2000
Chronicle of 1999

Sussex dentist Rob Hemingway, playing for St Peters against Horsted Keynes, became the first batsman of 1999 to hit a six through his own car windscreen. "It was quite nice to connect with the ball so early in the season," he said, "but then I heard the crack and thought, oops, whose car is that?" (*Sports Argus*, Brighton, May 1)

HOLED IN ONE 1999
Chronicle of 1998

At a celebration match to open the new pavilion at Buckie in north-east Scotland, Fraser McBean had his car window broken by a six from another player. When McBean batted himself, he hit a six into the hole that was already there. (*The Scottish Cricketer*, September)

SIX AND OUT 2001
by Derek Thursby

Alas, a large window, broken by a well-struck six, resulted in cricket being banned from the Shell Recreation ground [in Brunei Darussalam]. Two years earlier, the siting of soccer goals 15 yards from the bat at short mid-wicket had added an interesting dimension to the game. Although not proving as inconvenient as one might imagine, it was a sign of things to come.

REAR WINDOW 2001
DORSET v GLAMORGAN

Newell and Elliott put Glamorgan on course to their fourth-highest one-day total with 246, a county first-wicket record in one-day competitions: the previous best was 192 unbroken by Steve James and Hugh Morris against the same opponents in 1995. Newell, out in the 40th over, faced 123 balls for his 129, hitting three sixes and 15 fours. His first six crashed through the press-box roof; his third smashed the rear window of team-mate Croft's car.

DISPATCHES ON CATCHES

"Catches win matches" might be something of a cliché, but it's no less true for that. Spectacular catches lift a side, just as dropped catches can send morale plummeting. Not just on-field morale, either. "Desperate for an early breakthrough," we read in *Wisden* 2002, "England's prayers seemed answered next morning when Gilchrist, 13, edged Gough's first ball straight to second slip – where it bounced out of Butcher's hands, leaving him a distraught, crumpled heap." Butcher and most of the watching nation. "It set an ugly trend. Atherton spilled the simplest of Gilchrist's four reprieves – all off Gough – allowing him to make a typically aggressive 90."

It won't have helped the self-esteem of England's butter-fingered fielders when Australia's Mark Waugh finished off their second innings in that Lord's match by taking a typically unassuming slip catch that left him the leading catcher in Test cricket. By the time Waugh retired, he had held 181 catches in 128 Tests. Second and third on the list were also Australians, Mark Taylor and Allan Border.

Australians have always taken fielding seriously. George Lohmann, penning "a few words" in *Wisden* 1893, recalled that "The way some of the up-country teams fielded in Australia against Lord Sheffield's side was particularly smart. They also brought off a number of good catches, being more used to the glaring light than we were." Another Surrey man, the admirably named lob bowler, Digby Loder Armroid Jephson, bemoaning the standard of English fielding in the 1901 Almanack, didn't bother blaming the light when it came to his own dropped catches.

"Personally I shall never forget missing a well-known player through sleeping at extra slip. I missed him when 18, and he remained with us the rest of the live-long day, making nearly 300 with not a vestige of a chance. For several ensuing matches I endeavoured to keep awake."

Glad to hear it, Digby.

STICKY FINGERS 1930
by Lord Harris

Charles Inglis Thornton, my very dear old friend and comrade, was nicknamed "Bun and Jam" at Eton – afterwards abbreviated to "Buns" – because of an amusing incident when, as a lower boy, he was brought up to be tried in Upper Club. He was fielding long leg, close to the raised road, along which one of the "Cads" was passing with his basket or barrow of comestibles. Some say it was Bryan who wheeled a barrow and certainly purveyed buns and jam; others that it was Levi who carried a basket, but I do not remember his selling this particular edible. Thornton, in an interval when a wicket went down, bought a bun and jam, and commenced consuming it. It lasted long enough for play to be resumed. A high catch was hit to him, which I fancy he caught. What happened to the bun I never heard for certain. Some say he swallowed it, others that he dropped it, others again that he crammed it, jam and all, into his trousers pocket. Anyway it earned him his nickname. Years afterwards he was playing in a Whit Monday match at Lord's and got "spectacles", and Green Lubbock suggested he should in future be known as "Whit Monday Buns".

VICTORY IN HIS GRASP 1931

In the Gloucestershire and Surrey match of 1872 Mr R. F. Miles had a distressing experience, for the last Surrey batsman came in with two runs to win, and put up his first ball from W. G. Grace into the hands of Miles at mid-on. Victory, the chronicler says, was literally in the grasp of Gloucestershire but unfortunately it did not stay there and Surrey won by one wicket.

EASILY DISTRACTED 1925

Of the many stories that have enshrouded the Cobden match –
the Balaclava Charge of the cricket field [Oxford v Cambridge,
1870] – Walter Money contributed one of the best, telling how
Jack Dale, when reproached for allowing a simple catch at point
to go unheeded, apologised by saying, "I'm awfully sorry, Walter,
I was looking at a lady getting out of a drag."

NO, THANKS 1880
MIDDLESEX v SURREY

On the night of the Derby Day, and the following morning, a rain
storm of great length and violence fell over London and its
suburbs. This made Lord's ground so unfit for cricket that the
commencement of this match was compulsorily put back until
2.50. Even at that time the ground was so soft that it was difficult
to obtain a foothold. Surrey were first at the wickets with Jupp
and Mr Lucas. Messrs Stratford and Ford led the attacking
party. Mr Lucas played steadily, but at length gave a chance to
Mr E. Lyttelton at long-on, which that gentleman declined.

WHAT A GAS 1987

All who played with A. E. L. Hill will remember him as a beautiful field. It was typical of a charming and modest man that the
only story the writer ever heard him tell of his county career was
how he missed Fender (who went on to make 184) on the boundary at The Oval when he had made 22 and a kindly spectator
suggested that he would be more use on the top of the gasometer.
Typically, too, he did not bother to add what *Wisden* says: that
the sun was in his eyes at the time.

SOMETHING OF A DILEMMA 1982

The Worcestershire captain, the Hon. C. J. Lyttelton, seeing
Leonard Crawley coming out to open the Essex innings and
knowing that, given a chance, he would try to drive the first ball
over the screen, instructed the bowler, Perks, to give him one
slightly short of a length on the middle stump. Perks produced
just the right ball and Crawley's bat struck it when its face was

pointing straight upwards to the sky. The ball rose vertically to an astronomical height. A. P. Singleton in the gully put his hands in his pockets and said: "I'm not taking that." Lyttelton looked round in desperation and finally said to Singleton, "Sandy, you've got to take it," whereupon Singleton took his hands out of his pockets and held what in the circumstances was a fine catch.

WORTH A SHOUT 1886
MIDDLESEX v SURREY

Mr Roller, after making ten, was out to an extraordinary catch in the long-field. Mr Greatorex, running in from the deep field, took the ball with the right hand only about a foot from the ground, and this brilliant piece of cricket, which was, perhaps, the feature of the day, was received with loud cheering.

THREE OF THE BEST 1957
ENGLAND v AUSTRALIA, LORD'S
by Leslie Smith

England looked to be recovering from these two early disasters with Cowdrey and May batting well, but the first of three really brilliant catches in the match ended the stand. Cowdrey hit a ball with tremendous power, but Benaud, in the gully, flung up his hands and held on to it with everyone looking towards the boundary. The force of the ball knocked Benaud backwards.

Australia's long lead looked like being decisive, but great-hearted bowling by Trueman and fine fielding put England back in the game. First Cowdrey in the gully held a fine low right-handed catch, almost as good as that by Benaud, to break the opening stand. Harvey took ten off the first three balls he received and was out to the fourth, brilliantly taken at short fine leg by Bailey, who dived full length and held a genuine leg-glide with his right arm outstretched just off the ground.

A LORD'S SCREAMER 2003
ENGLAND v INDIA
by Lawrence Booth

Mongia and Tendulkar followed cheaply, before Ganguly fell victim to one of the greatest catches ever held at Lord's. Launching Giles towards wide long-on, he watched in horror as Kirtley hared round the boundary, dived at full stretch and clung on with his left hand an inch above the turf.

TEST TURNER 1931
ENGLAND v AUSTRALIA, NOTTINGHAM

England won the first of the series of Test matches shortly after half-past five on the fourth day by 93 runs. Australia, who were set to get 429 runs to win, had scored 60 runs for the loss of Woodfull's wicket overnight, and, with the England attack weakened [by the absence of Larwood with gastritis], made, thanks to Bradman, a very fine fight of it. Indeed, when shortly before three o'clock they had 229 runs on the board and only three men out, they possessed, with the wicket probably in better condition than at any previous time during the game, a reasonable chance of winning.

Bradman was well set and McCabe playing a bold and successful innings, but at that point McCabe fell to a splendid catch very low down at mid-on by [Syd] Copley, a member of the groundstaff at Trent Bridge, fielding as substitute for Larwood. Copley made a lot of ground, took the ball at full length and, although rolling over, retained possession. This catch, as it happened, turned the game in England's favour for, although Fairfax stayed some time and Richardson made a few hits, nobody after Bradman's dismissal at 267 offered any real resistance.

SLIPPERS 1932

Kotze could with perfect justice be included among the first half-dozen of the fastest bowlers seen . . . It is doing him no injustice to say that he did not like being punished, and on more than one occasion he got a little disheartened when he had catches missed off him in the slips. The ball, however, always went at terrific speed to the fieldsmen, and it is likely that had it been possible for him to field to his own bowling his opinions on the catching of his colleagues would not have been quite so scathing.

SOUTH AFRICAN STANDARD 1954
AUSTRALIA v SOUTH AFRICA, MELBOURNE

South Africa won by 82 runs. Their first victory over Australia for 42 years came as reward for superior all-round cricket. Endean and Tayfield played specially notable roles, but the whole side deserved praise for two fielding performances which drew favourable comparison with some of the best teams of the past. The spectacular catch which dismissed Morris set South Africa's standard for the first innings. A drive hit Cheetham's upflung hands close to the wicket but bounced away from him. Tayfield spun round, raced after the ball, and caught it in a full-length dive. Cheetham and McGlew made other excellent catches, and Endean, with his back to the iron fence, held a drive by Miller above his head.

BUSH-WHACKED 1938
by "Patsy" Hendren

A funny thing once happened to me when on an MCC tour in Australia. Between fixtures, I was journeying into the Bush by motor-car with a colleague when we stopped to watch a cricket match. One of the players, unaware of our identity, approached and asked if, as his team was a man short, one of us would play. I had already been in the field for two and a half days, but I yielded to persuasion and, rigged out in borrowed gear, was put in the deep field at the bottom of a pronounced slope, from where I could see nothing at all of the cricket. For hour after hour I fielded there, throwing the ball back at intervals until, at long last, I caught one. I ran to the top of the hill and announced with some satisfaction that I had made a catch. To my consternation, I was informed that the other team's innings had closed and that I had caught one of my own side!

AT LEAST HE CAUGHT IT 2000
MIDDLESEX v NOTTINGHAMSHIRE

After striking the first "free hit" at Lord's for four, Roseberry lofted another straight to Stemp, who, apparently uncertain what to do, held on to the ball so long that the batsmen completed a leisurely single.

NOTE: In 1999, the one-day National League introduced a free hit immediately after a no-ball. This had some spectator appeal, although some players took longer to get to grips with the novelty.

EXPENSIVE 1999
Chronicle of 1998

Chris Purdie of Tilford dropped Gary Cox off the first ball of his over in a match against Redingensians in Surrey, and went on to concede 40 from the over. The dropped catch went for four, and Cox hit the next six balls for six. This included a no-ball, when Purdie switched to bowling round the wicket without warning. (*Daily Telegraph*, September 4)

FASHION NOTES

LORD'S, LADIES AND GENTLEMEN
1870

That this, the most attractive match of the season, annually increases in popularity with the fair and fashionable portion of English society, Lord's ground bore brilliant testimony on Friday, the 9th of last July, on which day £100 more was taken at the gates for admission than was ever taken before in one day at Lord's. The weather was fortunately fine; the attendance was marvellous, both in numbers and quality; and the old ground, as it that day appeared, a fitting subject for a companion picture to Frith's "DERBY DAY". One writer described the Grand Stand as being "as gay as a bank of Summer Flowers", and so it was, for two-thirds of the occupants were THE LADIES OF ENGLAND whose gay, varied and brilliant hued attires pleasantly contrasted with the dark, sombre clad, dense mass of *he* humanity that thronged the seats and roof of the pavilion, a majority of whom "had been" Public School Boys, many of whom "are" distinguished members of the highest and most honoured Institutions of the Country. As many of the Drags of "THE FOUR-IN-HAND CLUB" as could gain admission to the ground were grouped together at the NW end of the pavilion. Around the ground, flanking the ropes, closely clustered (at most parts six deep) were 600 carriages of the nobility and gentry, each vehicle fully, most of them "fairly" freighted. The tops of the wood-stacks had occupants, so had the window sills of the Racket Court, and the top of Mr Dark's garden wall; and how vast was the number of visitors each day may be estimated from the facts that on the Friday, "about £770", and on Saturday, "nearly £500", was taken at the gates for admission money. In fact, the ETON and HARROW match at Lord's has now become one of the prominent events of the London Season; for years and years to come may it so continue to be, and thus materially aid in keeping alive the interest for the fine old game, at present so manifest and general, among its very best supporters, THE GENTLEMEN OF ENGLAND.

1894
ETON v HARROW

Uncertain weather and the strong counter-attraction of the meeting of Orme and La Flèche in the Eclipse Stakes at Sandown considerably affected the attendance on the first day, the company scarcely numbering more than 12,000, of whom 4,500 paid for admission at the gates.

NOTE: The Eclipse Stakes was won by Orme for the second year in succession; at Lord's, Eton won by nine wickets.

1943

Forty-nine matches were played at Lord's in 1941, many of them for Service Charities. Despite the fact that all Officers and men in uniform in the Royal Navy, the Army and the Royal Air Force were admitted free of charge, as in 1940, 89,612 spectators paid at the gate (6d.) during the season, as against 52,555 in 1940.

Notes by the Editor, *Wisden*, 1976

At the beginning of August when England and Australia were engaged at Lord's in an intriguing contest, it was hotter than in North Africa at 93 degrees Fahrenheit, the highest temperature in the London area since July 1948. The Australians were also here then, so perhaps there was some excuse for the streaker who, filled with Australian liquor, invaded the pitch while England were building up their second-innings total of 436.

National Village Final, 1986

September 1, 1985. Freuchie beat Rowledge by virtue of having lost fewer wickets with the scores level, so becoming, in the bicentenary year of Scottish cricket, the first Scottish village to win the final. Rowledge had won the toss and batted first, but against tigerish Scottish fielding the runs came slowly. Dunbar, whose 33 was top score of the match, and Offord were both run out by Andrew Crichton. Freuchie's captain and president, David Christie, saw the score to 134 for seven, when he was run out off the last ball of the 39th over, whereupon in great excitement in the gloaming of St John's Wood, the ninth-wicket pair played out a maiden 40th over to ensure victory. Freuchie, with kilts swirling and their piper skirling at their head, had marched into Lord's, where the national dress, including tie and jacket, was permitted wear in the pavilion.

1990
ENGLAND v AUSTRALIA

May 29, 1989. Australia won by six wickets. Toss: England. A loose second spell by Foster, during which Steve Waugh picked up two successive balls for six into the Tavern, tilted a close game irrevocably in favour of Australia. Played to a capacity crowd and in glorious weather, like its predecessors, the final match of the one-day series featured Gooch's and Marsh's seventh hundreds in, respectively, their 70th and 71st internationals; and the longest and easily most stylish "streak" on an English cricket ground, by a shapely young lady from the Essex-Suffolk borders. It started from the Mound Stand and finished by the Warner Stand and included an exultant cartwheel. Australia also showed their class, winning well despite an opening stand of 123 in 127 minutes between Gooch and Gower and an 11-ball 25 not out by Botham.

Notes by the Editor, *Wisden*, 1999

The replay screens at the Tests in England last year were sponsored by the car firm Citroën. And so, during intervals at the Lord's Test, the screen kept showing Citroën's current advert, which consisted of the model Claudia Schiffer descending a staircase and getting into a car while simultaneously removing every item of her clothing. She did this, in about twice life-size, in full view of the Lord's pavilion. It was a remarkable disjunction. At the time, a blocking minority of MCC had just ensured the continuation of the club's ban on women members.

Chronicle of 1999, *Wisden*, 2000

MCC issued new dress instructions to cope with the presence of women in the pavilion, following the decision to admit them in 1998. Ladies were instructed to wear "dresses, skirts or tailored trousers" and cover their shoulders. Leggings were to be specifically barred. (*Daily Telegraph*, February 15)

CRICKET DRESS
by H. S. Altham, 1941

Eighteenth Century

Three-cornered or jockey hats, often with silver or gold lace; shirts, generally frilled; nankeen breeches, silk stockings, buckled shoes. The Hambledon Club had sky-blue coats with buttons engraved "CC". The first uniform of the MCC was in azure blue.

1800–1850

From about 1810–15 trousers begin to replace breeches, though Eton and Harrow still wore the latter in 1830. Tall "beaver" hats, in black or white, became the rule. Shirts were no longer frilled, but were now worn with rather high collars and spreading bow ties; singlets instead of shirts were not uncommon. Wide braces often seen, especially on professionals. Black "Oxford" shoes universal. Belts, with metal clasps, for the waist.

Towards the end of this period the tall hat was beginning to give place to a soft and full flannel cap, generally white, or, less commonly, to a straw hat, often rather of a haymaker's shape. Short white jackets of flannel appeared as forerunner of "the blazer".

1850–1880

The beginning of this period saw the appearance of club cricket colours, under the lead of I Zingari (established 1845). These were often worn in ribbons round the white bowler hats which were now replacing the tall and straw hats of the previous two decades. Club caps date from about 1850; the Winchester XI first wore their blue caps in 1851, Harrow their striped cap in 1852. The Cambridge "blue" seems to date from 1861, the Oxford "blue" certainly from 1863. Many professionals played in black bowler hats.

Coloured shirts became common as uniform, e.g., a pattern of coloured spots, stripes, or checks on a white ground, as worn by the All-England elevens. The Oxford and Cambridge elevens for many years wore dark and light blue shirts. The Harlequins, founded 1852, originally wore blue trousers; Rugby School now present the sole survival of the coloured shirt.

The term "blazer" is said to have been evolved as a derogatory description of the very lively livery adopted by the boat clubs of Magdalen College, Oxford, or St John's College, Cambridge. The coloured cricket blazer seems to date from about 1860. The Oxford XI of 1863 are certainly wearing them. The Shaw and Shrewsbury team to Australia in 1884/85 wore blazers and caps to match.

Shoes tend to give place to boots, either brown or white with brown straps.

1880–1895

Coloured shirts disappear. White shirts, with starched or semi-starched fronts, now the rule. Ties not so common, but small bow ties in low turned-down starched collars common enough, and very smart they looked. Silk scarves in club colours increasingly fashionable for the waist.

White buckskin boots were first worn about 1882, but they only gradually superseded the old brown and brown-and-white type, which was still by no means uncommon in the nineties.

The modern "sweater", probably an evolution from the old "singlet", came in during this period.

1895 to date

Very little change. About the end of the century we find soft white hats, in felt or linen, possibly on an Australian model. In the last 20 years we may notice the disappearance of the silk scarf, due to the better fit of trousers round the hips, and the appearance of rubber-soled boots, now worn even by some bowlers in dry weather; also of sleeveless sweaters.

Umpires' white coats seem first to have been worn in 1861, but as late as 1882 the old uniform of the tall hat or "billycock" and black coat was by no means uncommon.

by Alfred Lubbock, 1909

Besides the great improvement in the wickets and the out-fielding ground, there are other changes which give a help to the present players. Not only do they have a great white tarpaulin behind the bowler's arm but the umpires are also clothed in immaculate white coats. Formerly they used to have black coats. I remember rather a good story about this. The batsmen used frequently to ask the umpire to stand further back, and one day old Jimmy Grundy, who had a somewhat portly figure, was kept being asked to stand further back by the batsman, with no avail, till at last the batsman said, "Perhaps if you stand sideways it may do." Old Jimmy, grinning to the bowler, said, "Don't make much difference which ways I stand, I am about the same both ways."

I remember once, I think it was in the Gentlemen v Players at Lord's, there was no tarpaulin and the bowler's arm was just in a line with one of the little trees that were waving about in the wind. I never had a ghost of an idea where the ball came, so was promptly shot out by what I was afterwards told was a regular long-hop. The pavilion at Lord's was a nasty background and people continually on the move. Now steps are taken to prevent this. We also used to go on playing when it was raining, and in the ten years I played in first-class matches I never remember the

---

SONS OF ABRAHAM 1923

Dr Arthur Abraham was at one time a well-known cricketer in Ireland, playing for Leinster against the South of England, when his resemblance to his twin brother led W. G. Grace to protest against him taking a second innings.

game being stopped on account of bad light, a thing often done in the present day, and to knock off the game for tea was a thing unknown.

by Lord Hawke, 1932

Here I must add something about the origin of the tea interval. Prior to its introduction, onlookers were used to seeing odd players leave the field for a few minutes, the fielding side continuing one short. Those absences were sometimes not beneficial only to the tea trade! The authorities weighed up this matter, with the desirable result that there was introduced a regular tea interval at a fixed hour. It is very rare now for a player to leave the field under any pretext, and that is, I think, one point at least to the credit of the tea interval.

MANNERS 1900
AUSTRALIANS v MIDDLESEX

On the first day the game was marred by an unseemly demonstration on the part of the spectators, happily without precedent at Lord's ground. Resenting the extreme caution with which Darling and Iredale were batting, a section of the crowd forgot their manners, cheering ironically when a run was obtained and at one point whistling the "Dead March in Saul". That his play was monotonous may be judged from the fact that Darling took three hours to get his first 38 runs. His explanation of this extreme slowness was that he was suffering from a painfully bruised heel.

WORD PLAY 1951
by R. C. Robertson-Glasgow

Time and a natural desire for novelty have brought in a few new names for fielding positions. "Leg slip" is perhaps simpler than "close fine leg". What used to be called "silly point" is now "silly mid-off" or "short mid-off". Short or silly, long or wise, what's in a name?

HEAD LINES

by "Patsy" Hendren, 1938

Then there was Albert Trott, one of the grandest cricketers of all time and the only man ever to hit the ball over the pavilion at Lord's. In his benefit match against Somerset at Lord's in 1907, he performed the hat-trick twice in one innings. He took four wickets with four balls and with the fifth dislodged a bail with a ball that went for four byes. In those days, the bail had to be *removed* before a batsman was out. Next over he sent back three men with following deliveries, making his analysis for the innings seven for 20. At the end of the innings Albert punched his own head and called himself names for finishing his benefit match early on the third day! Sammy Woods, captain of Somerset and one of the victims, gave him a straw hat with a hand-painted picture on the band of seven rabbits bolting into the pavilion. Albert wore it at a good many matches during the rest of the season – to the wonderment of everyone not in the know.

1963

In 1933 Hendren caused something of a sensation at Lord's when he batted against the West Indies fast bowlers wearing a special cap. Fashioned by his wife, this cap had three peaks, two of which covered the ears and temples, and was lined with sponge rubber. Hendren explained that he needed protection after being struck on the head two years earlier by the new-fashioned persistent short-pitched bouncers.

1937

Over six feet in height and finely built, Major Wynyard was a brilliant player of most games and excelled on the cricket field, where his commanding figure could not escape attention. In his Hampshire days he usually wore an I Zingari cap of polo shape balanced at the military angle with a strap under the chin.

Notes by the Editor, *Wisden*, 1981

Last year was the first in which helmets, or reinforced caps, became standard wear in first-class cricket. When, as more often than not, they have a visor attached, they reduce the batsman, or short-leg fielder, to wretched anonymity. I find it sartorially and aesthetically an objectionable trend. It has, furthermore, detracted from the artistry of batting. As you would expect, old cricketers deplore the sight of a helmeted batsman. Yet if their use saves cricketers from serious injury, they must be allowed. Had short-pitched bowling, over the years, not got so out of hand, they would not be necessary. But it has. The helmet, it seems, has come to stay – an unsightly adjunct to an increasingly dangerous game.

by Trevor Bailey, 1981

One of cricket's many charms used to be the way it was possible to walk into a ground and instantly recognise the batsman at the crease. Apart from his style, he was unmistakable because of his build, features, headgear or hair. Who could have failed to pick out Cyril Washbrook with his cap at a jaunty angle, or Jack Robertson, who wore his with the precision of a guardsman? Then again, there were the hairstyles of Herbert Sutcliffe, black "patent-leather" glinting in the sun, complete with the straightest of partings, the blonde waves of Joe Hardstaff, Reg Simpson's dark curls, and Denis Compton's, so unlike those Brylcream advertisements, forever unruly. Today, as often as not, it is impossible to tell who is batting without first consulting a scorecard, so many players being encrusted in helmets and camouflaged by visors. This gives them a space-age image, devoid of individuality and as dull as dirty denims.

PUMPING WILLOW
by H. S. Altham, 1941

The Bat

No dimensions were specified in the original Laws, when the bat was curved and much longer in the handle.

1774. Width of bat limited to 4¼ inches.
1840. Length of bat limited to 38 inches.
1853/54. Cane handles were patented by Nixon.
1880. Rubber handle-covers patented.

In 1773 the Pett family, Sevenoaks, a noted firm, sold the best bats for 4s. 6d. In 1836 Dark's bats were sold by Sadd of Cambridge for 8s. 6d.

by Norman Harris, 1985

Certainly at the highest level there is now a different style of batting, and it is clear that it has been influenced by changes in equipment – in particular, bats. In the mid-1970s the weight of bats had for long been standard, at something like 2¼ pounds; and the shape of the bat had altered very little since the early century. The parameters of length and width were, after all, laid down in the Laws of Cricket and the only area in which manu-facturers sought to gain a little advantage was in the "springing" of handles. Then, in 1974, the long-established bat-makers, Gray-Nicolls, cautiously introduced a bat which they probably feared would offend many traditionalists. The bat, which could be called by no other name than the "Scoop", drew its inspiration from the heel-and-toe-weighted golf putter invented by a South African, Dr Arthur Garner.

An Englishman named Barry Wheeler, who had some know-ledge of physics and was also the agent for an American golf-ball manufacturer, concluded that the perimeter-weighting principle could be applied equally well to cricket bats. By making the centre of the bat's back concave instead of ridge-like, the weight saved could be "pushed" towards the edges, thus effectively widening the bat's "middle".

The immediate consequence was that other bat-makers – and there were very soon more of them – began to think anew about the shape of cricket bats. Weight could be "spread" by other means than grooving out the back (for the "Scoop" had been patented). The hump could simply be flattened and pushed towards the edges. Weight could be moved from higher up the blade, including a fluting of the edges so that these were thicker at the bottom than near the shoulders.

Backing the bulge

Bats began to bulge at the business end. Heaviness seemed to become almost a greater virtue than balance, and thicker handles were made to help lift these bats. Some amused onlookers began to talk of "railway sleepers" and to wonder if bats were going to revert to the club-like shapes of the game's origins. It was recalled that in 1820, when William Ward made 278 at Lord's (a score not bettered on that ground for the next 105 years) he used a bat said to weigh over four pounds.

The heaviest of the new bats of the 1970s went above three pounds, which was nearly a 30 per cent increase. One was the 3lb 4oz Duncan Fearnley bat which Glenn Turner employed in his innings of 311 not out at Worcester in 1982. Turner, a relatively slight figure, argued that if a heavy bat was picked up straight it was less likely to go off line as it came down than a lighter bat might be. He thought of it as a heavy pendulum. Bigger men who have used heavy bats are Clive Lloyd, Ian Botham and Clive Rice. Some also employ the early backlift in which the bat is "up and waiting" as the bowler delivers. Accordingly, the ball has on occasion (and especially on Sundays) been hit very hard indeed – harder, in the opinion of some, than ever before.

Shot selection

In the process, a different range of shots has emerged. Fewer cuts, pulls and hooks – the hook, in particular – are made, but more are played in the arc between extra cover and mid-on. Indeed, sixes or one-bounce fours over cover are no longer a great rarity. Another popular sector is the one between square leg and mid-wicket. There is the shot off the legs which races along the ground and rattles the fence in that area; there is the pick-up over mid-wicket; and there is the drive which is mis-hit, but with sufficient power for the ball to "squeeze" through mid-wicket for runs.

These, of course, are shots which are made with a single, uncomplicated movement that is essentially downward. The wrists do not have to do much at all. Compare that with the movement required for what might now be regarded as the "old-fashioned" square-cut, for which the bat comes down on *top* of the ball. That shot is now much less popular than the other oft-termed "cut", which is simply a back-foot hit through the covers or square of the wicket – and which is much the easier of the two shots to play with a heavy bat.

LIGHT METAL
Notes by the Editor, *Wisden*, 1981

In Perth, Dennis Lillee, the great Australian, held up play for ten minutes in a Test match between England and Australia while he argued with the umpires and his own captain over the use of an aluminium bat in which he had a proprietorial interest. Technically Lillee had a point, there being nothing in the Laws at that time, though there is now, to say that a bat must be made of wood; morally, as he must have known, he should have done as the umpires asked him.

1933
KENT SECOND XI v SOUTH AMERICANS

Metal stumps were used for the first time but they were knocked out of shape and enlarged when struck by the ball. The experiment, tried because ash stumps are liable to split in some climates, was abandoned at lunch time on the first day.

SOCIAL REGISTER
1872
ETON v HARROW

The annually increasing attraction of this match among the upper crust of English Society is something wonderful. The amount of the receipts in 1871 was not made public, but those unerring calculators – "the tell tales" – told the following surprising tale as to the number of visitors to the ground in the course of the two days of last July: on Friday 13,494 and on Saturday 11,132 visitors paid and passed through the turnstiles on to the ground. Add to this 24,626 the members of MCC, their families and friends, *and* all who went to the ground in or on vehicles (600 carriages were estimated as being on the ground), then an idea can be formed of the vast numbers that composed "the fashionable crushes" up at Lord's on the 14th and 15th of July, 1871. The gatherings were as brilliant in rank as they were unprecedentedly large in numbers. Their Royal Highnesses THE CROWN PRINCESS OF PRUSSIA, PRINCESS LOUISE MARCHIONESS OF LORNE, and PRINCE ARTHUR with the Marquis of Lorne and a large number of the nobility honoured the match with their presence.

1873

The 85th ANNIVERSARY MEETING of the members of THE MARYLEBONE CLUB was held at Lord's ground on Wednesday, May 1st, when a ballot took place and the unprecedentedly large number of 90 *new members were elected*. Dinner was served in the new Tavern at 7.30 the same day, the president, The Right Hon. the Earl of CLARENDON, in the chair. What took place after the removal of the cloth will be best told by the following graphic report taken from *Bell's Life in London*: "After dinner the usual loyal toasts were given, and cordially responded to, the president making special allusion to the late illness of HRH the Prince of Wales, who, as patron of the MCC, had enlisted the sympathies and anxieties of the members during that trying period, his lordship adding that though uninitiated in the mysteries of medicine, he could recommend with confidence to HRH's medical advisers, as a thorough restoration, a gentle dose of cricket, to be taken weekly at Lord's."

1931

ENGLAND v AUSTRALIA

At Lord's, Monday, June 28, 1930. While in the end Bradman made most runs, very great credit was due to Woodfull and Ponsford who, when England's bowling was fresh, put on 162 for the first wicket. Curiously enough the partnership terminated almost directly after a break in the play while the members of both teams were presented to the King in front of the pavilion, Ponsford, who had batted very soundly, being caught at slip.

1948
ENGLAND v SOUTH AFRICA

At Lord's, Tuesday, June 24, 1947. South Africa followed on 227 behind and, with 15 scored, play was held up for 20 minutes while the cricketers were presented to the King and Queen and the Princesses, Elizabeth and Margaret. Upon the resumption Edrich bowled at a tremendous pace. His second ball flattened Melville's middle stump, and two overs later he sent Viljoen's middle stump flying.

NOTE: South Africa's Dudley Nourse recalled King George VI saying to Alan Melville, "I do hope I do not turn out to hold the reputation of my father. He was regarded as England's best change bowler, you know." As events proved, he was just as effective. Nor was Melville his first victim; this King had form going back to the New Zealand Test of 1937, when play was interrupted in the last session of the second day so that he could meet the touring team. Immediately after the resumption, Hedley Verity caught and bowled "Sonny" Moloney to end his partnership of 104 with Alby Roberts.

1953

HM KING GEORGE VI died at Sandringham on February 6 [1952]. He was Patron of the Marylebone, Surrey and Lancashire clubs. When Prince Albert, he performed the hat-trick on the private ground on the slopes below Windsor Castle, where the sons and grandsons of Edward VII used to play regularly. A left-handed batsman and bowler, the King bowled King Edward VII, King George V and the present Duke of Windsor [King Edward VIII] in three consecutive balls, thus proving himself the best Royal cricketer since Frederick, Prince of Wales in 1751 took a keen interest in the game. The ball is now mounted in the mess room of the Royal Naval College, Dartmouth. King George VI, like his father, often went to Lord's when Commonwealth teams were playing there, and invariably the players and umpires were presented to His Majesty in front of the pavilion. He entertained the 1948 Australian team at Balmoral, and in his 1949 New Year's Honours Donald Bradman received a knighthood.

Gordonstoun School, *Wisden*, 1980

BATTING	Innings	Not Outs	Runs	Highest	Average
*HRH Prince Andrew	9	0	212	74	23.55

BOWLING	Overs	Maidens	Runs	Wickets	Average
HRH Prince Andrew	26.3	9	50	11	4.54

* Denotes captain.

1996
Chronicle of 1995

Prince Charles was bowled first ball by ten-year-old Wajid Khan at a Kwik Cricket demonstration at The Oval. (*The Sun*, July 15)

SUPPLEMENTARY OBITUARY 1994

Dartmouth, William Heneage Legge, the 6th Earl of, who died at his home in Staffordshire, Patshull House, on March 11, 1936, aged 84, was President of MCC in 1893. Under his courtesy title, Lord Lewisham, he played a first-class match for an indifferent MCC team against Hampshire at Lord's in 1877. He also played for Shropshire and Staffordshire and was MP for West Kent and then Lewisham. His grandson married Raine McCorquodale, who later married Earl Spencer and became the Princess of Wales's stepmother.

1961
PAKISTAN v AUSTRALIA

At Karachi, December 1959. With Australia two wins ahead in the series and Pakistan beaten at home for the first time in a rubber, there seemed every chance of some lively cricket. In fact, play was drab for most of the time, with Pakistan taking eight hours 48 minutes over 287 in their first innings and eight hours over 194 in their second. Mr Eisenhower watched play on the fourth day and, as he was the first United States President to see Test cricket, his visit may well be remembered long after this disappointing game is forgotten.

2001

Film star Tom Cruise was taken to the Sydney Cricket Ground [on February 4, 2000] by director Sam Mendes to watch a one-day international. "He didn't know anything about cricket," said Mendes. "I told him about Warne and Tendulkar, how amazing Bradman was, and that Mark Taylor had declared when he was 334 not out, equal with Bradman's Australian Test record. Tom was so moved he was practically in tears. He enjoyed it so much he hired the box himself for a match the next day."

LADY IN RED 1994

MIDDLESEX v KENT

The most diverting moment came when Ramprakash complained that he was having difficulty sighting the ball because of the red sweater worn by a lady watching above the sightscreen at the Nursery End; she had to borrow a white cardigan.

CENTURIONS

What is it, this fascination of ours for milestones? Give a digit a couple of zeros and it takes on a significance beyond measure. Give a zed two noughts and you have a menagerie; put them after the figure one and we get a celebration. And why not? As Vivian Jenkins wrote in his 1951 *Wisden* profile, celebrating Les Ames's hundredth hundred, the world takes on a new look after even one three-figure innings.

Derek Underwood's unconfined delight in 1984 upon reaching his one and only century bears testimony to that. Underwood, in his fortieth year and, in his 22nd season, a fully paid-up member of the night-watchman's union, had more than 2,000 first-class wickets to his name at the time. Yet you felt on the day that he would have traded them all for this one magical moment as he raised his bat to acknowledge the genuine warmth of the applause. For bowlers, you see, as Jenkins also pointed out, "Valhalla is written in simple 'double figures'." Whoever said cricket was for batsmen knew what he was talking about.

When W. G. Grace became the first to reach a hundred hundreds, his contemporary, A. G. Steel, wrote of it in *Wisden* as "a performance which may be a record for all time". It wasn't, not by any means, although 18 years passed before Surrey's Tom Hayward matched it. *Wisden* commented that "The change that has come over modern cricket in the way of an extended programme of first-class fixtures is brought home to us by the fact that Hayward made his hundredth century in his 21st season. W. G. Grace began to play first-class cricket in 1865 – the year following his first appearance at Lord's – and it was not until 1895 that his hundredth hundred was obtained. Between the two batsmen, therefore, there was a difference of just ten years." On the other hand, as the accompanying table shows, the difference was only 37 innings, less than a season's cricket in Hayward's time.

THE HUNDREDTH HUNDREDS

	Career	Season	Score	Age	Inns for 100th	Career 100s
W. G. Grace	1865–1908	1895	288	46	1,113	126
T. W. Hayward	1893–1914	1913	139	42	1,076	104
J. B. Hobbs	1905–34	1923	116*	40	821	197
C. P. Mead	1905–36	1927	100*	40	892	153
E. H. Hendren	1907–38	1928/29	100	39	740	170
F. E. Woolley	1906–38	1929	176	42	1,031	145
H. Sutcliffe	1919–45	1932	132	37	700	149
E. Tyldesley	1909–36	1934	122	45	919	102
W. R. Hammond	1920–51	1935	116	31	679	167
A. Sandham	1911–37/38	1935	103	44	871	107
D. G. Bradman	1927/28–48/49	1947/48	172	39	295	117
L. E. G. Ames	1926–51	1950	131	44	915	102
L. Hutton	1934–60	1951	151	35	619	129
D. C. S. Compton	1936–64	1952	107	34	552	123
T. W. Graveney	1948–71/72	1964	132	37	940	122
M. C. Cowdrey	1950–76	1973	100*	40	1,035	107
J. H. Edrich	1956–78	1977	101*	40	945	103
G. Boycott	1962–86	1977	191	36	645	151
G. M. Turner	1964/65–82/83	1982	311*	35	779	103
Zaheer Abbas	1965/66–86/87	1982/83	215	35	658	108
D. L. Amiss	1960–87	1986	101*	43	1,081	102
I. V. A. Richards	1971/72–93	1988/89	101	36	658	114
G. A. Gooch	1973–2000	1992/93	102*	39	820	128
G. A. Hick	1983/84–	1998	132	32	574	†126

*Denotes not out.

†Hick's career hundreds to August 30, 2004.

NOTES: G. Boycott and Zaheer Abbas scored their hundredth hundred in a Test match.

G. A. Gooch's record includes his century in South Africa in 1981/82, which is no longer accepted by the ICC.

Not that innings became much more than an academic indicator once Don Bradman started pinging off hundreds at an average of one in every three. Only Denis Compton and Graeme Hick come close to that, with one in every five and a half innings.

When W. G. Grace hit his hundredth hundred, the *Daily Telegraph* instituted a testimonial to him and "Day after day," A. G. Steel noted, "one read of the flood of shillings pouring in." Steel was not best pleased. "One could not but feel a little alarm for the dignity of our great game." When Jack Hobbs followed his former opening partner, Hayward, to the landmark, Surrey gave him 100 guineas. *Wisden* doesn't mention how Surrey recognised Andrew Sandham and John Edrich's hundredth when they entered the list, but the 1983 Almanack contains a photo of Worcestershire's Glenn Turner pausing to celebrate his with a pre-prandial gin and tonic before marching on to a triple-century. When Hick in 1998 became the most recent to do the deed, yet another Worcestershire centurion, Tom Graveney, brought out a bottle of champagne, proving if nothing else that tipples change with the times. As for the next batsman to hit a hundred hundreds? It is tempting, looking in *Wisden* 2004 at the current runners, to wonder if anyone will. Then again they said that after Grace, 24 instances back down the line.

LES AMES Kent and England
by Vivian Jenkins, 1951

Leslie Egbert George Ames has joined the ranks of the immortals. He has scored a hundred centuries, a feat which raises him to the pinnacle tenanted only by the game's mastercraftsmen. Craft and art, let it be noted, are indissolubly linked. Hobbs still stands alone. Yet even the great Surrey master could not lay claim to the dual combination of talent which makes Ames possibly the foremost all-rounder the game has yet produced. Statistically, at least. Otherwise George Hirst might get some people's vote, and certainly that of all Yorkshiremen, though Hirst's tally of centuries amounted to no more than 60, and even 60 are insufficient. Depressing thought for anyone whose world has taken on a new look after even one three-figure innings.

Ames also kept wicket – superbly well. Well enough, for the benefit of those prepared to argue, to fulfil that role in the most discussed and not least successful team ever to leave England for Australia, Douglas Jardine's "bodyline buccaneers" of 1932/33. Ames's records in the stumped and caught department still stand alone as a target for successors to emulate. In 1928 he caught 70 batsmen and stumped 52, setting a new "high" of 122 for others to follow. Not content with that, he raised the total to 128 the following year, with 79 catches and 49 stumpings making up the "bag".

Ames has made many a hundred at Canterbury, but strangely enough never another one since 1932 during the "Week" itself, until the crowning effort against Middlesex last summer which occasions this article. It was a single to fine leg off dapper Jack Young which brought him to his goal and broke a tension which had existed over several previous unsuccessful attempts to reach that final century. Only a few thousand spectators were present on this last day of the match, but Ames has confessed that the reception they gave him more than made up for any lack of numbers. He admits, too, that a cold shiver went up his spine and he felt that catch in the throat that achievement of a supreme ambition brings to anyone. So much so that he broke out into a cold sweat for several seconds.

KENT v MIDDLESEX

At Canterbury, August 9, 10, 11, 1950. Kent won by four wickets within seven minutes of half-past three, the latest time for drawing stumps. During a great effort for his side, Ames made the hundredth century of his first-class career and put victory within reach. Going in on Fagg's failure without a run scored, Ames played a grand innings. Often running to drive while getting 131 runs out of 211 in two hours, Ames fell to that risk, Moss holding a hard drive close to the ground in the deep field. He hit two sixes and 17 fours. Hearn shared a stand that realised 110 in 75 minutes, and, with Pawson very free, 85 runs came in 35 minutes.

Evans received a blow on his right hand while batting in the first innings and Ames kept wicket in the Middlesex second innings.

Middlesex 249 (J. D. Robertson 40, J. G. Dewes 60, H. P. Sharp 62; F. Ridgway three for 86, D. V. P. Wright five for 61) **and 241** for three dec. (J. D. Robertson 54, J. G. Dewes 32, W. J. Edrich 77 not out, S. M. Brown 51 not out).

Kent 254 for six dec. (A. E. Fagg 88, L. E. G. Ames 4, H. A. Pawson 103 not out; J. J. Warr four for 67) **and 239** for six (L. E. G. Ames 131, P. Hearn 30, H. A. Pawson 57; J. J. Warr three for 57).

TWIN PEAKS 1936
BY PERCY PERRIN

Charles McGahey was a self-made cricketer without any tuition whatever. We were dubbed "Essex Twins" by Joe Armour, the Essex scorer for 44 years – a living volume of Essex cricket history. When I started, Joe Armour, in his quaint way, complained that he could not distinguish one from the other. McGahey's height was 6 feet 2 inches, mine 6 feet 3 inches. He suggested that one of "the twins" should wear a scarf round his waist so that he could get the runs down to the right man.

DENNIS AMISS Warwickshire and England
by Jack Bannister, 1987

The crisis-ridden career of Dennis Leslie Amiss is an object lesson to those lesser cricketers who, when faced with their first major hurdle in professional cricket, show a deficiency in technique and temperament which precludes further progress. But because Amiss's make-up is generously threaded with toughened steel, in his 44th year – 29 of which have been spent on the Warwickshire staff – he was able to step into the "hundred hundreds" club, as well as moving past Andrew Sandham into 12th place in the list of the game's most prolific run-scorers. He continued to parade a technique and level of concentration which, far from showing the first understandable signs of decline, were as impressively solid as ever.

For Amiss, the Holy Grail became the 21st entry card into batting's most exclusive club. It shone brightly enough at the beginning of the summer to draw in, in 17 innings, three of the four hundreds needed for glory, but then there was a tantalising wait as the hundredth century eluded him for 16 more innings, in three of which he topped 50. And although it finally came in slightly anticlimactic fashion – the extra half-hour of a "dead" game against Lancashire being taken to enable the last 36 runs to be scored – the innings marked the personal high-point of a magnificent career which survived at least four major crises.

WARWICKSHIRE v LANCASHIRE

At Birmingham, July 26, 28, 29, 1986. Drawn. Toss: Warwickshire. The match was notable for the hundredth hundred of Amiss's career. He became the 21st player to achieve this feat, thanks to the sportsmanship of Clive Lloyd, the Lancashire captain, who agreed to play out the last 20 overs, even though the result was certain to be a draw following the rain which prevented any play the previous day. Amiss batted for 114 minutes and faced 127 deliveries, from which he hit one six and 14 fours. Fifteen wickets fell on the Saturday.

Warwickshire 138 (D. L. Amiss 33, A. M. Ferreira 69 not out; P. J. W. Allott five for 55, M. Watkinson three for 48) **and 255** for three (A. J. Moles 67, D. L. Amiss 101 not out, G. W. Humpage 38 not out).
Lancashire 293 for nine dec. (G. Fowler 76, C. H. Lloyd 128; G. C. Small five for 85).

GEOFF BOYCOTT Yorkshire,
Northern Transvaal and England
by Harold Abel, 1978

For Australia to dispose of Boycott for a duck playing for Yorkshire at Scarborough must have looked fine at the time. Clearly it was likely to rebound, as it did with a century in the second innings. Then for McCosker to drop the Yorkshire captain when 20, at the end of three hours' painful acclimatisation on his return to the Test arena at Trent Bridge, was courting utter disaster. Instead of 87 for six, England remained 87 for five and, with the assistance of Knott, Boycott ensured that another 210 runs were on the board before the next wicket went down.

Boycott's influence on the series did not end there. He chose his own Headingley ground for his hundredth century, again with the help of a missed catch, albeit a difficult one, when 22, and went on to 191 before being last out. He just missed the opportunity of becoming the first Englishman to carry his bat against Australia in a home Test. The balance of power had been shifted by this one player who came from a three-year self-imposed exile to average 147.33 in five innings. Before his return there was little between the sides man-for-man. England held their catches more often.

by Geoffrey Wheeler, 1978
ENGLAND v AUSTRALIA
Fourth Test Match

At Leeds, August 11, 12, 13, 15, 1977. England won by an innings and 85 runs, completing a crushing victory at 4.40 p.m. on the fourth day to regain the Ashes. The completeness of their triumph, following wins by nine wickets at Manchester and seven wickets at Nottingham, left no room for doubt as to which was the superior side. It was the first year since 1886 that England had won three Tests in a home series against Australia.

A historic game was made more memorable by Boycott who, on the opening day, became the first player to score his hundredth century in a Test match. The Yorkshire crowd seemed to regard the achievement of this landmark as inevitable and Boycott batted with such ease and assurance that he gave his loyal supporters few qualms and the Australian bowlers scant hope. His was a remarkable feat, for he was only the 18th cricketer to reach this goal. Two of the others, Herbert Sutcliffe and Sir Leonard Hutton, were present for at least part of the match. A strong local conviction that cricket history was about to be made helped to fill the ground close to overflowing on the first two days when the gates were shut well before the start.

Boycott soon took the measure of the attack and apart from

one edged stroke off Walker, which nearly carried to Marsh, looked well nigh invincible. Partners came and went while he proceeded at his own measured pace. Thirty-four runs before lunch, another 35 by tea. He had been in for five hours 20 minutes when a full-throated roar from the crowd told those for miles around that the local hero had done it. An on-driven boundary off [Greg] Chappell, his 14th four from the 232nd ball he had received, took the Yorkshire captain to three figures and brought the inevitable invasion of the middle. Happily this did not cause a lengthy hold-up in play or cost Boycott his cap, which was sheepishly returned by a would-be souvenir hunter. When he was last out he had hit 23 fours in his second-best score for his country.

England 436 (G. Boycott 191, R. A. Woolmer 37, A. W. Greig 43,
    G. R. J. Roope 34, A. P. E. Knott 57; J. R. Thomson four for 113,
    L. S. Pascoe four for 91).

Australia 103 (M. Hendrick four for 41, I. T. Botham five for 21) **and 248**
    (G. S. Chappell 36, R. W. Marsh 63, M. H. N. Walker 30;
    R. G. D. Willis three for 32, M. Hendrick four for 54).

DON BRADMAN New South Wales, South Australia and Australia
by R. C. Robertson-Glasgow, 1949

Above all, Bradman was a business-cricketer. About his batting there was to be no style for style's sake. If there was to be any charm, that was not for the spectator to find or miss. It was not Bradman's concern. His aim was the making of runs, and he made them in staggering and ceaseless profusion. He seemed to have eliminated error, to have perfected the mechanism of stroke. Others before him had come near to doing this; but Bradman did it without abating the temperature of his attack. No other batsman, surely, has ever been able to score so fast while at the same time avoiding risk. He was, as near as a man batting may be, the flawless engine. There were critics who found surfeit in watching him. Man, by his nature, cannot bear perfection in his fellow. The very fact that something is being done which had been believed to be impossible goads and irritates. It is but a short step from annoyance to envy, and Bradman has never been free from envy's attacks. So when, first in 1930, he reeled off the centuries, single, double and treble, there were not wanting those who compared him unfavourably with other great ones – Trumper, Ranjitsinhji, Hobbs, Macartney. And Bradman's answer was more runs. Others, perhaps, *could* have made them, but they didn't. No one before had ever been quite so fit, quite so ruthless.

AN AUSTRALIAN XI v INDIANS

At Sydney, November 14, 15, 17, 18, 1947. Indians won by 47 runs, gaining their first victory of the tour over a side very little short of full Australian Test standard. The early stages went unfavourably, nine wickets falling for 229, but Kishenchand and Irani shared in a splendid partnership of 97. Bradman gave a glorious display in completing his hundredth hundred in first-class cricket, but, although he made 172 and Miller showed good form, the last six wickets fell for 38 and much of the home team's advantage was lost. Set to get 251 in two and a half hours, the Australians accepted the challenge but could not cope with the clever left-arm spin bowling of Mankad, who took eight for 84 in the innings.

Indians 326 (C. T. Sarwate 32, Gul Mahomed 85, V. S. Hazare 38, G. Kishenchand 75 not out, J. K. Irani 43; S. J. Loxton three for 70) **and 304** for nine dec. (M. H. Mankad 34, C. T. Sarwate 58, H. R. Adhikari 46, G. Kishenchand 63 not out, W. S. Sohoni 31; W. A. Johnston four for 71).

An Australian XI 380 (D. G. Bradman 172, K. R. Miller 86, R. N. Harvey 32; W. S. Sohoni four for 89) **and 203** (R. E. Rogers 31, W. A. Brown 30, D. G. Bradman 26, R. N. Harvey 56 not out, B. Dooland 31; M. H. Mankad eight for 84).

NOTE: Bradman made his hundredth hundred in his 295th first-class innings, at the time 384 innings fewer than the next fastest, 679 by Wally Hammond.

DENIS COMPTON Middlesex,
Holkar and England
1953

So much prominence was given to Denis Compton's loss of batting power in July and August and his omission from the England team that his temporary eclipse became regarded as the main cause of the Middlesex slide. Yet he was only one of a number of batsmen whose form departed at approximately the same time. Taking the summer as a whole, however, points to remember were that many cricketers would rejoice if, as Compton did, they came so near to a double of 2,000 runs and 100 wickets.

MIDDLESEX v NORTHAMPTONSHIRE

At Lord's, June 11, 12, 13, 1952. Middlesex won by 23 runs, with quarter of an hour to spare. In the first Middlesex innings Compton scored the hundredth hundred of his first-class career. Bowling and fielding of a high standard forced him to fight hard for runs but he showed top form. Edrich and Robertson also played with considerable skill. Northamptonshire began badly, but good innings by Greasley, twice missed, Jakeman, Barrick and Brown, who excelled with the drive, enabled them to go ahead. Rain in the night made the pitch favourable to bowlers and on the last day 20 wickets fell for 250. Edrich, frequently struck by balls which rose abruptly, saved Middlesex from collapse against Nutter's medium-pace bowling. Northamptonshire, needing 137 to win, lost six for 45 to the pace of Moss and the spin of Young, but good batting by Tribe delayed the end.

Middlesex 374 for seven dec. (J. D. Robertson 85, W. J. Edrich 94,
   D. C. S. Compton 107, A. W. Thompson 35; F. R. Brown four for 92)
   and 137 (W. J. Edrich 47, D. C. S. Compton 17; A. E. Nutter five for 47,
   F. R. Brown three for 46).
Northamptonshire 375 for eight dec. (D. G. Greasley 62, F. Jakeman 37,
   D. W. Barrick 76, F. R. Brown 73, G. E. Tribe 42 not out;
   D. C. S. Compton three for 98) **and 113** (G. E. Tribe 34; A. E. Moss
   three for 37, J. A. Young four for 37, D. C. S. Compton two for 21).

COLIN COWDREY Kent,
Oxford University and England
1974

Mention of centuries provides the introduction for Cowdrey. He went from strength to strength, particularly in the County Championship, and crowned a memorable summer with a triumphant week at Maidstone where previously he had never scored a century. He remedied that omission in the first game at Mote Park with his 99th hundred and, to the delight of the Kent fans, hit his hundredth century in the very next match – batting at No. 7.

KENT v SURREY

At Maidstone, July 4, 5, 6, 1973. Match drawn. Batsmen had matters all their own way on the first two days, a second-wicket stand of 132 off 45 overs between Howarth and Edrich paving the way for Surrey's big total. Howarth hit his highest score, 159, in four hours, including 21 fours, and he and Owen-Thomas added 128 in 90 minutes. Despite a steady fifty by Johnson, Kent lost half their side for 124 before Asif Iqbal and Cowdrey came to the rescue. Asif reached his hundred in two hours 40 minutes with two sixes and eight fours, and just after tea on the second day, amid scenes of great jubilation, Cowdrey reached his hundredth century. It was a fine innings containing 14 fours in two hours 20 minutes, during which time he and Asif had added 202. Rain curtailed play, and on the third day a more restrained but invaluable innings by Howarth saved Surrey as they struggled against the spinners.

Surrey 367 for six dec. (J. H. Edrich 59, G. P. Howarth 159,
D. R. Owen-Thomas 89 not out; J. N. Shepherd four for 85) **and 147** for eight dec. (J. H. Edrich 40, G. P. Howarth 42 not out; G. W. Johnson four for 57, B. W. Luckhurst three for 23).

Kent 326 for five dec. (G. W. Johnson 51, Asif Iqbal 119 not out,
M. C. Cowdrey 100 not out; Intikhab Alam three for 88) **and 102** for six (D. Nicholls 35, M. C. Cowdrey 9 not out).

A FAMILY AFFAIR 1936

"Parson" Crawford, as he was always called when well known as a cricketer, loved the game so much that all his children played from an early age. More than once a team of 11 Crawfords, including grandfather, his two sons, the Parson's two sons, daughters and a nephew took the field. His father, who lived to the age of 101, played for Gentlemen of England in the days when cricketers wore top hats. His brother, Major F. F. Crawford, who died in the South African War, captained Kent in the early 1870s and played for MCC in South Africa, India and elsewhere. Parson Crawford was the father of R. T., J. N. and the late V. F. S. Crawford, all of whom played first-class cricket with distinction.

JOHN EDRICH Surrey and England
1978

From the time the tactics of the bureaucrats delayed the reconstruction plans for The Oval, little had gone right for Surrey cricket. The standard of play deteriorated; disillusioned players did better elsewhere; a secretary handed in his resignation; and the club went across the river into Middlesex to find a coach.

The captain, Edrich, produced a rare moment when he recorded his hundredth hundred, but even then an occasion which should have riveted the attention passed almost unnoticed. It was nothing compared with the riotous scenes which greeted a similar milestone reached by Boycott a month later in the Headingley Test. The Oval was almost deserted and the game a certain draw when the Derbyshire captain, Eddie Barlow, signalled his willingness to continue into the extra time so that Edrich should have the chance of getting from 97 into three figures to put himself out of some considerable misery. Curiously Roope was the batting partner when first Edrich and then Boycott completed their hundredth hundred.

Edrich had been struggling mentally and physically for the century to add to his 99th, scored in his last match of 1976. Having succeeded, more flowed in each innings of the game against Kent, whereupon he went lame again, not to reappear until the last fixture. But at least Edrich had the memory of something well earned and well won to sustain him through his disappointing season. The award of the MBE in the Queen's Birthday Honours could not have been unconnected.

The century in each innings against Kent was the fourth such double recorded by Edrich, but even that match turned sour. The umpires cautioned the Surrey captain for "unfair play" when his bowlers reduced their output to eight overs in 40 minutes soon after Kent set off for a winning target. Such a happening was indicative of the season. If one thing went right, two went wrong. There seemed neither the will nor the skill to escape.

SURREY v DERBYSHIRE

At The Oval, July 9, 11, 12, 1977. Drawn. The big event came at 5.32 on the last day, but as the match was over as a contest then, and Derbyshire were staying on only as a gesture, much of the occasion was lost. The occurrence was John Edrich's hundredth hundred, for which he had waited since he scored his 99th on his last outing in 1976. Of the 16 players who had got to that mark before him, three were Surrey men, Tom Hayward, Sir Jack Hobbs and Andrew Sandham. Passing the milestone much relieved Edrich, not least of all as it helped him to forget that he had given Derbyshire first innings and seen Surrey struggle from the moment that Wright and Hill began to put together an opening stand of 152. Despite a century by Roope, of which the brightest part was a straight six which brought him to three figures, Surrey were contained for five and a half hours scoring 251. Derbyshire remained on top with the help of another century, this time by Harvey-Walker in his first match of the summer for the county. Surrey, set to score 321 runs in three hours, gave up when only 80 were forthcoming from the first hour, but Edrich continued to his successful conclusion.

Derbyshire 315 for four (100 overs) (J. G. Wright 86, A. Hill 77, E. J. Barlow 47, A. J. Borrington 51 not out, H. Cartwright 46) **and 256** for eight dec. (A. Hill 68, A. J. Harvey-Walker 101 not out; P. I. Pocock four for 65, A. Needham three for 65).

Surrey 251 for six dec. (J. H. Edrich 0, G. R. J. Roope 104, R. D. Jackman
53 not out; C. J. Tunnicliffe three for 44) **and 180** for three (J. H. Edrich
101 not out).

GRAHAM GOOCH Essex, Western Province
and England
ENGLAND IN INDIA AND SRI LANKA, 1992/93
by Peter Hayter, 1994

Certainly it was a strenuous tour physically and a stressful one
mentally. The mood of the party was not helped by the news they
received on arrival in Delhi, that Gooch's long-standing and
apparently solid marriage had foundered. At the start of a long
haul, during which players would be separated from wives and
young children in sometimes less-than-hospitable circumstances,
this may have affected some of them more than was at first
imagined. In the bar of the team's hotel on New Year's Eve, one
of the less experienced members of the party was in such distress
that he was already longing for home a mere four days into the
tour. The communal violence in the wake of the destruction of
the temple of Ayodhya that resulted in hundreds of deaths all
over India also created an unsettled atmosphere among the
squad.

In any circumstances other than dire necessity Gooch would
not have played [in the First Test] in Calcutta, and he did not in
Madras. Every member of the party went down with stomach
problems at some stage and all suffered from the 'flu virus that,
after he had witnessed at first hand the smog in the City of Joy,
led chairman of selectors Ted Dexter to announce a study into
the effects of air pollution on cricketers. Some suggested that, in
future, any player fortunate enough to be selected for India
should acclimatise by revving a car engine in a locked garage.

INDIAN UNDER-25 XI v ENGLAND XI

At Cuttack, January 23, 24, 25, 1993. Drawn. In contrast to the
previous 22 men who had reached the target, Graham Gooch
became the first batsman uncertain whether he had reached a
hundred hundreds or not. He made 102 in England's first innings,

just before his hundredth Test. Celebrations were somewhat muted since ICC was due to pronounce the following week on his century on the rebel tour of South Africa 11 years earlier. (Subsequently, ICC said this was not first-class but the decision was rejected by most statistical authorities, including *Wisden*.) Gooch retired at tea, allowing other players to get in some practice.

England XI 408 for four dec. (G. A. Gooch 102 retd hurt, A. J. Stewart 39, R. A. Smith 149 not out, M. W. Gatting 41) **and 146** for two dec. (M. A. Atherton 80 not out).

Indian Under-25 XI 273 (A. D. Jadeja 48, A. R. Khurasia 103, G. K. Pandey 54; I. D. K. Salisbury three for 77, D. E. Malcolm three for 3) **and 53** for one.

Notes by the Editor, *Wisden*, 1993

A first-class mess

I was starting to ruminate happily on these memories when news came through that the secretary of ICC had announced that he did not think the matches played on the rebel tours in South Africa before 1991 were first-class, which put many of the statistics in this and every other existing record book in doubt. His view was endorsed by the full ICC in the very week *Wisden* went to press. There was no time to alter the statistics in this edition; indeed a full year will hardly be enough.

I have never wavered in my view that the rebel tours were immoral. However, first-class status in cricket does not imply a moral judgment; in any case it is outrageous to make that judgment 11 years after the event. The matches palpably fitted ICC's own definition of what constitutes first-class cricket and *Wisden* strongly opposes any change in their status. Cricket's rulers did little to stop the tours when they were taking place. Now, when they are history, they have responded with a piece of vindictiveness that has a minimum effect on the players involved and a maximum effect on the integrity of the game's statistics. Do such details matter? I think so.

1994
CAMBRIDGE UNIVERSITY v ESSEX

At Cambridge, May 1, 2, 3, 1993. Drawn. When told that his hundredth first-class century, scored at Cuttack in January, was only reckoned to be his 99th by ICC, who did not recognise his matches for the South African Breweries XI as first-class, Gooch replied that he would have to get another against Cambridge. He duly passed the landmark with his second six and immediately walked off, disdaining the pretence of an injury; under Law 2.9, he was thus regarded as out.

Essex 323 (G. A. Gooch 105, N. Hussain 111, N. A. Foster 37; A. R. Whittall three for 85) **and 228** for four dec. (P. J. Prichard 54, N. V. Knight 94; R. M. Pearson three for 70).

Cambridge University 105 (J. P. Crawley 63; S. J. W. Andrew three for 47, T. D. Topley three for 15, J. H. Childs three for 11) **and 145** for three (J. P. Crawley 60, M. E. D. Jarrett 47).

W. G. GRACE Gloucestershire, London County and England
1896

No one interested in cricket will need to be told that Mr Grace last summer played with all the brilliancy and success of youth. In one respect, indeed, he surpassed all he had ever done before, scoring in the first month of the season 1,000 runs in first-class matches – a feat quite without parallel in the history of English cricket. As everyone knows, in the course of the month of May he made, on the Gloucestershire county ground at Ashley Down, Bristol, his hundredth hundred in first-class matches, this special circumstance being the origin of the national testimonial which was afterwards taken up with such enthusiasm in all parts of the country, and in many places far beyond the limits of the United Kingdom. It was not to be expected that Mr Grace would be able to quite keep up the form he showed in May, but he continued to bat marvellously well, and it is more than likely that, had the summer remained fine, he would have beaten his best aggregate in important cricket – 2,739 in the season of 1871. The chance of his doing this, however, was destroyed by the wet weather. He could not, at forty-seven years of age, overcome the difficulties of slow wickets as he might have done in his young days, and, though he again scored well as soon as the sunshine came back, there was no time left in which to break his previous record.

by A. G. Steel, 1896

Why has the name of W. G. Grace sunk so deeply into the hearts of all branches of the community? Firstly, because of the national love for the glorious game, and secondly, because of his wonderful skill and the unusual number of years he has maintained the position and name of "champion". It is as a batsman that he has earned this proud title, and it may be of interest to linger for a few moments on the characteristics of his style and play which in their combination have met with such phenomenal success. First of all, W. G. Grace obeys the fundamental rule of batting that is always instilled into young players as the first element of good batting; he keeps his right foot rigid and firm as a rock, and never does he move it during the actual stroke. (Alas! I never could grasp this rule myself or act up to it!) It is an exception, even to slow bowling, for W. G. to move his right foot. Once I remember (I wonder whether he does) him breaking this rule. During the compilation of one of his hundred centuries, in a match against the Australians at Lord's, he rushed out to hit the slow leg-break bowler (Cooper), missed, and after a somewhat undignified skurry back, just got the benefit from the umpire, a man subsequently not loved by the Australians.

GLOUCESTERSHIRE v SOMERSET

At Bristol, Thursday, Friday, Saturday, May 16, 17, 18, 1895. Though Fowler and Lionel Palairet opened the match by scoring 205 for the first Somerset wicket, Gloucestershire gained a brilliant victory by nine wickets. Everything in the game was dwarfed by Grace's big innings of 288, which was his hundredth three-figure score in important cricket. He was batting for five hours and 20 minutes without making a single mistake, his hitting at times being marked by all the vigour of his younger days. He was ninth out at 465, and among his hits were 38 fours, 11 threes and

29 twos. Townsend played a fine innings and helped his captain to put on 223 runs for the third wicket.

Somerset 303 (L. C. H. Palairet 80, G. Fowler 118; W. Murch four for 72, W. G. Grace five for 87) **and 189** (G. Fowler 33, H. T. Stanley 31, S. M. J. Woods 47; W. Murch eight for 68).

Gloucestershire 474 (W. G. Grace 288, C. L. Townsend 95, J. R. Painter 34; E. J. Tyler four for 160, S. M. J. Woods three for 145) **and 19** for one.

TOM GRAVENEY Gloucestershire,
Worcestershire, Queensland and England
1965

Worcestershire came within an ace of winning the County Championship in 1962. They even went as far as drinking their champagne, only for Yorkshire to ease them off the top in the very last match. This time [1964] they reserved celebrations on a sunny afternoon at Worcester on August 25 and it was two hours after their 16th win in 25 matches had been completed that news came from Southampton of Warwickshire's defeat. Only then did the corks pop again. The Championship had come to Worcestershire after 65 years of trying and a few months before the club became 100 years old.

Graveney enjoyed a glorious season with an aggregate of 2,385 runs, only 12 short of the best he has known in 16 years of first-class cricket. He played five three-figure innings, the third of which made him the 15th cricketer to hit a hundred centuries. In addition, he was twice out for 95 and played 14 other innings of 50 or over. He shared in nine of the side's three-figure partnerships.

by Sir Neville Cardus, 1965

Since Hammond's glorious reign, the character and economy have become tougher and tighter. Cricket everywhere, reflecting character and economy in the world at large, has tended to change from a sport and artistic spectacle to a competitive materialistic encounter, each contestant mainly setting his teeth not to lose. Batsmen not fit to tie Graveney's bootlaces, considered from the point of view of handsome, stroke-embedded play, have been encouraged to oust Graveney from Test matches stern and generally unbeautiful. "Style" has become a "corny" word everywhere, so it is natural enough that we have lived to see and extol an honest artisan such as Boycott building his brick wall of an innings, what time Graveney must needs content himself scoring felicitous runs for his adopted county.

Critics who think of Test matches as though they were of dire consequence to the nation politically, economically and what have you, have maintained that Graveney has on occasion "let England down". But nobody has claimed that Tom Graveney has ever "let cricket down". In form or out of form he has rendered tribute to the graces of cricket.

WORCESTERSHIRE v NORTHAMPTONSHIRE

At Worcester, August 5, 6, 7, 1964. Drawn. Rain interfered after Worcestershire had earned the two points which were to take them back to the top of the Championship table. Their big first-innings total reflected credit on Graveney, who hit his third hundred in six innings and in so doing became the 15th player to record one hundred centuries in first-class cricket. After a quiet start, he made some glorious strokes off both pace and spin, hitting 19 fours during an innings of just under five hours.

Worcestershire 309 for eight dec. (M. J. Horton 54, T. W. Graveney 132, R. Booth 51; D. S. Steele four for 65) **and 112** (R. G. A. Headley 36, T. W. Graveney 2; J. D. F. Larter five for 44, B. S. Crump four for 39).

Northamptonshire 212 (B. L. Reynolds 50, P. D. Watts 91; L. J. Coldwell three for 23, M. J. Horton four for 59) **and 142** for five (B. L. Reynolds 34, P. D. Watts 48).

FOR THE RECORD 1935

Going to Eton when ten as a colleger, Mr John Maude was there for nine years under three headmasters – Goodford, Balston and Hornby. His tutor was the Rev. J. E. Yonge. In his time he had three future bishops as fags – Welldon (Calcutta), Ryle (Liverpool) and Harmer (Rochester). He played in the Eton XI at Lord's as a medium left-hand bowler in 1868 and 1869.

WALLY HAMMOND Gloucestershire
and England
1936

The previous season, by consistently brilliant batting, Hammond secured the phenomenal average of 122. It was not expected he would repeat that performance [in 1935], neither was it anticipated that half the summer would go by before he scored a thousand runs. He came into his own again later on, and in the end his aggregate was greater than that of the previous year, but to secure it he took part in double the number of innings and they gave him an average of little more than a third of that of 1934. To begin with he seemed to be adapting his play to comply with the new lbw regulation, and it was only when he abandoned the effort that he scored with his old delightful ease and freedom.

GLOUCESTERSHIRE v SOMERSET

At Bristol, Wednesday, Thursday, Friday, June 12, 13, 14, 1935. Gloucestershire's victory by nine wickets – their first of the season – was rendered memorable by Hammond's hundredth hundred. Hammond had the utmost difficulty in scoring on a rain-affected pitch and he took four hours to achieve his great performance. At tea time on the second day he was 81, but he spent 70 minutes over the next 19 runs and meanwhile was twice missed. He hit eight fours in the hundred and altogether ten fours and a six. Between showers on Wednesday, Somerset were all out in two and a half hours. Gloucestershire finished only 34 behind with nine wickets in hand. Hammond was then 16 and next day, helped in turn by Sinfield and Neale, he went to the accomplishment of his feat.

Somerset 130 (J. W. Lee 31; T. W. Goddard five for 38) **and 223** (J. W. Lee 71, F. S. Lee 36, J. C. White 39; T. W. Goddard five for 69, C. W. L. Parker five for 89).

Gloucestershire 294 for six dec. (C. J. Barnett 57, R. A. Sinfield 31, W. R. Hammond 116, C. C. Dacre 31, W. L. Neale 39) **and 60** for one (C. C. Dacre 33, W. R. Hammond 6 not out).

TOM HAYWARD Surrey and England
1914

Hayward did not, in such a dry summer, have for him a remarkable record, but for a man of forty-two, who was in his 21st season for Surrey, an average of 34 with an aggregate of 1,326 runs must be considered very good indeed. As was only natural, he failed more often than he used to, but on his great days he was the real Hayward. During the season he and Hobbs beat the record in the number of first-wicket partnerships of over 100 runs.

SURREY v LANCASHIRE

At Kennington Oval, Thursday, Friday, Saturday, June 26, 27, 28, 1913. Left drawn, all in favour of Lancashire, this match went so much in the batsmen's way that 1,122 runs were scored for the loss of 26 wickets. The game was especially memorable for the achievement of Hayward in putting together his hundredth hundred in first-class cricket – a record which among all other batsmen W. G. Grace alone can claim. Surrey being engaged in a very uphill task all the time he was at the wickets, Hayward took four hours and 50 minutes to make his 139. On Thursday, when Lancashire scored 451 for six wickets, J. T. Tyldesley, batting with extraordinary ease and brilliancy, played one of the finest innings of his great career. He gave no chance of any kind during a stay of nearly four hours and a half. Hornby helped him to put on 176, and with the brothers Tyldesley [John and Ernest] together 177 runs were obtained. The two Tyldesleys had each played a three-figure innings earlier in the week.

Lancashire 558 (A. N. Hornby 86, J. T. Tyldesley 210, E. Tyldesley 110, R. A. Boddington 58 not out; J. W. Hitch four for 184, W. C. Smith four for 116).

Surrey 345 (T. W. Hayward 139, H. S. Harrison 39, C. T. A. Wilkinson 42, A. Sandham 33; R. Whitehead three for 93, W. Huddleston five for 76) and 219 for six (T. W. Hayward 7, J. B. Hobbs 61, E. G. Goatly 64, C. T. A. Wilkinson 30 not out).

"PATSY" HENDREN Middlesex and England
MCC TEAM IN AUSTRALIA, 1928/29
by S. J. Southerton, 1930

Hendren batted better than in any of his previous tours, his forward strokes which in most of his innings sent the ball careering past cover-point being a joy to see. At Brisbane [in the First Test] he gave a magnificent display of well-judged batting, playing carefully while the position was anxious and then hitting with tremendous power and certainty. His fielding, too, was uniformly brilliant.

MCC v VICTORIA

At Melbourne, Thursday, Friday, Saturday, Monday, November 1, 2, 3, 5, 1928. The run-getting powers of the MCC were further illustrated in the first match against Victoria, and the previously entertained ideas of the bowling being weak definitely dispelled. The match was drawn, rain interfering a good deal with the progress of the game, but England established a big advantage over their opponents. Batting first, Victoria were all out early on the second morning for 164 runs, their innings having lasted just over three hours. Light rain falling at intervals, the pitch, with the ball often getting up awkwardly, was entirely suited to Larwood's bowling, and he accomplished a great performance by taking the first seven wickets off the reel. With the score at 85, Larwood nearly did the hat-trick, getting Hartkopf and Scaife with following balls and, after almost bowling Ellis with his third, had him caught at second slip off the next . . . Woodfull carried his bat through the innings and gave a remarkable display. When only one, he was nearly bowled by Tate and near the end of the day he might have been run out; otherwise he made no mistake under conditions definitely against the batsman. Having disposed of their opponents so cheaply, the MCC proceeded to score runs with the utmost readiness and, batting until ten minutes to five on Saturday, put together in less than seven hours and a half a total of 486 . . . Hendren drove and hooked with great certainty during his stay of less than two hours and a quarter.

Victoria 164 (W. M. Woodfull 67 not out; H. Larwood seven for 51) **and 135** for no wkt (W. H. Ponsford 60 not out, H. S. T. L. Hendry 74 not out).

MCC 486 (J. B. Hobbs 51, D. R. Jardine 104, C. P. Mead 37, E. H. Hendren 100, A. P. F. Chapman 71, H. Larwood 79).

GRAEME HICK Zimbabwe, Worcestershire, Northern Districts, Queensland and England
1999

The happiest moment of the season occurred when Graeme Hick became the 24th player – and the second youngest – to complete a hundred hundreds, with his second century of the home match against Sussex at the end of May. Hick's early-season form, which brought him four hundreds in successive innings, earned him a Test recall after a two-year absence. But he could not deliver against South Africa. A century against Sri Lanka at The Oval was not enough to put him in the original winter Ashes party, though he was called up later to cover for injuries.

WORCESTERSHIRE v SUSSEX

At Worcester, May 29, 30, 31, June 1, 1998. Drawn. At 3.29 p.m. on the third afternoon, Graeme Hick, aged 32 years and eight days and playing his 574th first-class innings, flicked Robinson to mid-wicket. The two runs took him to his second hundred of the match (which he had achieved twice before) and his third in successive innings. It was also the hundredth of his career, a feat managed by just 23 others. Only one (Wally Hammond, by a fortnight) did it at a younger age, and only two (Bradman, 295, and Compton, 552) did it in fewer innings. Hick had announced his wish to reach the milestone either at New Road or in a Test. His exclusion from the squad for the First Test – announced that morning – may have spurred him to seize the first opportunity in front of his home crowd. Worcestershire president Tom Graveney, who had scored his own hundredth hundred on this ground in 1964, walked out to the middle with a bottle of cham-pagne and two glasses on a silver salver to toast the occasion. There had been less ceremony when Solanki, the batsman at the other end, reached his first Championship century two balls earlier, though it was, perhaps, the classier of the two innings. He and Hick put on 243 to help set a daunting target of 419. But after Sussex got to an unhurried 123 without loss, a lunch-time downpour ended any possibility of a late-afternoon run-chase.

Worcestershire 353 for nine dec. (G. A. Hick 104, T. M. Moody 48, D. A. Leatherdale 39, S. R. Lampitt 31 not out; J. D. Lewry four for 104) **and 343** for three dec. (V. S. Solanki 155, G. A. Hick 132).

Sussex 278 (M. G. Bevan 96, J. R. Carpenter 33, S. Humphries 43, extras 42; S. R. Lampitt five for 56) **and 123** for no wkt (M. T. E. Peirce 51 not out, W. G. Khan 53 not out).

JACK HOBBS Surrey and England
1924

Hobbs had, for him, a moderate year, but on occasions he was as clearly as ever the best bat in England. It is literally the truth to say that fortune was unkind to him. Whenever he gave a chance it was snapped up, and at times he fell to catches in odd positions in the field. Though less easily fatigued than in the previous year he had not the full physical strength that was his before his operation and illness in 1921. It struck one that not infrequently he lost his innings through his old fault of over-eagerness to turn the straight ball without waiting to get the pace of the wicket. At Bath in Surrey's second match he scored the hundredth century of his career, in recognition of which feat the Surrey club made him a present of 100 guineas.

SOMERSET v SURREY

At Bath, Saturday, Monday, Tuesday, May 5, 7, 8, 1923. A match full of incident was made memorable by the fact of Hobbs getting his hundredth century in first-class cricket. So bad was the weather that the first day's cricket was limited to three overs without a run, and on Monday Ducat alone saved Surrey from utter collapse. He was lucky in having two escapes, but played great cricket all the same. Not out 19 in Surrey's second innings at the close of play, Hobbs found an invaluable partner on

Tuesday in Hitch, the two batsmen putting on 121 runs together for the fifth wicket. At the wickets three hours and a half, Hobbs hit three sixes in his splendid innings. Fender took a great risk in declaring, as he left Somerset plenty of time in which to get the 168 runs required, but, as Surrey had been behind on the first innings, he went out for a win at all costs. So long as M. D. Lyon stayed, Somerset had a good chance of victory, but in the end Surrey won by ten runs.

Surrey 91 (J. B. Hobbs 0, A. Ducat 52 not out; E. Robson six for 59,
    J. C. White four for 27) **and 216** for five dec. (J. B. Hobbs 116 not out,
    J. W. Hitch 67).
Somerset 140 (M. D. Lyon 39; R. F. Lowe four for 51, W. J. Abel three for
    6) **and 157** (P. G. H. Fender four for 61, H. A. Peach three for 39).

LEN HUTTON Yorkshire and England
1952

Hutton took time to readjust himself from the heat and hard grounds of Australia to the bitter cold and soft turf of England in May. When acclimatised, he showed all his greatness in conditions compelling other batsmen to struggle for survival.

SURREY v YORKSHIRE

At The Oval, July 14, 16, 17, 1951. Drawn. This match was memorable for the performance of Hutton in completing his century of centuries. After Surrey had broken down when the pitch gave a little help to the bowlers, Hutton and Lowson took charge and at the end of the first day their unfinished stand had realised 112. Hutton then wanted 39 runs for his hundred and on Monday 15,000 people turned up. They were not disappointed and Hutton achieved his objective with a stroke worthy of the occasion – a superb drive off Wait sped past cover-point to the boundary. Altogether the opening partnership produced 197 and Hutton, who batted faultlessly for four hours 40 minutes, hit 12 fours. Surrey looked in a hopeless position when they batted again 275 behind, but Yorkshire dropped vital catches and finally found themselves wanting 43 in 20 minutes. In a hectic scramble for runs, they paid the penalty for hitting recklessly at every ball, and although they raced to and fro from the pavilion gate the task was beyond them.

Surrey 156 (T. H. Clark 47; F. S. Trueman three for 52, R. Appleyard three for 53, N. W. D. Yardley three for 28) **and 317** (M. R. Barton 39, B. Constable 47, L. B. Fishlock 89, A. J. McIntyre 32; J. H. Wardle three for 83, E. Leadbeater four for 112).

Yorkshire 431 for three dec. (L. Hutton 151, F. A. Lowson 84, J. V. Wilson 114 not out, W. G. Keighley 45) **and 30** for six (L. Hutton 5).

PHILIP MEAD Hampshire and England
1928

Philip Mead, as in so many previous seasons, proved the mainstay of the side in batting, once again making more than 2,000 runs for Hampshire and coming out on this occasion with the splendid average of 75. Still perhaps as difficult a man to bowl as any in England, he played some wonderful innings, showing remarkable skill and judgment and never allowing himself to be worried by any adverse state of the game. Often, indeed, the more anxious the position, the finer his cricket. His great period of success was between the latter part of May and the last few days of June, when in nine matches he played 14 innings, four times not out, and registered 1,257 runs with an average of 125. His scores during those five weeks included 187 against Gloucestershire, 108 not out against Kent, 200 not out against Essex, 183 against Yorkshire and 141 against Northamptonshire (at Southampton). In scoring 100 not out against Northamptonshire at Kettering in July, Mead attained the great distinction of completing his hundredth century in first-class cricket.

NORTHAMPTONSHIRE v HAMPSHIRE

At Kettering, Saturday, Monday, Tuesday, July 16, 18, 19, 1927. Mead made this match memorable by putting together his hundredth hundred in first-class cricket – a feat previously accomplished only by W. G. Grace, Hayward and Hobbs. He batted with unusual freedom to attain that distinction, his brilliant partnership with Tennyson on the last afternoon yielding 195 in 100 minutes, but the Hampshire captain, in delaying a declaration until half-past three, lost whatever chance there existed of forcing a win.

Hampshire 235 (J. A. Newman 80, G. Brown 49, C. P. Mead 34;
   V. W. C. Jupp six for 71) **and 358** for four dec. (J. A. Newman 62,
   G. Brown 34, C. P. Mead 100 not out, Hon. L. H. Tennyson 116 not
   out).
Northamptonshire 227 (C. N. Woolley 30, A. P. R. Hawtin 43;
   A. S. Kennedy five for 52) **and 28** for one.

VIV RICHARDS Leeward Islands, Combined
Islands, Somerset, Queensland, Glamorgan
and West Indies
by David Foot, 1990

At Sydney, in November 1988 against New South Wales, Richards became the first West Indian to complete a hundred first-class hundreds. In his previous innings – the first of the tour – he had fashioned his 99th, against South Australia. Clearly the procrastinations had gone on long enough. That particular landmark was overdue. In any case, he hated all the talk about records.

His inclusion, as No. 22 on the illustrious list, was always a matter of inevitability. Judged by his own expansive, often sublime, at times savage standards, the surprise was that the milestone took him so long. It was still achieved out of only 658 innings. Yet if the mind, the mood, the fitness and the circumstances had combined rather more felicitously, his statistics would have carried a greater dramatic eloquence. As it was, only Bradman (295), Compton (552), Hutton (619) and Boycott (645) had got there in fewer innings. Of that contrasting quartet, he would be most flattered to be compared with Compton, because of his impish disregard for reputation and his innate sense of adventure. There was a time, early in his career, when Richards was being dubbed "the black Bradman". It was an absurd analogy: their styles and attitudes were so dissimilar. Almost certainly the great Don kept a furtive eye on the scoreboard a great deal more than does Richards. I. V. A. could actually look fallible, and that was an integral part of his charm and his genius.

NEW SOUTH WALES v WEST INDIANS
by John Woodcock, 1990

At Sydney, November 11, 12, 13, 14, 1988. Drawn. On the third afternoon Richards became the 22nd cricketer to have scored 100 first-class centuries. "I'm not an individual who savours these things, but I'm proud to be the first West Indian to reach this particular landmark," he said. His 658th first-class innings lasted for 170 balls, contained 15 fours and a six, and pulled the West Indians round when they were struggling to find an adequate reply to New South Wales's large first-innings total. Once the tourists had saved the follow-on, there was no attempt to achieve a definite result.

New South Wales 401 for eight dec. (J. Dyson 79, M. A. Taylor 82, S. B. Smith 63, P. L. Taylor 50 not out, G. C. Dyer 33; I. V. A. Richards two for 46) **and 261** for one dec. (J. Dyson 100 not out, M. A. Taylor 49, M. E. Waugh 103 not out).

West Indians 329 (R. B. Richardson 41, I. V. A. Richards 101, R. A. Harper 46; G. F. Lawson five for 69) **and 156** for four (D. L. Haynes 52, K. L. T. Arthurton 57 not out).

ANDREW SANDHAM Surrey and England
1936

In getting 103 runs against Hampshire at Basingstoke, Sandham registered his hundredth hundred in first-class cricket, 64 of which he has made in the County Championship. It is worth recording that Sandham, who took his second benefit in the match against Kent and is approaching the end of his career, has scored at least one hundred against each county with the exception of Gloucestershire and Worcestershire.

NOTE: Sandham hit a hundred against Gloucestershire in 1937 when, *Wisden* reports, "He finished the season by hitting a hundred at Hove and then without any fuss or bother he allowed the county to announce his retirement. Associated with Surrey as far back as 1911, Sandham,

during his first-class career, scored 41,165 runs and hit 107 hundreds
with an average of 44.99 runs an innings. For 18 successive seasons he
made over 1,000 runs and eight times exceeded the 2,000 mark.
Always placing first the interests of his side, Sandham has been the
model professional." Three first-class games for Sir Theodore Brinck-
man's XI v All Argentine in 1937/38 took Sandham's aggregate to
41,284 runs, average 44.82.

HAMPSHIRE v SURREY

At Basingstoke, Wednesday, Thursday, June 26, 27, 1935. In the
first match to be played at Basingstoke for 21 years, Surrey won
readily by an innings and seven runs. The home county in both
innings had the worst of the wicket. Following storms on Tuesday night, Lowndes decided, with disastrous consequences, to
take first innings, and in an hour and three-quarters Hampshire
were all out, the one stand coming from Mead and Lowndes, who
added 33. Sandham and Gregory driving and pulling admirably
during an opening partnership of 84, Surrey took the lead without loss, and Sandham went on to complete his hundredth
century in first-class cricket. Batting three hours and a half, he
offered one chance and hit a six and 11 fours.

Hampshire 79 (A. R. Gover four for 21, P. G. H. Fender three for 27) **and**
    188 (J. Arnold 56, C. P. Mead 32; A. R. Gover three for 51,
    P. G. H. Fender four for 64).
Surrey 274 (A. Sandham 103, R. J. Gregory 51, L. B. Fishlock 56;
    W. L. Creese three for 43, G. Hill five for 46).

HERBERT SUTCLIFFE Yorkshire and England
1933

Sutcliffe, however, has probably never batted better in the whole
of his famous career [than he did in 1932]. Playing in Championship matches 35 innings as against 27 in the previous season, he
increased his aggregate from 2,049 to 2,624, and if his average fell
from 97 to 87 he shared altogether in 19 three-figure partnerships
– four with Holmes to bring up to 73 that famous pair's record
of putting on a hundred for the first wicket. Twelve times in

competition games he reached three figures, his triumphs including a score of 313 against Essex, when he and Holmes broke the first-wicket record at Leyton, putting on 555, and 270 obtained at the expense of the Sussex bowlers at Leeds. As he followed his huge innings at Leyton with one of 194 at Scarborough, his two appearances against the Essex bowlers yielded him 507 runs. Like practically all great batsmen, he was generally at much pains to play himself in, and at times his cricket – even when well set – proved rather more restrained than the situation warranted. But on most occasions he, no doubt, felt that a heavy responsibility rested upon him. How he could hit when he considered he might set about run-getting in light-hearted fashion, he showed in his 194 at Scarborough. Not only did he achieve such great things for Yorkshire but for the third year in succession he brought his season's aggregate in first-class matches to 3,000.

YORKSHIRE v GLOUCESTERSHIRE

At Bradford, Wednesday, Thursday, Friday, July 6, 7, 8, 1932. Declaring in each innings, Yorkshire defeated Gloucestershire by 133 runs but the victory was not obtained until what, in any circumstances, must have been the last over of the match. Holmes and Sutcliffe, despite indifferent light, put on 161 runs in the first innings and so registered their 71st three-figure first-wicket partnership. Hammond gave a glorious display for Gloucestershire, hitting up in two hours and ten minutes 147 out of 191 and having six sixes and 18 fours among his strokes. Sutcliffe, making his hundredth hundred in first-class cricket, played so brilliantly in the second innings that he scored 132 in 115 minutes. He gave no chance and hit eight sixes and eight fours. Yorkshire registered 240 runs at the rate of 125 an hour. Gloucestershire at six o'clock, with Hammond unbeaten, had five wickets to fall.

Yorkshire 472 for seven dec. (P. Holmes 81, H. Sutcliffe 83, A. Mitchell 177 not out, W. Barber 62) **and 240** for six dec. (H. Sutcliffe 132, M. Leyland 58; C. W. L. Parker three for 81).

Gloucestershire 404 (R. A. Sinfield 110, W. R. Hammond 147, C. C. Dacre 71 not out; G. G. Macaulay four for 103) **and 175** (R. A. Sinfield 36,

W. R. Hammond 71 not out; G. G. Macaulay five for 67, H. Verity four for 54).

GLENN TURNER Otago, Worcestershire, Northern Districts and New Zealand
1983

Turner opened up with his 99th century in the first match of the season, scoring an unbeaten 239 against Oxford University. On May 29, against Warwickshire, he completed his hundredth hundred with one of the greatest innings of his career. It had to be seen to be believed: 128 out of 181 for none at lunch; 254 out of 389 for one at tea; 300 in 336 minutes, and 311 not out out of 501 for one declared. Two more centuries took him past Don Kenyon's record of 70 hundreds for Worcestershire, and another against Kent at Hereford, in what proved to be his final Championship match, left him with a first-class average of 90.07 for the season. An appendix operation at the end of July cut short a season in which he felt he was batting as well as at any time in his career.

NOTE: Turner retired from first-class cricket at the end of the 1982/83 New Zealand season. He was the first to reach his hundredth hundred with a century before lunch on the opening day, and his 311 not out was the highest innings by a batsman reaching this milestone.

WORCESTERSHIRE v WARWICKSHIRE

At Worcester, May 29, 31, June 1, 1982. Drawn. Turner launched an amazing assault on the Warwickshire attack to complete his hundredth century in first-class cricket, going on to compile a career-best 311 not out on the opening day. His triple-hundred was a record for Worcestershire, beating Fred Bowley's 276 against Hampshire in 1914, and he became the first batsman to score 300 runs in a day in England since J. D. Robertson achieved the feat for Middlesex, against Worcestershire, in 1949. Turner reached his first 50 in 34 minutes, was 128 at lunch, and in all he batted for 343 minutes, hitting two sixes and 39 fours. But Kallicharran, with a career-best 235, ensured that Warwickshire avoided the follow-on, although in their second innings, needing 289 to win in 197 minutes, they were always batting to save the game as the spinners achieved increasing turn from the wearing wicket.

Worcestershire 501 for one dec. (G. M. Turner 311 not out, J. A. Ormrod 79, D. N. Patel 88 not out) **and 167** for six dec. (G. M. Turner 32, J. A. Ormrod 43).

Warwickshire 380 for nine dec. (D. L. Amiss 64, A. I. Kallicharran 235, K. D. Smith 31; R. K. Illingworth four for 85) **and 197** for five (A. I. Kallicharran 35, K. D. Smith 62 not out, Asif Din 39).

ERNEST TYLDESLEY Lancashire and England
1935

While advance in attack accounted chiefly for Lancashire's winning the title in 1934, batting remained the side's chief asset. For Ernest Tyldesley the season brought special distinction. Playing seven separate three-figure innings, with 239 against Glamorgan at Cardiff as the highest obtained for his county during the summer, Tyldesley placed a hundredth century to his name. Also he made 2,000 runs for the sixth time. To these unequalled accomplishments for Lancashire he added the further record of exceeding the aggregate of 32,267 runs scored for the county by his brother, John Tyldesley.

Few people with memories long enough to recall the special qualities of J. T. Tyldesley – an England batsman for many years – would go so far as to say that Ernest was superior. He has never possessed the elder brother's exceptional forcing powers, but ability in cutting and off-driving stand out as family characteristics, and Ernest, besides being the most consistent scorer and the most ready hitter of centuries, is now the most prolific run-getter of all time. He scored 835 more runs than in 1933, with an average increased by over 16. In view of such form at the age of 45 it came as a surprise that Ernest Tyldesley stated he would retire from first-class cricket. Happily he changed his mind, and at the dinner celebrating the Championship he modestly said he would play so long as Lancashire had room for him in the eleven.

NORTHAMPTONSHIRE v LANCASHIRE

At Peterborough, Saturday, Monday, Tuesday, July 7, 9, 10, 1934. For the second time in a week Northamptonshire were defeated by Lancashire in an innings. On this occasion the ultimate winners of the Championship had 68 runs to spare and were never in any way extended. The outstanding feature of the first day was the achievement by Ernest Tyldesley of scoring his hundredth century in first-class cricket. Drives, cuts and leg-side strokes brought him 13 fours in an innings noteworthy to a large degree by its sound defence. Still, he scored very quickly at times and his partnership with Paynter realised 227 runs in three and a half hours.

Lancashire 409 (F. Watson 39, J. Iddon 41, E. Tyldesley 122, E. Paynter 89, W. H. L. Lister 48, L. W. Parkinson 30; A. D. Matthews five for 74, T. A. Pitt four for 95).

Northamptonshire 200 (A. H. Bakewell 62, J. E. Timms 38, G. G. Tebbitt 41; F. M. Sibbles three for 43, L. W. Parkinson five for 31) **and 141** (A. H. Bakewell 50; F. M. Sibbles six for 47, L. W. Parkinson three for 53).

FRANK WOOLLEY Kent and England
1930

If their figures generally did not come up to expectations in 1929, Woolley and Hardinge accomplished some remarkable performances. Woolley made four consecutive centuries and took part with Hardinge in successive stands of 255 against Derbyshire at Chesterfield, 134 against Somerset, 239 against Yorkshire – both at Tonbridge – and 228 against Hampshire at Folkestone. In these games Woolley scored 155, 108, 131 and 117; altogether he scored seven separate hundreds in Championship innings.

MIDDLESEX v KENT

At Lord's, Wednesday, Thursday, Friday, August 28, 29, 30, 1929. Frank Woolley on the opening day of this match enjoyed the distinction of putting together the hundredth three-figure innings of his career. On a pitch off which the ball at times rose awkwardly, he showed all his well-known skill, freedom and finish and, apart from one chance from a big on-drive, made no real mistake. Fifth out at 302, he scored 176 of that number in three hours and a half with 18 fours as his chief strokes. Kent next day disposed of Middlesex cheaply but Legge, despite a lead of 212, did not make them follow on. Bryan, withstanding the Middlesex attack for three hours, carried his bat through Kent's second innings. Wanting 399 for victory, Middlesex made a highly creditable effort to accomplish the task, but lost by 87 runs.

Kent 380 (F. E. Woolley 176, L. E. G. Ames 31, L. J. Todd 44, W. H. Ashdown 34; N. E. Haig three for 95, R. W. V. Robins four for 82) **and 186** (J. L. Bryan 93 not out, F. E. Woolley 2; R. W. V. Robins four for 47, I. A. R. Peebles three for 33).

Middlesex 168 (R. W. V. Robins 37; A. P. Freeman five for 77, L. J. Todd three for 27) **and 311** (J. W. Hearne 49, E. H. Hendren 64, R. W. V. Robins 59, W. F. Price 31; G. G. Beslee four for 61, A. P. Freeman three for 118).

CORRECTIONS
BY THE EDITOR, WISDEN, 1935

Mr E. L. Bartlett, West Indies, of whom an obituary notice appeared in last year's issue of the Almanack, wrote from Bridgetown in March with the assurance "that I am very much alive and fit". It is a pleasure to publish this message sent to me.

1947

In the 1946 *Wisden* there occurred an error. The inclusion of Mr Frank Evershed in the obituary notices was incorrect. Mr Henry Ellis, of Burton-on-Trent, informed me of the mistake, to which I call attention, with the hope that Mr Evershed long may remain an active partner with Messrs Talbot & Co.

1983

The opening paragraph of the match report on the Fourth Test [Pakistan v West Indies, 1980/81] states that the start of play was delayed by the late arrival of an umpire. This is incorrect. Such a delay occurred at the start of play on the fourth day of the Third Test at Karachi.

ZAHEER ABBAS Karachi, Gloucestershire, PWD, Dawood Industries, Sind, PIA and Pakistan
by David Green, 1984

Zaheer, or "Zed" as he has been almost universally known since his association with Gloucestershire began in 1972, has already made well over 30,000 runs at an average of comfortably more than 50, and on December 12, 1982, his 215 for Pakistan against India at Lahore was his hundredth first-class hundred. By September 1983 he had made a century in each innings of a match on eight occasions, and on four of them one of the centuries was a "double"; both are feats unparalleled in the annals of the game. In Test matches he had scored his 4,000th run and was averaging 46.81.

Like all great players, he has an uncomplicated method. It is based first on correct footwork, so that he is positioned advantageously in relation to the length and line of each delivery. Secondly, though his backswing may not please the purist, the bat's downward path, which is much more important, is so strictly vertical as to satisfy the most pernickety geometrician. His power is derived from a high backlift, sweet timing and wristy acceleration of the blade at the moment of impact. It is this wristiness, together with the consequent free follow-through, that gives his batting its seductive bloom. When watching him, I am constantly reminded of Beldham's photographic studies of the heroes of cricket's Golden Age – of Fry, Trumper, Ranji and MacLaren.

by Qamar Ahmed, 1984
PAKISTAN v INDIA
First Test Match

At Lahore, December 10, 11, 12, 14, 15, 1982. Drawn. The match, though rain-affected, was a statistician's delight. Pakistan thrashed the Indian attack to the tune of 485 after Gavaskar had put them in. Zaheer's 215 was his hundredth first-class century – he became the 20th batsman to have achieved this great feat – and his ninth for Pakistan. He batted for five and a half hours, hitting two sixes and 23 fours. Mohsin Khan became the first Pakistani to complete 1,000 Test runs in a calendar year, his century being his fourth in Test matches, three of them at the Gaddafi Stadium, Lahore in 1982. Sarfraz took four for 63 in India's innings, having changed his mind about retiring. For India, Amarnath made his third Test century, reached in 383 minutes, and Gavaskar passed 7,000 runs in Tests, a feat achieved only by Boycott, Cowdrey, Hammond and Sobers. A draw became virtually inevitable after rain and bad light had accounted for 235 minutes on the first and third days.

Pakistan 485 (Mohsin Khan 94, Mudassar Nazar 50, Zaheer Abbas 215, Imran Khan 45; Madan Lal three for 101, D. R. Doshi five for 90) **and 135** for one (Mohsin Khan 101 not out).

India 379 (S. M. Gavaskar 83, Arun Lal 51, M. Amarnath 109 not out, S. M. Patil 68, extras 31; Imran Khan three for 68, Sarfraz Nawaz four for 63).

ANIMAL CRACKERS

"It was always our custom," Sir Compton Mackenzie recalled in *Wisden* 1973, "to talk of some famous cricketers by their Christian names – Archie MacLaren, Sammy Woods, Bobby Abel, Tom Richardson – and of others by their initials: L. C. H. and R. C. N. (Palairet), W. W. (Read) and of course the mighty W. G."

Wisden, by and large, has disdained too much familiarity. Until the 1980s, the Almanack mostly referred to players by their surnames in match reports, county reviews and the like, although amateurs, in the days of separate dressing-rooms, were sometimes given initials. First names rarely got a look-in, except for feature articles and obituaries. But then *Wisden* readers were familiar with the rubric; they enjoyed partaking in the freemasonry.

When it comes to nicknames, *Wisden* editors have generally and wisely confined them to the cutting-room floor. Occasionally there has been a "known in the cricket world as 'Tich' " – and it would have been a courageous sub who prevented Lord Harris from referring to his old friend, "Buns" Thornton. But there's no "Guy the Gorilla" Botham, "Goose" Willis or "Tiger" Lillee; not that I've noticed, anyway, although they may be lurking among the leaves somewhere. The feline Peter has an obituary in *Wisden*, but that other Lord's cat was always Philip, Phil or P. C. R. Tufnell. Never "The Cat" until he called it a day, whereupon he got a headline. Quite right, too. *Wisden* has gathered a useful little menagerie over the years, even if there have been a surfeit of ducks and all too few canards.

MONKEY 1926

A. N. Hornby, the famous batsman who captained Lancashire for nearly 20 seasons, and whose association with that county as a player extended over a period of 33 years, was born at Blackburn on February 10, 1847. Going up to Harrow in 1862, he played against Eton at Lord's in 1864 and 1865, his first appearance there taking place 13 days before that of W. G. Grace. At that time, Hornby was of such slight physique that he weighed ("bat and all" according to one account) less than six stone. For many seasons one of the leading English batsmen, Hornby had an attractive forward style and possessed splendid punishing powers which he used freely. In addition, he was a magnificent field, and as captain so firm, keen and genial that he could always get the best out of the men under his charge. His dashing methods, coupled with his obvious enthusiasm – he appeared thoroughly to enjoy every moment he was on the field – made him a general favourite wherever he went.

A characteristic tale of the famous batsman concerned the Gentlemen and Players match at The Oval in 1881. Hornby and W. G. Grace had given the amateurs a capital start when, from a powerful drive, Hornby was magnificently caught high up in the long-field by William Gunn, who stood some six feet three inches in height. "Bad luck, Monkey," said a friend as Hornby passed into the pavilion. "Yes," answered Hornby, "no one but a damned giraffe would have got near it."

TIGERS

by Rowland Ryder, 1980

Ernest James Smith – for over 70 years he had been known as "Tiger", although a few Warwickshire associates called him Jim – was born in Benacre Street, Birmingham; a street which has now disappeared, that area of Birmingham having been replaced by a series of ring roads, underpasses and flyovers near the centre of the city. But it used to be about a mile from the Edgbaston ground, and four months after "Tiger" Smith was born, Warwickshire played their first match at Edgbaston.

In 1902 Edgbaston became a Test match venue, and on May

31, thanks to Wilfred Rhodes, England bowled Australia out for 36. Young Smith was working at Cadbury's then, and two years later he offered his services to Warwickshire as a wicket-keeper, although he had lost the tips of two fingers in a works accident. For a time he was seconded to the MCC. It was during this period that he met W. G. Grace, and played in several matches for and against Grace's London County eleven. "Do you know what he'd do if he thought you weren't any good?" chuckled "Tiger". "He'd go out and buy a rabbit and put it in your cricketing bag."

1993

Bill "Tiger" O'Reilly was unquestionably one of cricket's great figures: as a player, as a character and later as a writer on the game. He bowled leg-breaks and, especially, top-spinners and googlies, backed up by an intimidating manner. It has been suggested that his action and the general commotion before delivery were born of frustration at not being able to bowl fast enough to knock the batsman down. Off the field, his gruffness was mitigated by his intelligence, erudition, wit and twinkling eyes.

O'Reilly was born in White Cliffs in the New South Wales bush into a large Irish family on December 20, 1905. His father was a small-town schoolmaster and young Bill was above average at several sports, including tennis, athletics and rugby. Cricket was harder to arrange. According to Jack Fingleton in *Cricket Crisis*, the four O'Reilly brothers played with a gum-wood bat and a piece of banksia root chiselled down to make a ball. In 1917 the family moved to Wingello. When he played his first match for Wingello Juniors, the team walked to the opposition's ground seven miles away in Tallong, with their dogs chasing rabbits along the way.

by John Arlott, 1970

The Nawab of Pataudi's autobiography, *Tiger's Tale*, "as told to Kenneth Wheeler", is of interest. It is the first book, so far as I know, to give an inside view of Indian cricket and some of its historic moments of the past decade. On the subject of his Indian background, Pataudi clears some misconceptions and misreportings, and the passage about his eye injury and its effect on his cricket is both revealing and free from self-pity.

THE BULL 1995

Jack Cowie played in only nine Tests, owing to World War II and New Zealand's limited international programme. But a couple of generations later his career might have been very different. He is widely regarded as New Zealand's best-ever bowler apart from Sir Richard Hadlee, with similar command of line and length for long spells, and the same ability to move the ball sharply at high speed. He also had something of Hadlee's aggression. Cowie was a very strong man known to his team-mates as "Bull" and his trade-mark was a hand-raised appeal-cum-roar of "Aaaaaa?" though his next remark to the umpire could be: "You know, I reckon it's getting a bit chilly. D'you think I could have my sweater?"

CATS AND DOGS

1964

Cat, Peter, whose ninth life ended on November 5, 1964, was a well-known cricket-watcher at Lord's, where he spent 12 of his 14 years. He preferred a close-up view of the proceedings and his sleek, black form could often be seen prowling on the field of play when the crowds were biggest. He frequently appeared on the television screen. Mr S. C. Griffith, secretary of MCC, said of him: "He was a cat of great character and loved publicity."

1987

A left-arm spin bowler, "Puss" Achong was the first cricketer of Chinese extraction to play Test cricket, appearing for West Indies in six matches against England and taking eight wickets at 47.25. Chosen to tour England in 1933, he played in all three Tests but with limited success, and in all first-class matches that season took 71 wickets. Essentially an orthodox slow left-armer, at Manchester he had Robins stumped by a ball which, bowled with a wrist-spinner's action, turned into the right-hander from the off and gave rise to the use in England of the word "chinaman" to describe such a delivery.

1962

Albert Charles Russell was the first English batsman to hit a century in each innings of a Test match. This he did against South Africa at Durban in 1923 when he scored 140 and 111 and played a leading part in England's rubber-winning victory by 109 runs. The performance was the more remarkable because "Jack" Russell, as he was generally known, "had", *Wisden* recorded at the time, "to battle against illness; when he started his second innings he ought to have been in bed rather than on the cricket field."

Son of Tom Russell, for many years Essex wicket-keeper, Jack was born near the county ground at Leyton. He assisted Essex from 1908 to 1930 and in all matches during that time he scored 27,358 runs, including 71 centuries, average 41.57, obtained 283 wickets with slow bowling for 26.90 runs each and brought off 313 catches, principally in the slips, where he excelled.

by Colin Bateman, 1990

Robert Charles (Jack) Russell was born in Stroud on August 15, 1963. He played cricket for his local comprehensive school and at Stroud Cricket Club with his father, John. As captain of the boys' team, young Jack – he has always been Jack – gave himself the honour of opening the batting and bowling. Then, two days before his fourteenth birthday, he saw a catch on television that changed his life. "McCosker ... caught Knott ... bowled Greig. Headingley '77." He reels it off as if it were yesterday. "Low down, one-handed, across first slip. Brilliant. I thought then that I would like to be able to do that. That's where it started, that was the inspiration."

Russell was soon a boy among men in Stroud's first team alongside his father, and within four years he was keeping wicket for Gloucestershire's first team. Derbyshire's England wicket-keeper of the time, Bob Taylor, soon saw a like spirit and talent in the quiet, slight lad with the West Country accent and gave Russell all the help he could. More recently Alan Knott has turned from being boyhood hero to friend and adviser, helping Russell toughen his mental approach for the five-day game, whether keeping or batting.

When he wants to relax, it is not with the headphones and lager can to which most of his colleagues turn. Rather it is an adventure out into the local surroundings, whether that be the tranquil banks of the Severn in Worcester or the teeming shanty towns of Bombay, sketchbook, pencil and camera in hand. Russell has discovered a penchant for drawing, and the hobby he took up to pass the time on rain-affected summer afternoons has become a second profession. His work has created such an impression that he has had books published and his work exhibited in a London gallery. Jack Russell, the keeper with drawing power.

BIRDLAND
1989

A 6ft 2in tall right-hand bat and fast-medium swing bowler, Hunter Hendry went straight from Sydney Grammar School into first-grade cricket, where his gangling build, especially his long legs, quickly earned him the sobriquet "Stork" from M. A. Noble, who as a young man had not been of such a different physique himself. Hendry made full use of his height, reaching into the drive or powerfully cutting and hooking the rising ball. His long arms made him an awkward bowler to judge, and he was an outstanding fielder. His combination with Gregory in the slips on the 1921 tour of England was described as "beyond praise".

by Doug Insole, 1995

On the South African tour of 1956/57, Peter [May] began with four consecutive hundreds. At a reception in Salisbury (now Harare), the city's mayor presented him with a live duck and expressed the patriotic hope that it might have a debilitating effect on his future performances. From that point on, he struggled to reach double figures. After getting out to yet another magnificent catch late in the Test series he came back to the dressing-room, threw his bat on his bag, and said, "That ———— duck." He did not often swear.

by John Arlott, 1989

"Big Bird" Flying High is the autobiography of Joel Garner, the impressively tall Barbadian fast bowler who made the ball rear so

high off a length that many of the best batsmen in the world found him uniquely difficult to play. His experiences in Barbados, in the Lancashire League, with Somerset and, above all, in Test matches for West Indies, are the theme of his book; and the final chapter consists of a conversation between Joel Garner and Big Bird on the subject of his leaving Somerset. "I had not really wanted to talk about the more disenchanting aspects of my stay with Somerset," he remarks.

1980

England's captain, Mike Brearley, itemised another advantage of Garner's height. "The trouble is that Garner's hand delivers over the top of the sightscreen, which makes him impossible to sight early. When you have one ball getting up chest high and another coming in at your toenails, it's jolly difficult to survive."

by Bruce Wilson, 1998

Friends who were there recall a day last year, deep in the Queensland bush "out the back of Longreach", on a pig-shooting weekend with the man they call "Pigeon" and the cricketing world knows as Glenn McGrath. The tall fast bowler had spotted a large boar, and he disappeared into the bush in hot pursuit. Three shots were heard, and McGrath came loping back into view, reached into the four-wheel drive, said "Out of ammo", and loped off again, all at the same relentless, steady pace. He got the pig. It is a story many who have played against him will recognise uneasily; wild boar or batsman, Glenn McGrath tends to get what he is hunting.

WELL, I DECLARE 1996

Easterbrook was a much-loved member of the press corps with a puckish humour. He claimed that while covering a match from the old Lord's press box, he leaned out of the window to throw away his pencil shavings and the Nottinghamshire batsmen walked in, thinking it was the signal to declare. Once he phoned his office to dictate his copy, announced his name to the telephonist – "Basil V. Easterbrook" – to be greeted by the response, "What league is that in?"

HEROES AND VILLAINS

Sport can be notoriously fickle when it comes to herocs, and cricket is no exception. "W. G. – Champion and Rotter" touted *Wisden*'s front cover in 1998: "Geoffrey Moorhouse on a flawed master." And this on the 150th anniversary of the old boy's birth to boot! No wonder Sir Donald Bradman kept going till he was 92. He must have relished holding off the jackals and the jack-asses who were waiting to drag him down from the pedestal he never asked to be set upon.

Topping the tall poppies says more about us, our human nature, than it ever says about the heroes we try to diminish. There's more to it, too, than merely wanting to keep our heroes' feet on the ground. We're a prurient society, and boy do we believe in scratching that itch in public. It is not an edifying sight.

We make heroes of sportsmen when they do things most of us only dream of. They fulfil our fantasies. But heaven forbid if they fall below our expectations, revealing their own human frailties or, worse still, having them revealed in the tabloid press. Over-night we downgrade them from hero to zero. Poor us. What sad lives we must lead. Poor heroes, having to live the life we demand of them. Unhappy villains, left wondering what they did that was so out of character as to be so wrong.

HAROLD LARWOOD
1927

Standing only 5ft 7½in high, and weighing 10st 8lb, Larwood, who began life as a miner, is despite a somewhat frail appearance very strong physically. He gets great pace off the ground, probably because he has a perfect run-up to the wicket, and at times makes the ball come back so much that he is almost unplayable. Except that he drags his right foot and is inclined to stoop slightly at the moment of delivery, his action is all that a fast bowler's should be. Under the tuition of James Iremonger, now coach at Trent Bridge, his powers have developed amazingly. Only twenty-two years of age he should have a big future.

1934
THE MCC TEAM IN AUSTRALASIA

Successfully as at times Allen, Voce and Verity acquitted themselves, it was the opinion on all hands that to Larwood belonged chief credit for England winning the rubber. Sharply divergent views will probably always be held as to the desirability of the method of attack he employed. This, however, is not the place to discuss that thorny subject. Suffice it to say that his fast leg-theory bowling, with three or four fieldsmen close in and others deeper on the leg side, enabled him to establish an ascendancy over practically all the leading Australian batsmen that continued until the end of the tour. Whatever may be thought of this type of bowling, no possible doubt existed that Larwood proved himself the ideal exponent of it. Stronger probably than on the occasion of his previous visit to Australia, and very judiciously "nursed" during the matches by Jardine, he not only maintained an extraordinarily accurate length necessary for this form of attack but kept up a tremendous pace. In his own way Larwood obviously must have bowled magnificently. His record of wickets and the standing of his victims prove this, and in match after match Australian batsmen clearly gave the impression of being overawed.

The Bowling Controversy, 1934

And now, what of this fast leg-theory method of bowling to which not only the Australian players themselves, but a vast majority of the people of Australia, took such grave exception? With the dictum of the MCC, that any form of bowling which constitutes a direct attack by the bowler on the batsman is contrary to the spirit of the game, everyone must unquestionably concur. D. R. Jardine, on his return to England, stated definitely in his book that the bowling against which the Australians demurred was not that of this description, and Larwood, the chief exponent of it, said with equal directness that he had never intentionally bowled at a man. On the other hand, there are numerous statements by responsible Australians to the effect that the type of bowling adopted was calculated to intimidate batsmen, pitched as the ball was so short as to cause it to fly shoulder and head high and make batsmen, with the leg side studded with fieldsmen, use the bat as a protection for their bodies or their heads rather than in defence of the wicket or to make a scoring stroke.

Notes by the Editor, *Wisden*, 1935

No greater disservice was ever done to English cricket than when Larwood was induced to dash into print and become responsible for statements which put him beyond the pale of being selected for England. I think I am right in saying that he would have been chosen for the Test match at Lord's – to mention only one – but for the article under his name which appeared shortly before that game. No selection committee worthy of the name could possibly have considered him after that, and the backing which unfortunately he received in the press from certain quarters merely added fuel to the flames of controversy about this unhappy incident.

DENNIS LILLEE
by John Thicknesse, 1976

When Thomson and Lillee were bowling, the atmosphere was more like that of a soccer ground than of a cricket match, especially at Sydney, where England's batsmen must have experienced the same sort of emotions as they waited for the next ball as early Christians felt as they waited in the Colosseum for the lions. Passions were additionally roused by the fact that during the season Lillee had published *Back to the Mark*, a book in which he openly admitted that when he bowled a bouncer he aimed to hit the batsman and make him think twice about the wisdom of going on batting.

No fast bowler had been as explicit as that in print (although it stands to reason that a bouncer has to be straight to be effective) and there was no doubt that the comment played its part in provoking the exultant chants of "Lill . . . lee, Lill . . . lee" from the jam-packed Hill that accompanied him along the 30-yard walk to his mark, and up to the first half of his run-up . . . to be followed by an expectant hush as he neared the bowling crease.

It would have needed umpires of much self-confidence to have interfered with this Roman holiday, and Brooks and Bailhache – a fledgling of twenty-seven – did not possess it. It was a very difficult series to umpire and the Australian Board of Control did nothing to relieve the burden by appointing the pair for all six Tests, so that they were never out of the thick of it. Yet when all their difficulties are added up, it must still be said that their umpiring fell short of required standards. The lack of protection afforded to England's batsmen prompted a re-examination of Law 46 at the Test and County Cricket Board's spring meeting.

TONY GREIG
1976
AUSTRALIA v ENGLAND

At Brisbane, 1974. Edrich, dropped at one off Lillee, and Greig batted through the 110 minutes to stumps, when England were 114 for four. Edrich was out early on the third morning, caught at slip off Lillee an over after being rapped hard on the top hand. Knott and Lever followed, but Greig found a determined partner in Underwood and, having faced the prospect of a three-figure deficit, England cut Australia's lead to 44. Greig's hundred was a memorable mixture of brilliant off-side strokes, wild passes, and continual attempts to rattle Lillee by shadow-boxing underneath the bouncers. He batted five hours and hit 15 fours. His hundred was only the second for England at the Woolloongabba ground; M. Leyland scored 126 there in the 1936/37 series. E. Hendren scored 169 at the Exhibition Ground in 1928/29.

Notes by the Editor, *Wisden*, 1977

Twelve months ago I commented in these Notes that Tony Greig, while not the greatest tactician, possessed many splendid qualities, and the success in India of such emphatic proportions brought out his better points. No cricketer plays the game with more dedication, and no doubt his self-confidence and enthusiasm inspired a party of uncertain standard when they embarked on their mission to the East. Greig, in a sense, was on trial himself following so many Test setbacks. England had not won a match since he took over the leadership from Michael Denness midway through 1975 and this, allied to his own lack of success with both bat and ball, made some people question his suitability for the job.

But everything came off for Greig on the Indian expedition. He regained his form with several praiseworthy innings, including a priceless century in the Second Test at Calcutta under a merciless sun while running a temperature of 103 degrees. As captain, he received the unstinted support of his players and there was no more popular personality with the Indian multitudes.

1978

Not for many a year had a season opened with such justifiably high hopes of success. Players, committee and followers of the club felt that Sussex would win one of the competitions, and the captain, Tony Greig, spoke confidently of the splendid spirit right throughout the camp. There was the right approach and a very good side, he emphasised . . . Then came the Packer affair.

The Australian TV tycoon visited the Hove County Ground and conferred with Greig in the captain's room at the top of the pavilion. Greig followed by holding the most extraordinary press conference ever likely to be staged on the ground, and the Sussex boat was then well and truly rocked. Just what an adverse effect the whole business had on the club we do not yet know. But with Greig obviously Packer's right-hand man over here, foremost in his recruitment policy and talking with such enthusiasm of the opportunities opening out for cricket and players – plus the fact that Snow and Imran Khan had also signed up for Australian duty – Sussex were closely involved. There was uncertainty in the air, and the earlier spirit of hope and confidence disappeared.

by Gordon Ross, 1978

On May 13, The Cricket Council issued a statement at the end of an emergency meeting to the effect that Greig was not to be considered as England's captain in the forthcoming series against Australia. The statement went on: "His action has inevitably impaired the trust which existed between the cricket authorities and the captain of the England side." F. R. Brown, chairman of the Council, added: "The captaincy of the England team involves close liaison with the selectors in the management, selection and development of England players for the future and clearly Greig is unlikely to be able to do this as his stated intention is to be contracted elsewhere during the next three winters."

THE RAIN MEN 1909

SUSSEX v HAMPSHIRE

Restricted to one day's cricket which naturally led to no definite result, this match was rendered noteworthy by an altogether unpardonable course of conduct on the part of the Sussex team. Continuous rain precluded any possibility of cricket on Thursday but, although the weather continued very wet during the night, the pitch was fit for play at half-past eleven next morning. At that hour, while the Hampshire men were in attendance, only two or three members of the Sussex eleven had made their way to the Priory Park [Chichester]. Fry and Vine arrived some time later, but the majority of the side did not put in an appearance until between three and four o'clock in the afternoon. Preparations were then made for a start but the weather, always showery, turned wet again and the game was not entered upon until Saturday. Had the Sussex team arrived at the proper hour, comparatively little cricket would have been possible but that was no excuse for the non-appearance of the men. The only attempt at explanation urged was that as rain fell heavily 20 miles away, where the majority of the Sussex team stayed for the night, the cricketers concluded that no play could take place.

GEOFFREY BOYCOTT
by Bill Bowes, 1965

In 1963, his first full season of county cricket, Geoffrey Boycott, Yorkshire opening batsman, scored 1,628 runs at an average of 45.22 an innings and was elected "The Best Young Cricketer" of the year. Less than 12 months after becoming a professional cricketer he was chosen to open for England against Australia. He finished second in the England averages with 291 runs at 48.50, scored his first Test century in the Fifth Test at The Oval; for his second season's work he could point to 2,110 runs at an average of 52.75 an innings.

He is ruthlessly dedicated to the job of scoring runs, analyses his own game, and takes the trouble to learn about the others'. Cricket for him is an all-absorbing occupation and in Yorkshire, where they expect 100 per cent effort, he caused an uplift of eyebrows prior to the start of the 1964 season, when he gave up his job as a wages clerk earlier than the county authorities demanded, attended the Yorkshire Schoolboys practices in the morning, stayed for the Colts and senior coaching classes in the afternoon, and then left the Headingley ground in order to join evening practices with the Leeds club. He had four sessions of net practice each day and regretted he could not get more.

1972

The new captain, Boycott, responded to his duties in the one way he knew best – he scored more than 2,000 runs for an average of 109.85 for Yorkshire and became the first Englishman to average more than 100 in all matches for the season. But he failed to bring the team along with him and this was a reason for disappointment.

1979

The manoeuvring behind the scenes involved a rearguard action by the anti-Boycott lobby, who seized on a welcome run of good results under Hampshire and devalued it by using it as a weapon in the captaincy argument. Thus, by the middle of June, the county was split by the suggestion that the team did better under

Hampshire, whose batting also prospered as he deputised for the injured Boycott.

The climax came at the end of September when the Yorkshire committee dismissed Boycott as captain after eight years in command. He was replaced by John Hampshire. It had been a shattering week for Boycott. He had been passed over as vice-captain of the England team to visit Australia, the honour being given to Bob Willis, and only four days before the Yorkshire decision his mother, with whom he lived, died after a long and painful illness.

by Derek Hodgson, 1988

In 1987, Geoffrey Boycott published an autobiography, reviewers generally regarding it as a long, somewhat tedious attempt at self-justification. "A sad book" was an almost universal comment, a wry reflection on Boycott's own influence on the publication, for his helper, Terry Brindle, is one of the most humorous of cricket writers. Nor is Boycott himself without humour, taking and giving the dressing-room horseplay with some relish. But he could also, in his time as Yorkshire's captain, make the dressing-room feared, almost hated, by young Yorkshire players.

So the paradox continues. Once asked to name his closest friend, he could not find one he was confident to nominate. Abominated by great Yorkshire contemporaries, he was found by many outside the game to be utterly charming. Perhaps he was unfortunate to be born in an age when the public interest is served by a media intent on prying and prising loose every single item, good but preferably bad. Had he lived in Victorian times he might have been regarded as one of the great eccentrics; "an intensely private man" is a phrase that might have been used.

IAN BOTHAM
Notes by the Editor, *Wisden*, 1987

Botham, it might be argued, is irresponsible; some wouldn't even bother to argue. But his lack of responsibility is more to himself than to his fellow-man. He bats and bowls not with concern for averages or place but for the joy of playing and the stimulus of competition. He, too, is a "guerrilla fighter impatient of discipline. A devotee of action who thrives on challenge and crisis." Those are words used to describe Winston Churchill in the 1930s: a man at times as much loved or loathed as Botham has been in recent years.

Botham may not be everyone's ideal hero, but as Carlyle said, the hero can be poet, prophet, king, priest or whatever you will, according to the kind of world he finds himself born into. To a society that cries out for any extravagant gesture to alleviate the mediocrity, Botham by his deeds has indeed become a hero. In August he presented the Leukaemia Research Fund with a cheque for £888,000 as a result of his great walk from John o'Groats to Land's End in 1985.

Botham's absence from the England side for all but the last Test match of last summer was due to his suspension by the TCCB from all first-class cricket from May 29 until July 31. His misdemeanour was bringing the game into disrepute by admitting to using cannabis (in a newspaper article on May 18), denying in the past that he had used cannabis, and making public pronouncements without the clearance of his county.

SHANE WARNE
by Vic Marks, 1994

Ominously for Test batsmen of the 1990s, Warne is not yet the complete wrist-spinner. His googly is not so penetrating or well-disguised as Mushtaq Ahmed's, which is one reason why he employs it so infrequently. His flipper is lethal if it is on target, but it often zooms down the leg side. But he is the most prodigious spinner of the ball of the last three decades, a gift which causes deceptive in-swing as well as deceptive turn. He is also remarkably accurate, but if ever his control is threatened, he can regroup by bowling round the wicket to the right-handed batsman, thereby restricting him to just one scoring stroke, a risky sweep. Hence in the Ashes series his captain, Border, was able to use him as both shock and stock bowler.

On a broader scale he has triggered a mini-renaissance in the art of wrist-spin bowling. In the summer of 1993 young village cricketers could be spied on the outfield, no longer seeking to emulate Curtly Ambrose or Merv Hughes but attempting to ape the more subtle skills of Warne. For that we should all be grateful.

by Mihir Bose, 1999

The original accusation was that the Australians Shane Warne, Tim May and Mark Waugh had been approached by Salim Malik, who allegedly offered them $200,000 bribes to throw matches in October 1994. This first alerted a dozing cricket world to the heavy illegal betting going on in the subcontinent and Sharjah, and to the possibility that players were being bribed to rig matches.

More than four years later, it finally emerged that Warne and Waugh had their own involvement with subcontinental bookmakers and that the Australian Cricket Board knew about this and had covered it up all the time. The revelation was that [in Sri Lanka in September 1994] Waugh and Warne had been approached by an Indian bookmaker identified only as "John", who had asked them to begin giving him apparently innocent information about the weather and the state of the pitch – less, said the players, than they might routinely give free to journalists. For this Waugh was paid A$6,000 (about £2,500) and Warne A$5,000. The players had admitted this after making their original allegations about Malik to the Australian Cricket Board, which then fined them slightly more than John paid them (A$10,000 for Waugh and A$8,000 for Warne).

The news incensed the Australian public, and Waugh was booed during the Adelaide Test against England. Warne escaped this because he was injured. But letter-writers to Australian papers demanded that both be drummed out of the game. Warne and Waugh admitted being "naïve and stupid" but insisted they had not been involved in match-fixing in any way.

THE 2003 WORLD CUP
by Simon Wilde, 2004

Hours earlier, Shane Warne, Australia's match-winner in the semi-final and final of 1999, had returned home after failing a drugs test taken during the VB Series in Australia the previous month. Warne's "A" sample – later confirmed by the "B" – showed he had taken two banned diuretics, hydrochlorothiazide and amiloride. Warne said he got them from his mum and took them out of vanity, wanting to lose weight before his return to the Australia side after injury. But diuretics can also mask steroids, which could have expedited Warne's swift recovery from a dislocated shoulder. A fortnight into the tournament, he was handed a one-year ban. It was the highest-profile drugs case to afflict cricket and sent shock waves through the game but, as with everything else, the Australians rode them well.

BRIAN LARA
by Tony Cozier, 1995

The unparalleled glut of batting records that fell to Brian Lara between April and June 1994 amazed the cricket world and gained global attention beyond the game's narrow confines. It also prompted an outpouring of national pride in his native Trinidad & Tobago where he was showered with honours and gifts. Yet, while there was understandable joy, there was no real surprise among many of his countrymen at the left-hander's achievement, simply the feeling that his inevitable date with destiny had arrived rather more suddenly than expected.

Trinidadians craved the arrival of a batting superstar they, alone of all the territories that comprise West Indies cricket, had lacked; and Lara had long since provided unmistakable signs that he would fill the void. Even the most cock-eyed optimist could not have foreseen his virtually simultaneous eclipse of Sir Garfield Sobers's Test and Hanif Mohammad's first-class records, but those who had followed his development from the time he first played organised cricket were never in any doubt that it was within the potential of his talent and ambition. There was even talk, not entirely prompted by the euphoria of the moment, that

Lara himself would surpass his own standards by the time he was through.

But Lara is from the island renowned for its carnival, and he knows how to enjoy himself beyond the boundary. Like Sobers and so many other cricketers, he has become addicted to golf, which he plays right-handed and increasingly well, and is an avid fan of horse-racing. His boyish good looks and easy-going manner, not to mention his fame and fortune, render him a vulnerable bachelor.

There is another more threatening consequence of his sudden success and stardom. It places on him an awesome responsibility that not all celebrated young sportsmen can properly handle. With satellite television now spanning the globe, Lara has become cricket's first truly international megastar. Public expectation will be excessive, and the non-cricketing demands on him persistent. Temperament, as much as talent, is now likely to dictate Brian Lara's future.

by Tony Cozier, 2000

In spite of a career embroiled in controversy, Lara finally ascended to the West Indian captaincy in January 1998, replacing the much admired Courtney Walsh. Straight away, he led the team to victories over England in both Tests and one-day internationals. When he carried a team without Curtly Ambrose and Walsh, its two great and long-serving fast bowlers, to the final of the Mini World Cup in Bangladesh, there were signs Lara was presiding over a welcome revival.

Within days, such optimism was shattered. Instead of assembling in South Africa for the start of West Indies' first tour there, the players convened in a hotel at London's Heathrow Airport. They refused to budge until the West Indies Cricket Board sent its president, Pat Rousseau, to discuss their grievances. If Lara was not the instigator of the crisis – it was initiated by the Players' Association, whose president was Walsh – he was at its centre as captain. Confronted by an unprecedented uprising, the WICB reacted hastily: they dismissed Lara and vice-captain Carl Hooper and fined the remaining players while ordering them to leave for South Africa. But Rousseau was eventually obliged to cave in; he flew to London and negotiated. Lara and Hooper were reinstated, the fines were withdrawn and the South African tour proceeded.

Cancellation might have been preferable. All five Tests were comprehensively lost, and a solitary win in the seven one-day internationals was negligible consolation. Well before the end, Lara was a forlorn and seemingly broken man, unable to energise the team with either his batting or his leadership. Humiliated by the climbdown at Heathrow, the WIBC might have appreciated the chance of retribution; there was enough public condemnation of the performance to make it possible to dismiss Lara without an outcry. But, lacking an obvious successor, they placed him on probation for the first two Tests of the home series against Australia that followed. A statement castigated his "weaknesses in leadership that contributed to poor performances".

WEST INDIES v AUSTRALIA
by Mike Coward, 2000

At Port-of-Spain, 1999. Compounding the humiliation of the infamous whitewash in South Africa, West Indies truly reached their nadir when they were dismissed for 51 – their lowest score in 71 years of Test cricket. Their previous worst was 53 in Faisalabad in 1986/87, and their lowest at home 102 against England in 1934/35. Only Jacobs reached double figures – the next best was six, by Ambrose. Astonishingly, they lost their last 17 wickets for 69 runs in 31.4 overs, to be ridiculed by critics and crowds alike. The prime target for the vitriol was captain Lara (out second ball). Even doting followers in his native Trinidad showed signs of disaffection, if not anger. When the match ended, after lunch on the fourth day, there were renewed and loud calls for his head.

by Tony Cozier, 2000

The transformation that followed was immediate, incredible and entirely inspired by Lara. The team, he told the press, needed someone to "star with the bat" and he was that someone. Words come easily. But Lara was true to his word. Within three weeks, he had fashioned two innings which, given the circumstances and their bravado, were fit to rank among the finest ever played by a West Indian.

His 213 at Sabina Park and 153 not out at Kensington Oval were the basis of successive victories over Australia and lifted the gloom that had descended over the whole English-speaking Caribbean. Suddenly there was new optimism and heightened interest, even among the young whose attention had been turning to the alien sports they watch on the ubiquitous American satellite television. It was a busy Tuesday afternoon as Lara ushered West Indies to their remarkable one-wicket victory at Bridgetown; but everywhere rush-hour traffic came to a standstill, shoppers went unattended and telephones unanswered. Cricket was back where it belonged, in the hearts of a people fast giving up on it.

HANSIE CRONJE
SOUTH AFRICA v ENGLAND
by Neil Manthorp, 2001

At Centurion Park, 2000. History was made on the final day when a match apparently reduced to the deadliest of finishes, following three consecutive playless days, was brought back to life by the captains. For the first time in Test cricket, innings were forfeited and this produced a memorable, entertaining climax. When play resumed, with South Africa still in the first innings, the many hundreds of travelling English supporters and a few hundred hardy locals had every reason to expect the worst. What they were treated to was a gripping finale that saw England win with five balls and two wickets remaining.

Five months after the match, however, came the bitterness of deceit when Cronje, South Africa's captain, admitted receiving 53,000 rand (around £5,000) and a leather jacket from a bookmaker, who had urged him to initiate a positive result, rather than let the match peter out as a draw. At the King Commission inquiry into match-fixing, which opened in Cape Town in June 2000, he insisted that his motives were "for the good of cricket", but the fact that financial reward formed a part of his motivation tainted the match for ever. History would also record that it was the first Test in which "fixing" was proven.

Some 30 minutes into play on the final day, the first rumour of what was about to happen reached the media. Cronje had approached his opposite number, Hussain, half an hour before the start and offered to "make a game of it". His offer was a target of 255 runs in 73 overs, based on the premise that South Africa could score another 100 runs in 30 overs on the extended final morning, followed by a double forfeiture of innings – England's first and South Africa's second. Hussain declined. "The wicket might have been sweating under those covers for three days. It might have been unplayable. I couldn't take that chance," he said later. Ten overs into the session, however, having seen how well the pitch was playing under sunny skies, he left the field and sought out Cronje. "Is the offer still open?" he enquired. The answer was "Yes."

Inevitably, some wondered whether Test cricket had been contaminated, even belittled, by the contrived result. Cronje was adamant that, should the game's administrators at the ICC be among those showing disapproval, he "wouldn't want to be part of cricket any more. What is wrong with trying to make a game of it?" he said afterwards. But his previous dealings with bookmakers, as revealed at the King Commission, had forced him into that position. It was the first, albeit oblique, evidence of what had become a sadly corrupted outlook on the game and his responsibilities. "Test cricket needs to do everything it can to advertise itself and be competitive in a busy sporting market," he went on. "It hurts to lose – we lost a 14-match unbeaten run because of this – but it was a fabulous game in the end and people deserve to be entertained."

Hussain, understandably delighted, paid special tribute to Cronje at the time. "It was a very special thing that Hansie did and I hope he gets the credit he deserves. It certainly was a great finish to be part of." But later, when it emerged that corruption had played its regrettable part in the shaping of the final day, he would write in his newspaper column that England's win had been ruined. "We can't get away from that," he said. "It will always be remembered as a Test that was fixed."

INDEX OF KEY PLAYERS, TEAMS AND TOPICS

Page numbers in *italic* refer to the authors of articles